PC Mod Projects:

Cool It! Light It! Morph It!

About the Authors

Edward S. Chen was raised in Queens, NY, and currently resides in Albany, NY. He is a web programmer for AOL/Time Warner, one of the largest media and entertainment companies in the world. Edward designs and maintains database backends for the numerous web ventures in the Albany, NY, affiliate.

Philip Mansfield lives in Cambridge, England, and has worked in computers all of his adult life; he finally became fed up with beige boxes a couple of years ago. Since then he has modified his own PC cases and undertaken some customwork to design replacement drive bays for other people.

Carl Mixon is at the heart of the case mod industry, having helped found PcMods.com; he has been immersed in case modding for the last three years. By being involved in the case mod industry from its inception he has either created, improved, or helped to create many products that are common case mod devices. Creating a computer case from scratch, as he did for this book, is the pinnacle of case modding enjoyment.

Grace A. Punska is a components buyer for arcade games, computer modding, and military projects. A mother of two, this self-professed geek likes nonviolent computer games and is the author of the novel *Sands of Ice*.

About the Tech Editor

Mark Knoch was born in Southern California, schooled in Oregon, and now resides on the beautiful central coast of California with his wife, Shannon. A geek by nature, he was naturally drawn to all things "computer" from a very early age. He started his company, Wahoo Computers (www.wahoocomputers.com), which specializes in high-end custom system and case modding, in 2000 and has never looked back. Since the company's inception, Mark has been involved in hundreds of custom modding projects. He enjoys fishing, golfing, hockey, and, of course, PC gaming.

PC Mod Projects:
Cool It! Light It! Morph It!

Edward Chen
Philip Mansfield
Carl Mixon
Grace Punska

McGraw-Hill/Osborne
New York Chicago San Francisco Lisbon London Madrid Mexico City
Milan New Delhi San Juan Seoul Singapore Sydney Toronto

The McGraw-Hill Companies

McGraw-Hill/Osborne
2100 Powell Street, 10th Floor
Emeryville, California 94608
U.S.A.

To arrange bulk purchase discounts for sales promotions, premiums, or fund-raisers, please contact **McGraw-Hill**/Osborne at the above address. For information on translations or book distributors outside the U.S.A., please see the International Contact Information page immediately following the index of this book.

PC Mod Projects: Cool It! Light It! Morph It!

1234567890 QPD QPD 019876543

ISBN 0-07-223011-8

Publisher
Brandon A. Nordin

Vice President & Associate Publisher
Scott Rogers

Acquisitions Editor
Franny Kelly

Project Editor
Jennifer Malnick

Technical Editor
Mark Knoch

Copy Editor
Bill McManus

Indexer
Rebecca Plunkett

Composition
Carie Abrew
Tara A. Davis

Illustrator
Kathleen Fay Edwards
Melinda Moore Lytle
Lyssa Wald

Series Design
Jean Butterfield

Cover Series Design
Tree Hines

This book was composed with Corel VENTURA™ Publisher.

Thank you to all who believed in me.
"We have stopped for a moment to encounter each other.
To meet, to love, to share. It is a precious moment,
but it is transient. It is a little parentheses in eternity.
If we share with caring, lightheartedness, and love,
we will create abundance and joy for each other,
and this moment will have been worthwhile."
(Deepak Chopra, M.D.)—Ed

To my wife, Joan, for loving and supporting me,
both throughout this project and
our life together.—Philip

This book is dedicated to my wife, Katarzyna.
Thanks for having the courage to take chances.—Carl

To my grandfather, who taught me the value of tools.—Grace

Contents at a Glance

Table of Contents

Acknowledgments

Ed

Thank you to Franny Kelly and the entire staff at McGraw-Hill/Osborne for all their hard work and belief in this project. Thank you to one of my *biggest* supporters, Jeanette Moy, for her motivation, energy, and confidence in me. Thank you also to my parents and Suzanne, for all their unconditional love and devotion. Finally, to my staff at GideonTech.com, for their efforts and ideas.

Philip

Many thanks to everyone at McGraw-Hill who gave me the chance to work on this project.

Carl

I would like to extend my thanks to several vendors who provided parts for this mod. PcMods contributed nearly everything mod-related, including fans, a motherboard tray, standoffs, window materials, power supplies, edge molding—the list goes on and on. Wahoo Computers was kind enough to donate a Danger Den water-cooling rig. IOSS provided the cabling for the system, in the form of two single-device IDE cables and a matching super-shielded audio cable. I greatly appreciate their assistance (and knowledge) while I created our super case.

This mod has a family who helped bring it to life. When you mod your case, you will find that it's fun to put your ideas into reality, but you probably won't do it alone. Modding is much more fun when you have a co-conspirator, and I'd like to extend a heartfelt thanks to Pete Cupial on the PcMods staff for his enormous efforts in helping to cut the case, for his photo skills in taking the pictures for the system, and for all of his efforts in helping to create the Gas Can case. It would have been much harder (and less fun) without him.

Grace

I'd like to thank Guy Muff and Bob Garrity for their assistance during this mod. The extra help went a long way. Thanks, guys—I couldn't have done it without you.

Introduction

Chances are, if you are a computer fanatic, you have already upgraded your computer to make it more useful. Once they have mastered basic upgrades, most people find themselves drawn to further improve their computer by modding it. Why mod the case? It's the most interesting part of your computer. Certainly, it's what most people see first.

So what is the difference between an upgrade and a mod? Upgrades are simple things like adding a hard drive, adding RAM, or even changing the operating system. Standard upgrades scare many people, who pay too much money to have a single stick of ram put in a slot. After your computer stops being a magical device that you don't understand, you can start upgrading your computer regularly, and very soon after that you are building your own computer system. Once many people reach that comfort level, they start looking beyond basic improvements. Advanced improvements are then needed to make the computer an advanced system. That's when you are ready to begin modding.

"Modding" refers to any improvement that is outside the normal focus of computer upgrades (RAM, HDDs, OSs). Examples of these kinds of improvements could include increasing the performance of your computer past manufacturer limits by overclocking it and putting on a high-performance heatsink, making your computer look cooler by painting it, or increasing the functionality of your computer by adding more controls in the front.

Case mods fall into two distinct categories: function and style.

Many mods are designed to make your case more functional, and there are two aspects of improving functionality. The first is performance, which includes adding fans, fan controllers, and other devices that make your case perform better than a "stock" case does. The second aspect of functional mods is convenience. The addition of front USB ports, front audio controls, or case handles does not make your computer perform better, but it does add convenience to your life. The amount of functional improvements you can make is simply amazing.

Your case has the most room for improvement out of all the components in your computer—and the options for improvement are almost infinite. Improving the style of your case—including painting your case, adding lights and windows, LEDs, and more—is almost an art form. And, since the style of your case is a reflection of yourself, it becomes a statement that you make to others.

Some people are good at improving style; some people excel at adding functionality; the best mods are those that incorporate both. It's a challenge to find ways to make your functional mods fit in with the aesthetic looks of the case. When you fully integrate great style with fantastic functionality, you then have a case that will meet the highest expectations. You create a showcase, one that can be displayed at LANparties or entered into case mod contests. *Your mod should be both highly functional and extremely cool. And that is what we are going to show you in this book.*

The simplest examples of having style and functionality together can be seen in many standard mods. This includes installing LED fans on a case window, painting a tornado around a fan duct opening, or putting tubing around PSU wires to improve looks and airflow. These excellent examples fall short in one important way: they are just one part of your case that is modded. For your case to look truly fantastic, you have to have all of your mods integrated together.

How do you do this? The answer is simple: stop playing by the rules. The modding of stock cases has been thoroughly explored by hundreds of thousands of people. It's no longer enough to take a standard steel case and build it out into a supercase. People are turning to new mods, and putting motherboards where they have never gone before. You have to break the rules—do not use a stock case like everyone else has. You have to use a completely different enclosure for your PC. This enclosure defines what mods you will have and how they will work, and requires you to plan ahead so that everything fits perfectly. We can help you do that.

Project 1: Installing a Water-Cooling System

Building a computer used to be something very mysterious and difficult. Hardware and software have changed so that this is no longer true: hardware has become much easier to work with. For example, most motherboards do not require special jumper settings—you just plug in your parts and go. And software has become much easier. If you install a new piece of hardware, most computers will detect it and install it, often without any interaction from you.

Because the technical side of building a computer has gotten easier, system building isn't as fun as it used to be; that's why case modding is enjoyable. The time we used to spend putting things together is not spent customizing our case. So when we were building this system, we decided to build from scratch whenever possible. This is more challenging, more fun, and (as you will see) looks much better than a boring beige case.

These days, people are very passionate about cars and computers, so, when we were building our case, we wanted to show off our interest in cars by making the "skin" of the computers something very car-oriented.

The result is something we could never have purchased at a local computer store, as you will see in Chapters 1–5.

Project 2: Adding Lights

Adding lights to a computer case was one of the earliest and most popular modding ideas; modders show no signs of slowing down in using lights in different and unique ways. It's safe to say that lighting is practically mandatory if you want a cool case worthy of showing off. The mod presented in Chapters 6–10 features lights aplenty, in every side of the case, in different styles, colors, and brightness. We'll show you how to choose lights for different locations in the case and how to install them for maximum effect.

Project 3: Morphing the Case

Creating your own case is a feat in itself, but creating your own case out of crystal-clear acrylic is distinctly individual. No beige case will be able to display your hardware like an acrylic case. The acrylic displays interior lighting with incredible ease and will cause the novice as well as an advanced computer users and modders to turn their heads. The whole idea of creating your own case is to give you complete originality and freedom over how your case appears. With the steps in Chapter 11–15, you will be able to achieve your desired case.

Project 4: Epiphany in Blue

In Chapters 16–20, we'll take a case that already looks pretty good and enhance it further. The modder's dictionary doesn't include the word "stock," so there's plenty of work to be done on the case. Windows, lights, LCD screens, and TFT screens will all be called on to play their parts in transforming this case into something unique.

So open it up and have some fun. Good luck!

Project 1

Installing a Water-Cooling System

Chapter 1

Planning the Mod

This project focuses on installing a computer system in a container that was never meant to hold a computer—in this case, a WWII jerry can (see Figure 1-1). Jerry cans are meant to hold fuel, so they have no ventilation. Unlike modern aluminum cases, the steel of the jerry can has no special heat dissipation properties. In short, this can is a computer chip's worst nightmare, but we are going to mod it to make it a chip's dream home.

Figure 1-1 WWII jerry can, unmodded

One of the reasons that we chose this type of can is that it is big enough for a full-size ATX motherboard. We could use a microATX system, but we prefer the full-size ATX over the microATX because microATX motherboards usually forego some features to get the smaller footprint. We want this system to be powerful. Also, the full-size ATX system meets all of our requirements: it looks great, performs better than most systems out there, is easy to upgrade, and is fully compatible with anything that we want to put into it.

TIPS OF THE TRADE

Does it Have to Be a Jerry Can?

Just about anything the size of a jerry can will work for a PC case, such as a camp stove, a briefcase, or even a milk crate! A good place to start your search is to consider objects associated with your favorite hobby... if you have one other than computers, that is!

Overcoming the Obstacles

We have two obstacles to overcome when using this mod: case design and cooling. We have to plan ahead to figure out how to do this with style.

Case Design

Because we are using a jerry can for a case, we have to decide how to secure everything in the case. For example, there are no 5.25-inch drive bays for us to conveniently put a DVD-ROM drive into.

The devices we need to include in the case are a DVD-ROM drive, the motherboard and its cards, and a hard drive. We are not going to install a floppy drive in this case because they are rarely used anymore and it would be very hard to integrate into the look and feel of the system.

To install these items, we are going to use a variety of seldom-used methods, all of which are easy to do. These include using hard drive standoffs from an acrylic case, using rivets as fasteners, and creating our own DVD-ROM brackets. When we create the brackets, we will use scrap aluminum because it is light and easy to work with—always an important consideration.

But we're not going to reinvent the wheel for every aspect of our design; we are going to include a removable Lian Li motherboard tray to ensure compatibility with any motherboard we may want to use in the future. This tray is available at various online stores, but you don't necessarily need to buy anything. You can hack apart your ugly OEM computer case—the one that you may be throwing away because you are building your new supercase—so that you can use various pieces in your new case. We haven't totally turned our back on the standardized PC case, but what we are going to use will be hidden from view.

Since we do not have a drive bay to put the DVD-ROM drive into, we are going to install a slot-loading DVD player (see Figure 1-2) instead of a drawer-style DVD player. Slot-loading DVD players are much less commonly available on the market, but using one in this design enables us to make our DVD-ROM drive less obvious so that it won't take away from the basic look of the case. Our DVD-ROM drive has only one purpose: as an input device. It's not a part of the style statement that we are trying to achieve, so we're going to hide it as much as possible. When it comes time to install this device, we'll be able to just cut a slot in the case, which will be very unobtrusive.

Figure 1-2 Slot-loading DVD-ROM drive

TIPS OF THE TRADE

Stealth Drive

There aren't many slot-loading DVD-ROM drives on the market compared to drawer-style DVD-ROM drives. If you want to use a drawer-style unit, you may have to cut a hole in your case and attach a piece of metal from the hole onto the front of the DVD-ROM drawer. This is called a "stealth drive" mod; check it out on the Internet!

Using Water Cooling

Because a jerry can is a type of gas can, the biggest problem that we have to deal with is cooling. Gas cans are designed to be airtight, so this case has an enormous cooling problem. If we put fans all over the can, the case will lose a lot of its identity. So we want to avoid using fans whenever possible, for style purposes. Therefore, we are turning to a cooling method that has grown much more popular recently: water cooling. By using water to cool the system, our ventilation system will be less obvious, both visually and from a noise perspective. Both of these are big pluses.

As you are probably aware, most computer systems are air-cooled. However, if we look around, we'll find other industries that have started with air cooling and then transitioned to water cooling as their cooling needs grew more complex. A great example is the automobile industry. Two well-known German automakers originally designed their cars with air-cooled engines, and now, 30 years later, both use water to cool the engine. Granted, the cooling requirements are somewhat different in cars than in computers, but many of the same benefits apply. Another example, which is closer to home, exists in console video game systems. All early console video game systems were air-cooled, but at least one of the newer gaming systems has a packet of liquid on top of the processor, with cooling tubes to drain the heat out of the chip more effectively. With water being a very popular cooling medium, it was inevitable that this technology would work its way into computer systems.

Because water cooling is so drastically different than air cooling, it will take some time to discuss the differences and the risks.

Your basic air-cooled system is very simple. Case fans circulate fresh air into the case, and individual, smaller heat sink and fan combos are positioned on specific hot components like the CPU and graphics card core. The benefits of using air cooling are that it is less expensive and much simpler to install. Air cooling will get the job done as long as you are not doing any extreme overclocking.

But air cooling has some negatives. The most obvious negative is noise. Air-cooled machines are noisier due to airflow in the case—the more powerful the fans are, the more wind noise they generate. This has led to the development of fan-controlled devices, which reduce the noise the fans make when the system is not running hot. Stock air-cooled systems may have as many as six OEM fans cooling the case. This leaves a lot more openings for dust to come into the case. The last and biggest argument against air-cooled systems is that air is not as efficient in removing heat. We'll discuss this in more depth shortly.

What are the risks with air cooling? Fan failure is one of the major reasons why a chip might burn up quickly. Most fans have a long lifespan and become very noisy as they reach the end of their life, so you know a problem is on the horizon long before the fan fails. The most frequent problem with air-cooled systems is airflow restriction due to fans or vent holes being covered up. Airflow restriction in any system can reduce the life of your chip. This may go unnoticed for a period of time, and many people don't even know that that is the reason their computer failed.

Water cooling, on the other hand, is better at cooling your system. If you aren't familiar with water cooling, an example of how a water-cooled system looks can be seen in Figure 1-3. Water keeps your chip somewhat cooler than air does, because water absorbs heat more efficiently. It's easy to understand this concept by considering a real-world example. Suppose that you walk outside and it is 60 degrees Fahrenheit. You are near a pool, which, coincidentally, has a water temperature of 60 degrees. You can probably stand outside all day long and be comfortable, but as soon as you jump in the water, the water sucks all the heat out of you almost immediately.

Figure 1-3 Example of a water-cooled system

There are additional benefits to water cooling—it is much quieter than air cooling, because a radiator cools the water down. Radiators are very efficient, but the key is that any fan that moves air through the radiator spins much slower than a heat sink fan. The slower a fan spins, the less noise it generates, all other things being equal. Quiet PCs are becoming more and more important now that PCs are such a big part of our lives. If you spend a lot of time next to your computer, chances are you could do without the incessant humming of the fans. Water cooling is a great step toward making your PC quieter.

The downside of using water cooling is that it is more complicated and more expensive than air-cooled solutions. Water cooling costs a lot more than air cooling, so for many people water cooling can't be cost-justified. And, if you don't install the system correctly and the system leaks, you could end up with ruined equipment. As stated earlier, ventilation is not an option in this mod, so we are going to install a water-cooling setup despite the increase in the cost.

Water cooling can be very reliable, and many companies now sell kits to help you water-cool your system. Some companies even sell cases that have built-in water-cooling systems, and some custom-system builders provide ready-to-go water-cooled computers right out of the box. It's apparent that water cooling is here to stay.

TIPS OF THE TRADE

Water-Cooling Parts: Make or Buy?

Although retail water-cooling parts may look expensive, don't rush into making your own waterblock. It is possible to make your own, but companies are spending more and more R&D money to make better water-cooling products, so it's unlikely yours will perform as well unless you are a thermodynamics wizard.

There is one other important element of a water-cooled system: the peltier, a popular device, which is shown in Figure 1-4.

What is a peltier? Simply put, it's a wafer-shaped electronic cooling device. The circuit inside transfers heat from one side to the other, making one side cold and one side hot. In simple terms, you are putting a refrigeration unit directly on your computer chip, but this refrigeration unit generates heat of its own.

You can use a peltier with an air-cooling system, but there is a problem: air is less efficient than water in removing heat. If you don't pull the heat off the hot side of the peltier efficiently, the hot side heats up the "cool" side, reducing efficiency. If you are really serious about getting the temperatures down, use a bigger peltier. The peltier will generate more heat than the air-cooled heat sink can pull off. Efficiency is then lost. For this reason, peltiers are most often used with water-cooled systems, which are able to pull off more heat.

Figure 1-4
A peltier

Peltiers come in different wattages. You can start off with a less powerful one and increase the power as you become more comfortable with them. Using a peltier, it is possible to get your chip down to freezing temperatures. We'll talk a little more about peltiers in Chapter 4. For more information on selecting the right size peltier, visit some of the many overclocking web sites on the Internet. Peltier selection varies widely from system to system.

HEADS UP!

You don't need to have a peltier to make a water-cooling system work. The peltier is an additional improvement in cooling power.

TESTING 1-2-3

- ❑ In this chapter we covered the basics of our mod as well as how water cooling works. Many of the parts and tools that we need to complete the mod are not standard household equipment, but we are not building a standard household computer system. The good news is that none of the tools that we need are too expensive or hard to find, and thus will not increase the cost of our system significantly.

- ❑ Now that we have decided the basic plan for our mod, it's time to get to work on the specifics. The next thing to do is to decide where everything will go and start cutting the case.

Chapter 2

Prepping the Case

Tools of the Trade

Electric jigsaw
Nibbler
Electric drill
Dremel (electric rotary tool)
Tin snips
Hand-held riveter
Pencil
Four-inch can
Small washers
Gas can
Motherboard tray
Tygon tubing
Masking tape
Assorted rivets and screws
Small switch
Acrylic sheet
Rubber molding (grommet)
Slot-loading DVD player
Water pump
Laptop hard drive
Scrap aluminum
Brass standoffs

In its current form, the metal gas can that we propose to use as the case for our computer system fails to be a good computer case in several ways. To convert the gas can into a good computer case, we need to make several modifications. This chapter discusses all of the structural changes required to transform the gas can into a computer case.

This project is about constructing a computer in a nonstandard container of any kind—we're using a gas can, but the same lessons apply if you are using a camp stove, a tool chest, or any other container. No matter what kind of container you have chosen to mutate into a PC case, you need to consider two things: how you will keep your case cool; and how you will install everything in the case. By choosing to mod something as radical as a gas can, we expose ourselves to problems that the average computer enthusiast doesn't have to think about. The can is airtight, so there is an enormous airflow problem. The can is also very small, so we can't fit much in it. Fortunately, we have some great solutions for you no matter what kind of enclosure you want to use.

As discussed in Chapter 1, we are going to resolve the cooling problem by using a water-cooling setup. While the water-cooling system solves the airflow problem perfectly, it actually makes our space problem much worse. This setup has two large components that an air-cooling rig does not: a radiator and a water pump. We also need to make sure to consider where the water pipes are going to be routed. Since our gas can is smaller than the average computer case, it's going to be hard to fit everything in the case. This is a trade-off that we can afford, but only because we are planning ahead so that we know where everything is going to fit.

The big challenge that we have ahead of us is the installation of all the parts. This container isn't very big, so we have to make the most out of the space that we have. One of our core philosophies is to modify the can only where necessary. We want to make as few cuts as possible so that the finished product will look clean and simple. If your case has too many holes, it will look cluttered, disorganized, and less appealing. By choosing a gas can, we haven't chosen the easy route, and we will have to break a few rules before we are done.

HEADS UP!

Before you start any case cutting, you need to know where everything will go. Start by making a list of all the parts that you'll need to install, so that you don't forget any along the way.

The main parts we have to consider during the install include the following:

- ❑ Motherboard (with chip, ram, and video card)
- ❑ DVD drive
- ❑ Hard drive
- ❑ Water pump
- ❑ Radiator
- ❑ Window
- ❑ Power supply

Configuring the Can

The first step that you should take when trying to figure out where things will go is to put them inside your case or, if you can't get inside it, on top of the case. Move them around into various configurations so that you can see what will work the best. You may want to make a drawing of the case and sketch in where you will put the parts. This is just one way you can plan ahead so that you don't end up making a big mistake somewhere along the way.

After test-fitting several items and sketching locations on the case, we recognize that it would be impossible to make everything fit inside the case. To make things easier, we have to consider what could be mounted on the exterior of the can to create more space. The radiator stands out as the best choice—it is chromed, so it looks good on its own. Also, by installing the radiator on the outside of the case, we can take advantage of the cooler air. The interior of the case is sure to be hotter than the room's air temperature, and the radiator will perform much better on the outside. The radiator we will use is shown in Figure 2-1.

HEADS UP!

The easiest thing to forget when you are installing this type of system is that you will need to have pipes running water to all the components. Make sure you leave room for the pipes.

Figure 2-1 Radiator for water-cooling system

The fact that the can is completely sealed except for the gas cap area makes it impossible to physically test-fit parts without opening the case up. So, to make it easier to design the case, we will make two cuts before we settle on a final configuration. These cuts are the motherboard cutout and the window cutout (which are discussed in detail in the following two sections). By cutting these holes, we will have plenty of room to move around inside the case and test-fit the other components.

The motherboard placement is the easiest decision. The gas can has rounded walls and a rounded top, so having a side installation would not look very good. There is only one place to put the motherboard: in the bottom of the can.

TIPS OF THE TRADE

Window Safety

Although the rule "bigger is better" applies to windows, don't ruin the integrity of your case. Our can is made out of steel and is welded into one piece, so it is safe to cut a big window into it. If your enclosure has several pieces, try checking the construction of the enclosure before you start. You don't want it to fall apart before you finish your system!

Window placement can be the easiest part of planning your case mod. As a rule of thumb, the bigger the window you put in, the happier you will be with the results. Small windows are hard to install and don't provide much of a view of the inner workings of your system. With this in mind, our recommendation is to put the biggest window possible on your case.

Before we actually cut the case, let's talk about the variety of case cutting tools out there. There are a lot of options, so let's see what we are going to use, and why.

Case Cutting Tools

Case cutting seems like a scary thing to people who fear making a mistake. In reality, case cutting is not very difficult as long as you plan ahead. The process can be very slow at times. In a sense this is good, because when you proceed slowly, there is less chance you will make a mistake.

When we cut this case, we will generally use two different cutting tools. The primary tool we will use is an electric jigsaw. This tool is fast and efficient, and poses little risk of slipping and putting an ugly scratch on your case.

The other tool that we like to use is a nibbler, a hand-held tool that "nibbles" or "bites" a small piece of metal each time. The nibbler is painfully slow to use, but will easily give you a nice, straight cut. As a side benefit, your grip will get stronger with prolonged use. The slowness of the nibbler forces you to take your time, and reduces the chance that you will make a mistake. The number-one benefit of a nibbler, however, is the price. A router, jigsaw, or Dremel® will easily cost you $50 or more, and the cutting bits may not be included. The nibbler rings up at an affordable $10. If you will have no use for the power tools after you complete your mod, the nibbler is the right choice for you.

In addition to the nibbler and the electric jigsaw, we also have a pair of tin snips and a Dremel handy. Tin snips are heavy-duty scissors that can cut metal and are great for making quick cuts. We use the Dremel, which is good for small details and highly maneuverable, for deburring holes and straightening cuts.

You don't need all these tools to mod your case—each one has distinct advantages and disadvantages. The nibbler is cheap and accurate, yet slow; the tin snips are effective but not good for detailed work; the Dremel is easy to get into tight places, but can slip and mar your case easily; and the jigsaw and router are fast but cannot get into small places.

Cutting the Opening for the Motherboard Tray

Before we talked about the tools, we mentioned that we were going to cut the motherboard tray opening and window hole as an intermediary step before determining the final configuration of components inside the case. We're going to use a Lian Li PC-30 motherboard tray, shown in Figure 2-2. A motherboard tray is the piece of metal that you attach your motherboard to. Most motherboard trays are permanently attached to the case. This one is designed to be removable, which makes it a great component for our system, because otherwise it would be very hard to service the motherboard after installing the entire system. Normal cases have doors, making a removable motherboard tray less important. Our case is anything but normal—it is airtight. If we want to add a stick of RAM, we will want to remove the motherboard tray from the gas can completely. By using a removable motherboard tray, we will not have to remove the window or create an access door.

Figure 2-2
Lian Li PC-30 motherboard tray

To install the motherboard, we have to cut out most of the bottom of the gas can. We want the opening to be the perfect size so that the motherboard doesn't shift around. It needs to be held firmly in place. The first step is to cut a slot in the bottom of the gas can that is exactly as tall and wide as the motherboard tray. We are using the electric jigsaw to cut the slot because it is good for nice, straight lines.

The best template for the hole is the motherboard tray itself. Place the motherboard tray against the bottom of the can so that it rests on the curved walls. Trace around the tray with a pencil.

HEADS UP!

Before you start cutting, put on protective eyewear. Whether you are dealing with plastic or metal, shavings are hazardous. If one gets in your eye, your eye could get painfully scratched, or you could suffer a permanent injury.

In addition to the protective eyewear, we highly recommend that you perform your cuts on a flat surface that is easy to clean, such as the concrete slab floor of a garage. This will make it easy to clean up the metal shavings using a vacuum cleaner. Metal shavings easily get embedded into the sole of your shoes and get carried around your house, where they can damage things or be a health risk. We vacuumed our work area (including the inside of the can) after every cut was finished.

The next step is to drill a starter hole. Using an electric drill, we cut a hole in the area that is going to be removed from the case so that we have a place to start the jigsaw blade. When you use a jigsaw or a nibbler, a starter hole is required, since neither tool can create the hole on its own. Routers and Dremels are capable of starting their own cut because of how they operate.

HEADS UP!

To make things easy, drill the edge of the starter hole so that it touches the line you are going to cut.

In this case, we drill a hole that is exactly as wide as the slot we want to cut. Then we carefully cut along our pencil line using the jigsaw. The jigsaw does not reach the corners, so we use the tin snips to cut as close as possible and bend the edges back into the case. The cutting of the motherboard slot is shown in Figure 2-3.

Figure 2-3
Cutting the motherboard slot

Next we fit the motherboard into the slot we just cut. When we slide it all the way into the slot, we see that the frame around the PCI brackets is obviously too big. We expected this, because of our test fitting. We can resolve the problem by drilling out the rivets that hold on the external frame. This will decrease the footprint significantly.

Now the tray is completely inserted into the gas can, and the PCI slots are flush with the bottom wall of the can. Once again, using a pencil, we outline the area where the back plate and PCI slots need to go. After removing the motherboard tray, we start cutting again with the jigsaw and the tin snips. The top-right corner is still keeping the tray from sliding all the way in. To make it smaller, we first nip off the top-right corner with a pair of tin snips. Next we turn our attention to the main motherboard tray, which still has to be lowered a few millimeters. The way this tray is constructed, all four edges of the tray are folded down at a right angle. The motherboard actually rests on these folded-down edges. To drop the tray a few more millimeters, bend these edges up underneath the tray. Now the motherboard tray fits perfectly—it's a snug fit, and it doesn't rattle in the case. The motherboard tray looks perfect, as if it were always meant to be there.

Our motherboard tray is very snug, so we've avoided having to further secure the tray. You may have to make a retention clip if your tray is loose. This can be done by bending a piece of scrap metal into a "c" shape and riveting it to the case. Then the tip of the tray can be caught under the clip.

Any time you cut metal, make sure you remove the metal burrs and dull down the sharp edge you just created. These edges can give you a nasty gash. The best tool for doing this is a special deburring tool. It makes the deburring process quick and painless. We don't have one of those in our toolbox, so we will use the Dremel to sand down the edge to make it safe.

After you have finished deburring, test-fit the motherboard tray again. After some trial and error, we were able to tweak it so it fit just right. The result is shown in Figure 2-4.

Figure 2-4 Motherboard tray installed

Cutting the Window Hole

The second big cut is the window. After this, we can plan out the rest of our case. Our case window is going to be relatively small compared to many case windows, because the gas can is relatively small—a standard ATX motherboard barely fits in it.

It would be difficult to find a store-bought window kit that is the perfect size and shape, so we are going to create our own custom window. This is very easy to do. To start, you need to determine the shape of the window you want—we are going to have a window that is almost a perfect square. Although we could use a round window, a lot of viewing area would be lost, and bigger is better. Square windows are also much easier to cut and install.

TIPS OF THE TRADE

Hip to Be Square

The primary purpose of putting a window into your case is to allow people to see the interior of the case. Square windows are usually the best because they have the most viewing area.

If you prefer to have a windowpane that is another shape (triangle, round, oval), the window will tend to distract attention from the rest of your rig. As long as you want your window to be the center of attention, this is fine, but we want the inside of our case to be what people really notice—we want the actual window itself to take a back seat to the rest of the design, since our rig has so much else to look at.

Now that we have decided the shape for our window, we need to decide where on the case we want to put the window. Both sides of our gas can have the letter X indented into them, which is very common for this type of can. This makes the metal uneven, and makes a window installation harder.

The most obvious thing to do is to make our window larger than the X. By taking some quick measurements, we realize that to remove the X, the size of the windowpane has to be roughly 9×10 inches. Now that we have established the size, we are ready to measure it out on the case and then cut it out.

HEADS UP!

You don't have to make the acrylic windowpane exactly the right size. As long as you get the window approximately the right size, it will still work, because the windowpane will define the size of the hole that you cut.

Using a right angle, which has a ruler on it, we quickly sketch out the basic square shape of the window on a piece of bulk acrylic. We recommend that you use a corner of the acrylic, so that two sides are precut for you. You know that they will be straight, and it will save time.

Bulk acrylic usually comes in 4×8-foot sheets, but, fortunately, Lowe's hardware store sells precut pieces in several different-sized squares. You won't find a good selection of colored acrylic, but otherwise Lowe's selection is very good. Our acrylic is ¼-inch thick.

Now it is time to trace the rounded corners, which can create problems with your mod if you don't design them correctly because a rubber strip, usually called window molding, holds the windowpane in the hole you are going to cut. If the corner radius is too tight, the molding will not lie flat, and will buckle. We happen to have lots of extra acrylic windowpanes lying around to use as a template, but if you don't have another window to use as a template, find a jar or can that is four inches from rim to rim. Place this on the acrylic where the corner needs to go, and trace around one-quarter of the way. Do this in all four corners.

If you've traced everything correctly, you should have a piece of bulk acrylic with a square traced on it, with rounded corners. Acrylic is easy to cut, and the electric jigsaw works like a dream on acrylic as well as metal. Acrylic comes with protective backing to keep it from getting scratched; this also helps prevent the acrylic from cracking as you cut it.

After you cut your acrylic windowpane, you can use it to trace the opening on the case. The double-sided molding requires about a quarter inch of clearance. It is called "double-sided" because it has a slot on one side for the metal of the case, and a slot on the other side for the acrylic pane.

TIPS OF THE TRADE

Ask for Grommet

Molding is a slang case-modding term for grommet. If you are looking for a molding supplier near you, ask for rubber grommet—otherwise you might get a blank stare. Molding normally comes in black, but you can find it in translucent, blue, red, or green.

To provide the quarter inch of clearance that we need, the easiest thing to do is to use a round metal washer to trace around the acrylic window pane. We purchased a bag of washers for less than $1 at a hardware store (they were marked #8). It is important to make sure the acrylic windowpane is exactly where you want it and that it does not slip while you are tracing. The best thing to do is to hold the windowpane down firmly with one hand and then place the washer next to the pane with your other hand. Then put the pencil inside the washer (see Figure 2-5) and carefully trace along all four sides, skipping the corners.

HEADS UP!

You may find that the washer slips under the window frequently. If this is the case, try stacking three washers on top of the pencil tip.

You can now see why we recommend a custom window. The acrylic isn't hard to cut, and you can use any shape that you can trace on the case, as long as you get the corners right.

After you have traced all four sides of the windowpane, go back and trace the corners of the pane. The most important thing is to not get lazy with the tracing—try to make sure that you are always at the shortest point between the washer and the pane. Don't ride up on the sides of the washer as you get to the end of your trace. If you do, your lines will not be straight. Use your trusty jigsaw to cut out the window hole after you drill a starter hole for the blade.

Don't forget to deburr the hole! You're going to install a window in a few minutes, and if you slip you don't want to get cut.

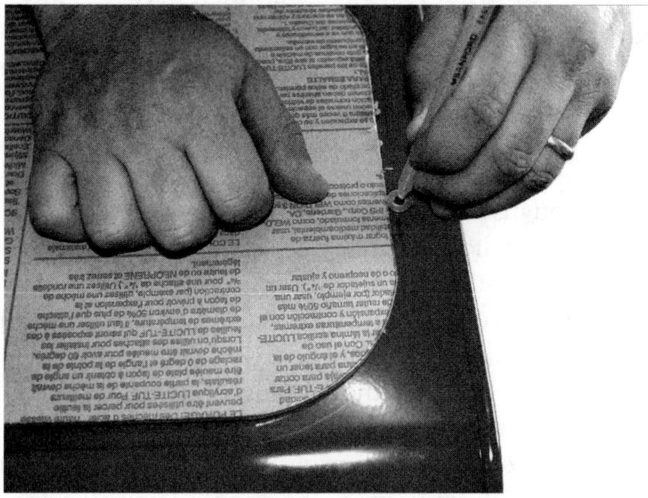

Figure 2-5 Tracing around the windowpane

HEADS UP!

Before you start, you may want to put masking tape around the hole. We're going to do this on our case because we received the case with a nice, glossy red paint job. By putting masking tape around the hole, we can prevent the jigsaw from scratching the paint, and we won't have to repaint the case later.

If you've never installed a case window before, this next step can be the most frustrating. With the hole for the window finished, pick up your windowpane and molding and get ready to learn how to install a window in a computer case. Molding is very difficult to use the first time. Many new modders swear that perfectly good molding is faulty, not realizing that the true problem is that they don't yet have the skill to install the window. If the window hole is too big, the pane will simply fall out. If the window hole is too small, you will never get the molding in. This is why you have to be precise when you trace the windowpane and make the cut.

Always start by suspending the pane in the window hole to see how much clearance it has. There shouldn't be much space between the pane and the metal.

Before you make any changes to the hole you just cut, you should try to install the window to see how difficult it is. It is very hard to judge this the first time you do it—it always seems harder than it should be. In fact, if you have never installed a window using molding in your life, it may be a good idea for you to try it on another case (or piece of scrap metal) before you try it on your supermodded rig.

After we go over some techniques, we'll talk about your options if you didn't cut it right.

Stick one hand in the motherboard hole and use your other hand on top of the window pane to feed the molding in; try to gradually massage the molding in. The first half of the window installation will be the hardest part. After you get more than half of the molding in, and it's still holding together, the rest is a little easier to get in.

It is much easier to install a window in a case door than in a gas can. When you install a window in a case door, you put the door on a table and use the table to help hold the molding and window in place. This works because the molding that is massaged between the pane and the door is compressed against the table. Here we are trying to install a window that is floating in midair, so it is much more difficult. It may be best to get another person to help you. With two people trying to install the window, one person holds the window in place while the other person slips the molding in.

Not sure where to get started? Start at the bottom of the window and put one end of the molding in the middle. Cover the entire corner of the window cut with the molding, and slip the pane into its groove. Continue to push the pane into the groove as you work the molding around the window pane, slipping it between the acrylic and the case. You are forcing the molding to compress as it slips through the tiny gap between the acrylic and the metal. Make sure that the molding goes completely through and lies flat on the other side of the pane.

The first half of the window installation is the hardest part. After you get the first half of the window in, stop trying to push the windowpane into the molding on the side, and worry more about keeping the windowpane from moving up or down. You'll feel like you are working against your helper as they squeeze in the molding.

After enough tries, you will get the window in (we promise) and it will be very snug. If you do it perfectly, you will not even need the locking strip that comes with most molding. The locking strip is included to allow you to fill the groove on the other side of the molding, but on a good installation, the molding is so tight that the locking strip is unnecessary.

Fixing a Bad Cut

What if you didn't cut the window right? Well, you aren't the first. If the window is just way too tight, you may have to make the window hole slightly larger using a dremel or a rasp. Most people think that the window is too tight when it's not, so don't jump the gun. If the window falls out easily after it is installed, you've made the hole too big. You don't have to get a new gas can; you just have to cut a piece of acrylic that is slightly larger. Whether the hole is too big or too small, you should have been able to tell that you were going to have trouble when you suspended the windowpane in the hole without the molding being there.

HEADS UP!

Be very careful about using any solvents to lubricate the window. Some alcohol-based solutions will make your window brittle and it will crack. And anything that helps the window go in will also help the window to pop back out. We do not recommend using a lubricant during installation.

Now you have proven that the window cut was made correctly, which can only be proven by installing the window. Unfortunately, we can't leave the window in because we need the opening we just cut to help us to do more of the work on the case. So you should carefully remove the window by applying pressure to the center of it and pulling the molding out. If you just spent 45 minutes installing it, you might think this is crazy, but you don't want to have to fix your window cut later after you've put in the components.

By cutting the motherboard tray and window holes, we have made it enormously easier to work inside the case. This is one of the few situations in which putting a window in is almost required. Without a window, installing the rest of the hardware would be extremely difficult.

Installing the Rest of the Components

It's time to finalize where the rest of the components will go. These components include the radiator, hard drive, water pump, DVD-ROM drive, and power supply. We had a very good idea where they would all go before we cut the holes, but now we can actually put the components in place to see how they relate to each other.

We have already decided to put the radiator outside the case, where it will be more efficient at cooling the water because it is surrounded by fresh air. After considering several placements, we elected to put the radiator on top of the gas can handles. This also allows us to show off the water-cooling aspect of the case by having the water tubes go out of the gas cap. This will make the case extremely eye-catching.

One of the things that made this decision much easier is that our radiator, a Black Ice model supplied by Wahoo Computers, arrived chromed, so it will look very nice mounted outside the case.

In addition, by moving the radiator outside of the case, we have more room inside the case to put the rest of the parts. We'll discuss in more detail later how the radiator will be attached, when we install our water-cooling system.

The rest of the components are slated to go inside the case. In the next pages, we will discuss the final locations we chose for our DVD player, water pump, and hard drive.

DVD Player Installation: Phase One

In this project, the DVD player provides the biggest placement challenge because it is long and square. The DVD player actually is a perfect fit horizontally. Unfortunately, the corners of the gas can are rounded, so the DVD player doesn't fit flush to the front of the case horizontally—we wouldn't be able to reach the DVD after we hit the eject button.

To mount the front of the DVD player flush to the wall, we have to turn it vertically. When we do this, it becomes obvious that the best spot would be on the front of the can, where we could easily access the DVD.

Mounting the DVD player requires a lot more creativity. The DVD player has to be installed in such a way that it "floats" in the middle of the case. The only way to accomplish this is to create a custom bracket to hold the DVD player.

After some research, the best solution we found is to mount the DVD player directly onto the motherboard. This is accomplished by using some one-inch standoffs and a custom bracket. The four standoffs that will hold up the drive are from an acrylic case kit, but they are available separately as spare parts on some web sites.

While the standoffs hold the DVD player up, there still is no way to attach the DVD player to the standoffs. Using some scrap Lian Li aluminum, which is light and easy to work with, we were able to fashion a bracket, shown in Figure 2-6, that will hold the DVD player. This required some measuring, marking, bending, and cutting.

Figure 2-6
Custom DVD player bracket

When we bent the bracket into a U shape to hold the DVD player, we bent the far side of the bracket (as seen from the bottom of the can) over the top of the DVD player. This way it clips over the top of the DVD player. By putting this "lip" on the far side, we only have to screw in the one side of the DVD player. We attached the bracket to the standoffs with screws. These standoffs have a male end and a female end. Now our DVD player is ready to be installed securely in the case.

DVD Player Installation: Phase Two

Phase one of the DVD player installation is now complete. We have a nice, secure mounting surface for our DVD player where none existed before. To finish the DVD player installation, we need to modify the case to accommodate the slot for the DVDs and the eject button to eject the DVD.

The slot in which to insert and eject DVDs is going to be cut right into the case. As we mentioned, the DVD player is a slot loader, not a drawer loader, so the case will look much cleaner.

This is the most painstaking cut that we have to make on the case. If the cut is a little high or a little low, the slot effect will be ruined. When you find yourself in this situation, measure everything twice.

The first step in the measuring process is to put the DVD player into the bracket and slide the motherboard tray in. Then, using your pencil, trace a line on the inside of the can wall, around the top and sides of the DVD-ROM housing. Next remove the motherboard tray and DVD player.

Next we need to find out how far down the slot is from the top of the DVD player, so that we can cut the slot in the case at the same height as the slot on the DVD player. We won't need the plastic bezel on the front of the DVD drive, because the DVD will be almost completely hidden. There are four little teeth that hold it on, and by pushing these in and popping off the bezel, we now have a faceless DVD player. We measure the distance between the top of the DVD-ROM drive and the loading slot. In this case, it is half an inch.

To make sure that the slot is in the right place, we measure half an inch below the pencil line on the inside of the gas can, and drill a starter hole.

Now is the time when the nibbler really shines, as shown in Figure 2-7. Coincidentally, the nibbler is about ¼-inch wide, and this is a good width to make our slot. We use a ¼-inch drill bit to make the hole, but the hole is round and the nibbler head is square, and we can't put a square peg in a round hole. The answer to this dilemma is the Dremel, with a metal routing bit. The Dremel is small enough and maneuverable enough to square off the corners of the round hole so that the nibbler will fit in.

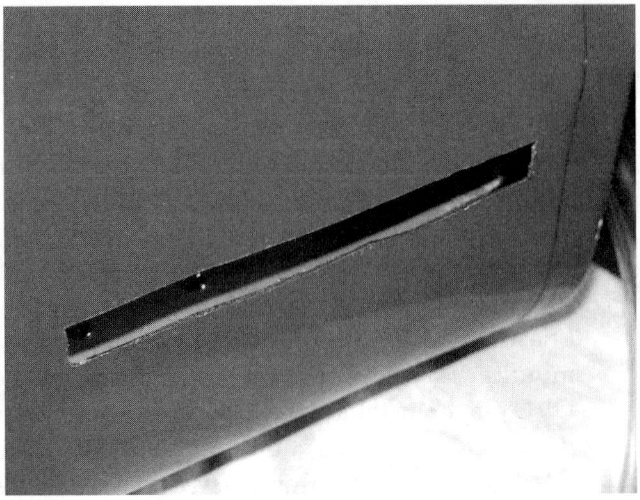

Figure 2-7
DVD slot being cut

To make sure that everything is done correctly, slide the motherboard tray with the DVD drive back into the computer. Push the DVD drive back half an inch. You don't need to worry too much about shavings damaging your components, because the nibbler cuts much larger pieces of metal at a time. So, starting with the square hole, use the nibbler to cut all the way to the left and right, using the DVD player on the inside of the case as a guide. The nibbler will cut a straight line very well, but you must make sure that the nibbler's cutting bit is pushed flat against the metal it is cutting, or watch the flat head to make sure it is even. It is slow work, but you will have a nice, clean, ¼-inch slot when you are done.

HEADS UP!

Bare metal edges do not look professional and are a safety hazard. To make the case look better and reduce the possibility of getting a cut when using the DVD player, use rubber-edge molding around the DVD slot. This will also help cover up any minor cutting blemishes.

Things are really moving right along now. The last challenge we have with the DVD player is to figure out how to accommodate the eject button. But aren't we forgetting something? What about the volume knob and other controls? Although these might be useful to some people, we don't intend to use these controls, so we have no plans to make it possible to use them. We think that the multiple controls will clutter the appearance of the case and make it less appealing, and because we intend to use only the eject button and are building this case from scratch, we can tailor it to our needs.

There are four options with the eject button. First, we could cut a hole over it and use our pinky finger to press it. We do not like this design because people would be able to see the gray button through the hole. The second option is to use the eject command in our file management program to open the drive. To do this, we would open Windows Explorer, right-click the DVD player icon, and choose Eject. While this is a nice option, it is really more difficult than we would like, even if we create a hot key for it. The third option is to use a program to open it. There is some freeware available on the Internet that will allow you to control basic functions of your CD/DVD player from your system tray. All of these options have their advantages and disadvantages. We're all about modding our case, so we will be doing something different.

To be able to understand what we are going to do next, it's time to do one of our favorite things—void a warranty! Take the DVD player and cut through the warning sticker and remove all four screws on the bottom. You can see that the switch to open the drive has four connections to the DVD player's main PCB (printed circuit board). This kind of switch is called a momentary switch. A good example of a momentary switch is a doorbell—when you press it in, it makes the doorbell ring and automatically resets itself when you let go. By wiring in a line to the momentary switch on the board, we can have a remote switch that will open our DVD-ROM drive, as shown in Figure 2-8.

Figure 2-8 Hacking the DVD player's main PCB

We're going to go over the exact wiring in Chapter 5, since we are really working on cutting the case right now. We have to cut a hole for the remote switch before we can move on with our project.

Using parts from other computers is a foundation of our project, and we are going to use a small black rocker switch for our momentary switch. This black rocker switch is very thin, and came from a PCI switch for a cold cathode unit. This isn't a true momentary switch, but it will make and break the connection and thus will work. The best thing about it is that it is very small yet has a nice, OEM look to it.

Next we have to find a suitable location for the switch. We can put this switch anywhere we want on the case, and our preference is for the switch to be on top of the case. So, the switch will go right next to the gas cap on the can. The switch is only ¼-inch wide, so we are going to follow the same procedure that we followed for the DVD slot. We'll start with a quarter-inch hole, then square it off with the Dremel, and lastly cut the slot to length with the nibbler. Once again, you may want to tape off the area around the proposed switch hole to avoid scratching the paint (see Figure 2-9).

Figure 2-9 Cutting the switch hole

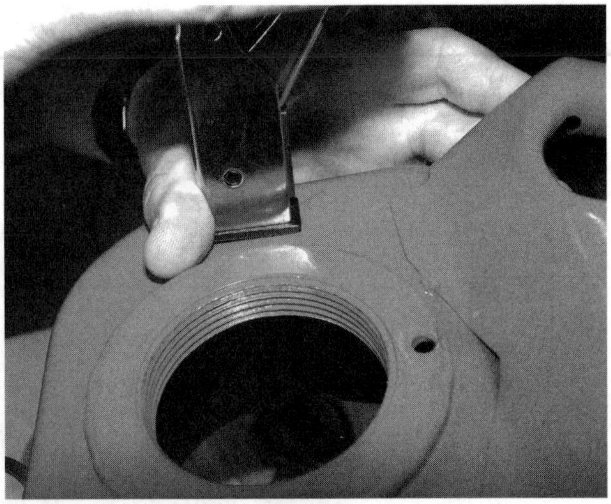

HEADS UP!

The last thing you want is a loose switch, so test-fit the switch almost every step of the way. By testing it after every nibble or two, the switch snaps into place tightly and firmly.

Water Pump Installation

The gas can has a nice shape for our water-cooled system. Because the can rises up in the back, there is a wonderful place to hide any components that we don't want people to see. We really don't want people to see the water pump, which is manufactured by Eheim, because it isn't customized and doesn't look very high-tech.

The location we've selected for the water pump is in the top of the case, with the rear of the pump shoved up into the concealed corner. The inflow is then facing the main processor, and the outflow is facing the DVD drive slot.

There are many ways we could attach the water pump, and we're going to choose a way that not many people use. Rivets are the most under-used fastener in case modding, but they are really enjoyable to work with (see Figure 2-10). There are several reasons for this. First, the finished product has a very OEM look to it—a rivet looks better than a flathead screw, for example. Second, the rivet is removable—all we have to do is drill through it, like we drilled through the motherboard tray rivets. If we were to glue the water pump to the case, we wouldn't have to drill any holes, but it might be much harder to remove if we ever needed to. The last reason to use rivets is that a handheld rivet gun costs only about $20, is easy to use, and is faster than using a screw and nut assembly. Rivets are a semipermanent installation, and we'll explain more about how to use them shortly.

Figure 2-10
Riveting the water pump to the case

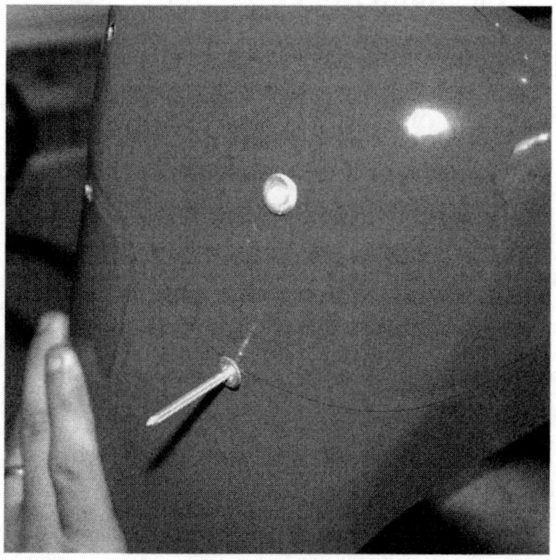

The important thing is to get rivets that are the size of the screw slot. The way that the rivet will fasten is that it will bulge out at the end that is inside the case. If the bulge isn't big enough, the water pump will simply fall off. Test-fit several different size rivets into the water pumps bracket. After you know what size rivet you are going to use, select a drill bit that is exactly the size of your rivet. In this project, we are using 3mm rivets, but the size you need may be different. The rivet gun we are using came with a package of assorted rivets. If you need to buy rivets, we suggest you buy six or so of the size that you need.

Before we can continue, we first have to remove a thin tube that's in the top of the can. The tube is there to allow air to enter the can when gas is being poured out. This air intake helps the gas to pour smoothly, without the can gulping air. It's welded to the top of the case, but by flexing it back and forth, the tube snaps off of the weld spot without much resistance.

With the way cleared, we can start marking off the holes for the water pump rivets. The first hole is the most critical. With all the other hardware out of the can, hold the water pump into place by hand. Then, in one of the screw slots that the water pump has, make a mark with your pencil. Remove the pump and drill the hole out using a small bit.

Now hold the pump up to the outside of the can, mirroring where it would be on the inside. Mark off the three other holes with your pencil and drill them out. You are ready to rivet the pump to the side of the case.

If you plan to paint your case, do not rivet the water pump in at this time, unless you want the rivet heads to be painted too. If that case, make sure you protect the pump from overspray.

Push the head of the rivet (the end with the ball on it) into the case. If you push all four rivets in, the water pump should hang on without a problem. It helps to have a second person hold the water pump in place to make sure it doesn't slip.

TIPS OF THE TRADE

Use a Washer

The water pump is made of plastic, which can bend under the pressure of the rivet. To provide an extra level of security, put a washer on the end of each rivet. This eliminates the possibility of the plastic weakening and the pump falling off.

With the water pump, rivets, and washers in place, it's time to secure the pump. Place the rivet gun over the "nail" portion, which is sticking out of the can, and ratchet the handle down. You want it to be nice and tight, so release the rivet after each stroke so you can reseat the gun to get it tighter. After three strong pulls, the "nail" portion of the rivet will break off, leaving the rivet tight and secure. Do this with all four rivets. The finished product looks great and is extremely secure, as shown in Figure 2-11.

Figure 2-11
The water pump, riveted into place

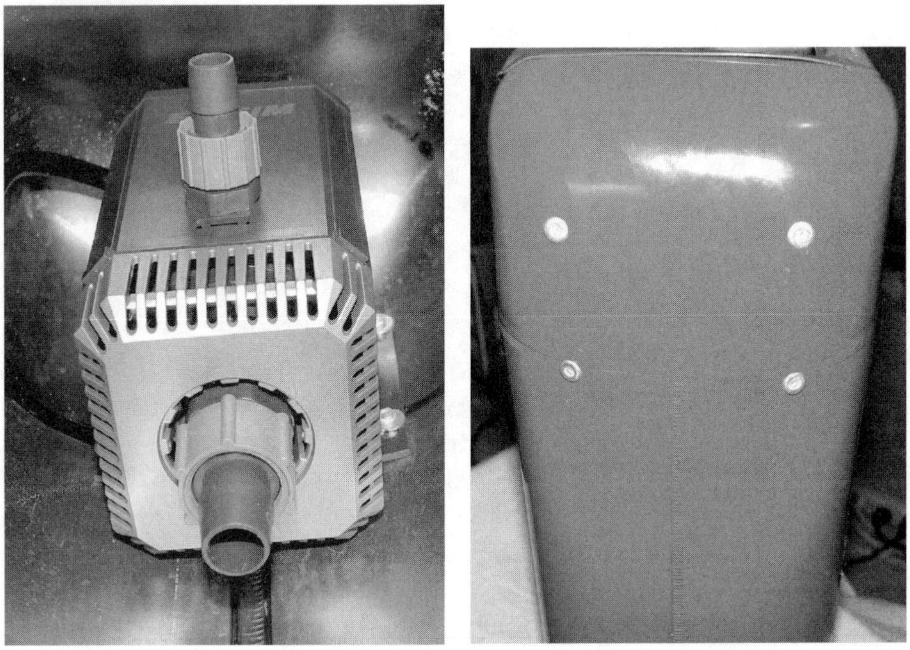

Hard Drive Installation

For the hard drive, we are going to cheat again. As discussed, we are going to use a laptop hard drive. One of the reasons we have decided to do this is that the case is extremely cramped on space. Laptop hard drives don't use standard IDE cables, so we have an adapter that will make it compatible with IDE. This allows us to use one dual-device IDE cable for both the HDD and DVD player.

HEADS UP!

When buying electronics equipment, look at the board you are buying. If it's a quality product, there will be no wires attached directly to the PCB. All wires should terminate into a socket that can plug into a receptacle on the board. The adapter we are using is not of very good quality because the wires attach directly, as shown in Figure 2-12. We will use it anyway, as it is the only adapter that was available.

Figure 2-13
Laptop hard drive to IDE adapter card

We have the same problem with our hard drive that we had with our DVD player—we have to create a place to put it. Our standoffs worked remarkably well with the DVD drive, and they will work even better with the laptop hard drive. The laptop hard drive has screw holes in the bottom four corners, and our standoffs were made, coincidentally, with hard drive threads. So the standoffs will attach right to the bottom of the hard drive with no problem whatsoever. There will be no need for a bracket.

To finish fixing the hard drive on the motherboard, we place it where it will go, trace around the standoffs, and drill four holes for the screws to go through. Now our motherboard tray is starting to look cluttered, as shown in Figure 2-13.

Figure 2-12
HDD installed on motherboard

Cutting Holes for the Water Pipes

As we mentioned earlier, the radiator is on top of the case, and everything else is inside, so we need to find a way to pipe the water in and out. We decided early on that the water pipes would come out of the gas cap, side by side, and arc up to the radiator intakes near the back of the case. This is a signature element of the case, and will be an eye catcher.

The tygon tubes that we will be using are surprisingly big. They are about one inch in diameter. These tubes do not kink easily, which is good, because a kink in your tubes can fry your chip. The drill bit we need to use to cut these holes in the gas cap is very large—it's a little over one inch in diameter.

HEADS UP!

To keep the drill bit from traveling away from the spot where you want to cut the hole, create a dimple using a punch and a hammer. The drill bit will be more likely to stay put when you first start drilling the hole.

The metal of the gas cap is by far the thickest metal we've cut yet, and it takes a sharp drill bit to get through. The best way to cut the cap is to tighten it on the can, and then have someone hold the can very tightly while you drill. When the drill bit first starts going through, it will tend to bind and make the can "spin," so make sure you have it tightly secured! Don't forget to deburr the metal around the holes so that they don't cut you later. The finished product is shown in Figure 2-14.

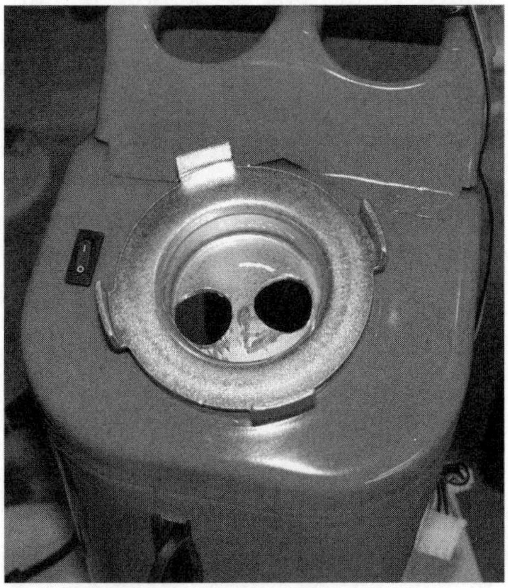

Figure 2-14 Gas cap with holes in it

Wrapping Up the Details

The majority of our cutting, drilling, and riveting is now finished! We've installed the DVD and hard drive onto extra space on the removable motherboard tray, we've riveted the water pump into the case, and we've cut a slot for the DVD and its switch.

Does it seem as though we have forgotten something? We never found a good location for the power supply—what we have on hand is a 300W Enermax 1U PSU. It's made for rack-mounted servers and is just over an inch tall. We selected it because of its low profile, hoping that it would fit in the case somewhere. It would fit in the case—either over the DVD drive or in the area of the water pump—but the case is getting very crowded and we don't want the view through the window to look cluttered. We had considered mounting this on the outside of the case—perhaps on the back or the side—and trying to make it look like a cyborg gas can, with wires and tubes coming out of it. But that also seems like it would be too cluttered.

In the end we have decided that the best option is to have the PSU be an external PSU, with a very similar look to that of most laptops. Specifically, the PSU will sit outside the case on the floor. There will be one cord leading up to it and one cord leading away. We're going to mod the PSU in Chapter 5.

Cleanup Time

The last step in any project is cleanup. If you haven't cleaned up as you worked, there are going to be shavings everywhere—inside the can, on your work bench, and all over the floor. Use a shop vacuum to clean up all the metal and acrylic bits. It may be necessary to wipe some surfaces clean with a damp disposable cloth. Our gas can was new, but it had an oily film on the inside that made the metal shavings stick to it. Cleaning up now will keep these shavings from accidentally getting into your computer hardware and wreaking havoc, as well as reduce your risk of personal injury.

TIPS OF THE TRADE

Chrome as a Special Touch

Chroming your case is a fantastic way to make your case stand out from the rest. Look in the yellow pages for companies that can chrome things for you. If we were to chrome this case, it would look great with the chromed radiator on top. Chroming isn't cheap: expect to pay a few hundred dollars to get the job done right. But it isn't common either, and if you are looking for a special touch to distinguish your case from the rest, this may be a great option for you.

TESTING 1-2-3

- ❑ Now that we have finished all of the prepping to the case, there is one final decision to be made. In the process of cutting your case, you may have scratched it, or maybe your case is old, dented, and rusty.
- ❑ This would be an excellent time to paint the case. Our case is already painted a stunning fire-engine red, so we won't be painting it. When painting your case, there are several concerns, including having paint scratch easily or chip off. If you are not knowledgeable about painting, it may be better to find a small paint and body shop and see if they will paint it for cheap.

Chapter 3

Building the Water Window

Tools of the Trade

Syringe
Dremel
Some books or other heavy objects
Two soft cloths
Jigsaw
Pencil
Scissors
1/8-inch vinyl hose (air tubing)
Plumber's waterproof epoxy/adhesive
A sharp screw
An inline coupler
A small aquarium pump
Water additive
Some newspaper

When you are building a supercase, it's important to find a theme for the case and stick to it. For example, your theme may be an H.R. Giger case—you may choose to decorate it in the style of your favorite first-person shooter (game), or you may use a chromed motif. The important thing is to make sure that all elements of your theme tie together. If you do this correctly, the whole theme is often cooler than the sum of the individual mods.

For our case, we started with a gas can, which defined our theme. We then modded it to be able to add a water-cooling system. Our next step is to add a water window to the case.

What is a water window? This is an obscure mod that is rarely seen. Recently, a manufacturer came out with an aquarium panel as a part for its case, complete with plastic fish. Plastic fish are amusing, just like the "duck pond" game at carnivals, but "amusing" is not what we are shooting for. We want to give the impression that the "gasoline" inside our case is boiling out of control, and may blow up violently at any moment! This effect will tie in very well with our overall theme.

In this chapter, we are going to demonstrate how to make your own custom water window from scratch, for any size case that you need. We will start with a regular window, mod it to be able to hold water, add a bubbling effect to it, and install it in our case.

Inspecting the Parts

You may have noticed from our parts list that we now are installing a second pump inside the case. While this may seem redundant, it is not: one pump pushes the water through the cooling system while the other pump pushes the air through the water window. We are creating two different systems in the case, and we can't mix the two.

One thing that we were tempted to do was to use the water window as a reservoir for the water-cooling system. Reservoirs make it easy to bleed the air out of the water-cooling system, and to keep them topped off. The biggest reason we didn't do this was because of space constraints. You don't want to have any air in your water-cooling lines, and the window is very small. Because of this, we couldn't create a "tank" that would keep the bubbles away from the air line. Using a water window as a reservoir would be very neat, and we encourage you to give it a try.

Building the Window Reservoir

The main task in building a water window is to create a reservoir that will hold the water. If you do not build a waterproof reservoir, any leaks that develop are sure to create serious problems for your computer. This is not a mod for the weak of heart.

The basic concept of this mod is to create a reservoir that looks like a sandwich. On the front and back there will be ¼-inch acrylic. In the middle will be sandwiched tubing that will act as a gasket. This will prevent leaks, as well as provide our bubbling effect.

Once again, our can appears to be slightly too small to install such a device. This time, however, the culprit of the space problem is new. We installed our window kit as a test fit after we cut our window hole. To be able to see how much space we would have, we installed the window and all of the electronic components to see how much clearance we had. Because we included our components this time, we had our nice, fast 128MB video card to contend with. This card is so large that it only left approximately half an inch between the windowpane and the top of the video card. This means that our water window has to be less than ½-inch thick.

HEADS UP!

Test fitting is very important. When you are working with limited space, you will want to measure everything before you start. Plan ahead.

Cutting the Rear Wall of the Reservoir

To get started, we cut a matching piece of acrylic for the rear wall of the reservoir. We are going to do this by placing our existing window on a piece of bulk acrylic and tracing around it. After this is done, it's back to the jigsaw as we cut out another windowpane.

When we are cutting the pane, we have to make sure that it is cut as accurately as possible, on the inside of the line, if you can. If you use your thumb to help steady the jigsaw, as shown in Figure 3-1, this may help you considerably.

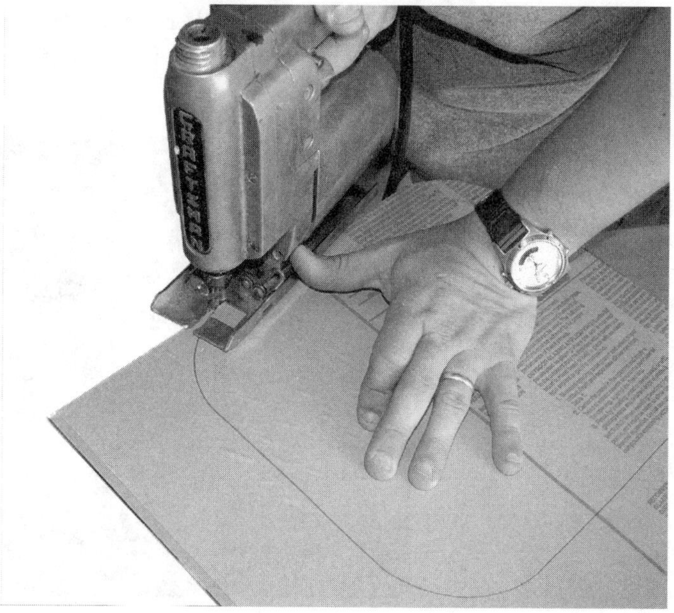

Figure 3-1 Steadying the jigsaw as it cuts

Once we are done cutting the rear wall of the reservoir, we pull the protective paper (or plastic) backing off of one side. We leave the protective backing on the other side until we are almost done with the mod. We do the same to the front wall of the reservoir—the window that we cut in Chapter 2.

HEADS UP!

Be very careful with the uncovered acrylic. The sides that are exposed are going to be on the inside of the reservoir and there will be no way to clean them when you seal it up. Make sure you don't leave fingerprints.

Now that we have two identical pieces of acrylic, we are ready to get started with the fun part.

Prepping the Water Window Air Line

The air line that came with the kit is going to be our main "gasket." We will compress the two acrylic panes on either side of the tube to create the basic reservoir. The air line will maintain the distance between the two panes of acrylic and keep it from collapsing; it will also provide the bubbling effect to the window as we pump air into it. It is the key to the success of the mod, so please treat it carefully. Before we can continue, we will have to prepare the air line to perform these various duties.

The first thing we have to do is to insert a plug into the end of the air line, so that the air will be forced out of the holes and into the water. We are going to accomplish this by squeezing a little bit of our plumber's epoxy into the end of the tube, as shown in Figure 3-2—but before you get started with the epoxy, you need to take some precautions.

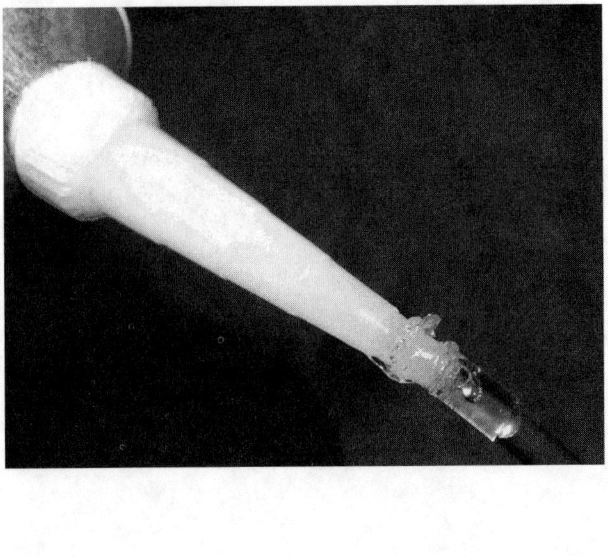

Figure 3-2
Creating a plug at the end of the airline

First, when using the epoxy, make sure you work in a well-ventilated area. It has a harsh odor, which can't be good for you to inhale. Second, not all sealants are the same, so be careful when you select one. Some strong adhesives can create a chemical reaction that melts some plastics.

TIPS OF THE TRADE

Epoxy Is not Super

Before using any sealant, test it on some scrap material first before you actually use it on your mod. Also, stay away from super glue–type products entirely. For this mod, you want to use a sticky, thick epoxy that will create a nice watertight seal.

Our plumber's epoxy, made by GOOP, was purchased at our local Lowe's hardware store. It is easy to use and is like many other epoxies in the way that it is applied. Unscrew the cap and break the seal on the tube. Then screw on the applicator. The applicator has a plug at the end—we'll cut this off with some scissors. The important thing to do here is to make sure that when you cut off the plug on the applicator, you cut off as little as possible. If you cut off too much of the applicator, it will be hard to inject the epoxy into the skinny little tube that we are using as an air line.

Squeeze in just enough of the epoxy to fill up about half an inch of the tubing. This epoxy will take 24 to 72 hours to cure completely, taking less time in warmer temperatures. You can expect it to start tacking up within an hour or so.

TIPS OF THE TRADE

Quick-Drying Tip

You can use an ordinary hair dryer, at low heat, to speed the drying time. We recommend only using it to speed the "tacking up" of the epoxy, and still allowing the epoxy to cure overnight.

Now it's time to lay out the tubing on the rear reservoir pane. Our tube seems to have kinks in all the right places. The bottom of the pane is on the right side of Figure 3-3. We have laid out the tubing so that it exits at the top of the window.

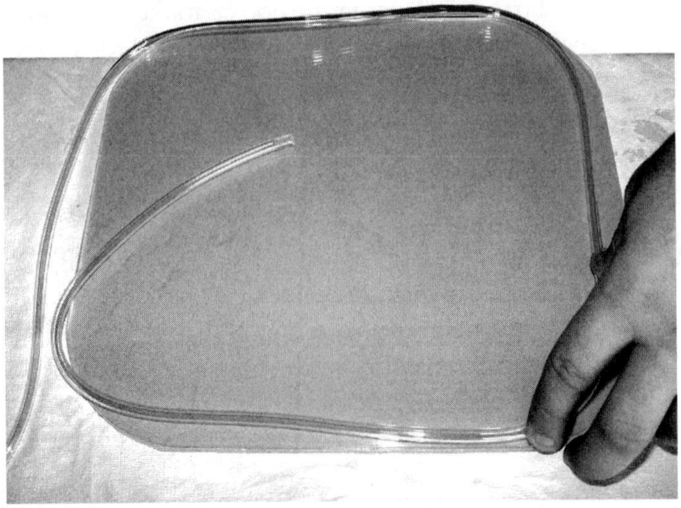

Figure 3-3
Laying out the tubing

Once you figure out where the bottom of the window is going, you can put holes in the tubing for the air bubbles to escape out of. Mark off the left and right side of the bottom of the tubing. The air bubble holes will be punched out between these marks.

Next take a screw (or other sharp implement) and start to punch holes every few millimeters in the hose. One every 3 to 4 millimeters is sufficient. There are two things that are very important with this step.

First, make sure you do not punch straight through the hose and create a leak on the other side. If necessary, angle the screw so that it is not pointing to the opposite wall. The opposite wall of your tubing (the outside wall) is going to be one of your defenses against the water getting into your case.

Second, make sure you punch the holes in a perfectly straight line, as shown in Figure 3-4. If you do not, then some of the holes may be covered by the window and not bubble correctly, which will make your water window look bad.

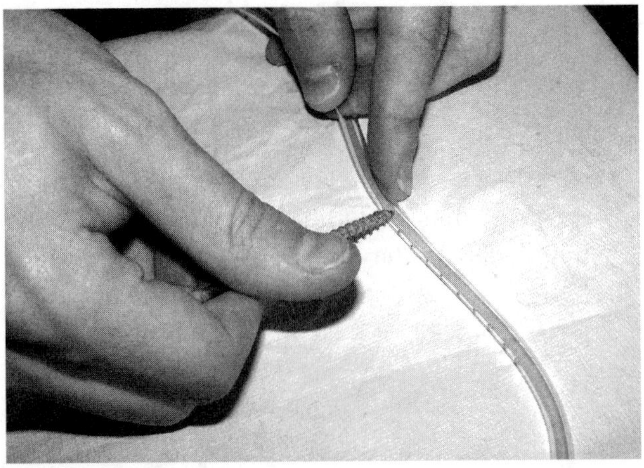

Figure 3-4
Punching out the bubble holes

When this is complete, the "bubble" part of the hose is ready to go. Before we rush into the installation, it's time for more testing! After we epoxy the window together, it will be impossible to go back and fix the holes, so we need to make sure we get them right before we move on.

Take the water pump and the hose, and find an aquatic testing chamber. In this case, we are using a recently vacated fishbowl, because it is clear. We can see what is going on very easily from the side. (We wouldn't be able to see whether it is working right if we were looking at it from the top down.) The important thing is to make sure that the tube can lie straight, so that the bubble holes are not kinked. You want to see exactly how it will look in the window.

It took several tries to get the holes just right. The vinyl resists being cut and tries to "heal" itself, so it may be necessary to turn the screw as you poke it in so that the holes it creates are more substantial. We want to have a steady flow of bubbles streaming out of our "air curtain," as shown in Figure 3-5.

Figure 3-5
Testing the air curtain

There is another device out on the market that you may want to use for the bubbles, which costs about $4 and is called a bubble curtain. We recommend the tube-style bubble curtains. These bubble curtains will give you very nice bubbles, and have the added advantage that they can be cut to size, but they are thicker than our vinyl tubing, so we could not use them in our mod. They are available at most better aquarium stores; you can easily make your own by punching holes in the vinyl tubing as we have done. You will have to use some vinyl tubing in your mod if you use a bubble curtain to connect all the parts.

Now that we have our bubble curtain prepared and tested, it's time to build the window.

Epoxying the Window Together

This is the critical part of the mod; we need to make sure that we cure the epoxy as required. We do not want to rush this section, because otherwise we may create flaws that allow the window to leak.

The vinyl tubing will not want to stay where you put it, so it will be necessary to "tack" it to the acrylic using some epoxy. Place the top of the reservoir in a safe place where it will not get scratched. Then, using your epoxy, start drawing a thin bead of epoxy down the first side of the acrylic window pane, as shown in Figure 3-6.

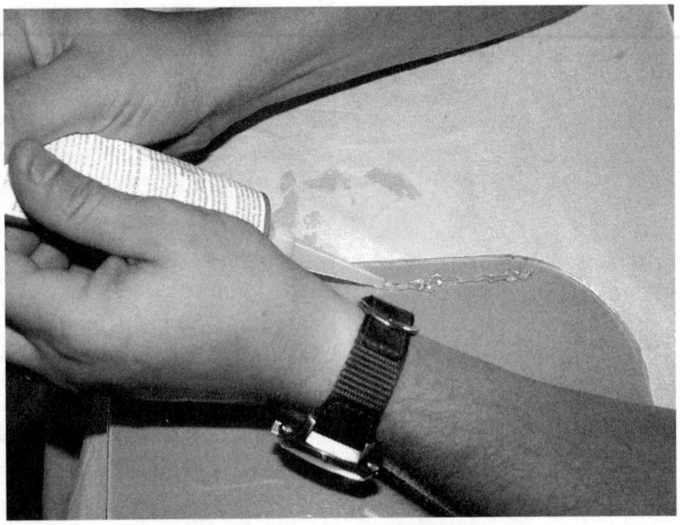

Figure 3-6
Starting the bead

How far in from the edge should you put the epoxy? This depends on what you are using to secure your window. We are using translucent molding (grommet). We need to make sure that there is a channel between the windows for two reasons. First, for the grommet to work effectively, it has to be able to grip one of the acrylic panes. Second, we need plenty of space to inject the epoxy, so that there are no leaks. So we are going to stay away from the edge of the window by a quarter of an inch or so.

We are doing one side of the window at a time so that we can arrange the epoxy on the bead while it is still very fresh. The critical step to watch at this point is to make sure that the section of tubing that has the bubble holes is along the bottom of the pane, with the holes pointed straight up at the top of the pane. If you didn't punch the holes in a straight line, this is also your last chance to try to fix the tubing.

We put the plugged end of the tubing in the corner of the window, with the air supply line almost meeting it, as shown in Figure 3-7.

Figure 3-7
Arranging the tubing

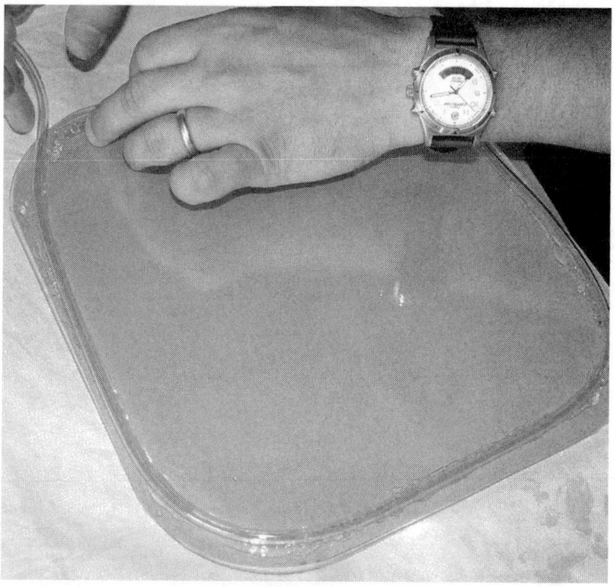

We are almost done arranging the tubing. We cannot make the window completely airtight on the top: the air is being pumped in through the supply tube, and the plug in the end of the tube is forcing the air through the holes that we punched. The air has to have an outlet so that it can escape the window. We left a small gap for an exhaust tube.

HEADS UP!

If you do not add an outlet for the air to escape, the pressure inside your water window will build up quickly and create a leak.

We chose a small piece of the same size vinyl tubing for the exhaust, as shown in Figure 3-8. The basic idea is that we want the air to be able to escape in the same volume that it entered the window. Although our air bubble holes are not scientifically calibrated, there are enough of them that we are confident that no pressure will develop.

TIPS OF THE TRADE

Crank Up the Pressure

If you do a really large window, you may notice that the air does not bubble out of the last few holes in the supply line. If this happens, the air pressure in the tube is not great enough. You will have to upgrade your pump to fix this problem.

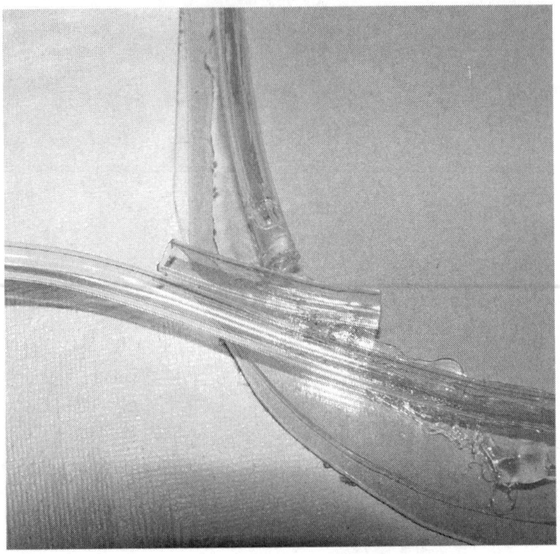

Figure 3-8
Configuring the air outlet

The water window reservoir is now halfway completed! Before moving on, get a clean, damp cloth and wipe down any fingerprints that you may have put on the inside of the window that you just worked on, and also on the reservoir's top panel. We are now ready to epoxy the top piece of acrylic to finish our "sandwich." If you've made any accidental marks are on the inside of the water window, they will be there forever, so wipe off any fingerprints before moving on.

HEADS UP!

For the purposes of picture taking, we have removed the protective backing from the other side of the top acrylic piece. We have done this only so that you can see the process better in the figures. We recommend leaving the protective backing on, unless you feel that it will help you to see what you are doing. If that is the case, then you will have to clean up more fingerprints later. If you get any epoxy on the unprotected pane, you may have to start over!

Take the tube of plumber's epoxy and cut the applicator nozzle to allow more epoxy to flow through at a quicker rate. We want to get a nice even bead of epoxy, and if the applicator is too small, we will have to put on many extra coats of the epoxy.

Insert the tube into the groove that is between the two windows, as shown in Figure 3-9, and start squeezing the epoxy so that it completely covers the vinyl tube and the gap between the tube and the acrylic panes. It will bond the two panes and the air tube together.

Figure 3-9
Applying the epoxy

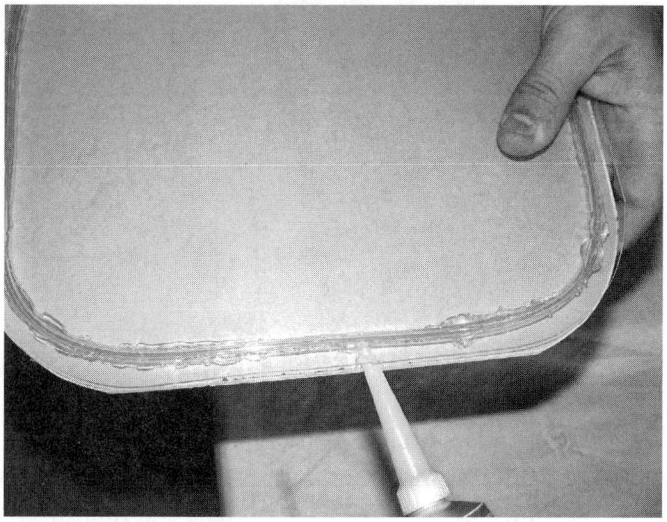

Before moving on to the next step, squeeze some epoxy between the air supply and the air outlet, and between the air outlet and the plugged end.

Curing the Window

Now that the first layer of epoxy is done, it is time for the curing process. If you live in a cold climate, where it is damp, the curing can take up to three days. This is an enormous amount of time, as we are going to cure two separate applications. As mentioned earlier, a hair dryer will speed the curing. Even with the use of a hair dryer, we strongly recommend that you cure the window for at least 12 hours to provide a good, firm bond.

To cure the window, we placed the epoxied pieces on a soft cloth. Next we put a soft cloth on top of the assembly. Then we placed a sheet of metal (to even out the load distribution), followed by approximately 12 pounds of stuff that we had lying around, as shown in Figure 3-10. The window sat with this weight on it all night.

Figure 3-10
Curing the window

The next day, after the curing was complete, we repeated the epoxy application. This time, we tried to smooth out the epoxy with our finger (you can also use a nail head). We don't want the groove to be overfull, so that it will still fit in the molding. By smoothing out the epoxy, we also force it into small nooks and crannies that we may have missed somehow.

After this, it is another 12 hours of curing (under pressure), and we're ready to test the water window for use in our case.

Testing the Window: The Water Test

We now have another water device in our supersystem. It seems like we're just temping fate, doesn't it? Perhaps we are, but if we follow some simple precautionary steps, we can feel more confident about installing it.

Now that the window is completely cured, it's time to put it through the water test. The window is supposed to be airtight; we'll put it through a test to validate this.

Using a syringe with no needle, we filled the water window with water. To make it easy, we squirted some water into the air inlet tube and then connected the small aquarium pump so it could push the water into the window. Then we got the bubbles going, as shown in Figure 3-11. We put our bubbling contraption over some newspaper and waited several hours to see if it leaked at all. You can put it over anything that will plainly show any water leaks. Newspaper is good because even if water leaks out and then dries, there will be a permanent water mark on the paper.

Figure 3-11
Performing the water test

Now that we are sure the window is watertight, we have to drain the window, because it cannot be installed while it has water in it. Then it's time to reinstall the window in our case. With the motherboard out of the case, reinstall the window in the grommet.

We had a little too much difficulty, so we used a Dremel on the rear panel of the water window and made it smaller than the front panel. This was a tricky thing to do, because we didn't want to make a leak. But by making the rear pane a little smaller, the grommet fit easier.

Aside from any minor trimming, we will install the window in the same manner that we did the first time (only now it's thicker). If you left the protective backing on the acrylic, you may have to peel it about half an inch back from the edge.

We prepared the water mixture using some water and a small amount of bleach. The bleach will prevent microorganisms from growing in the water. A tablespoon of bleach per quart of water is all that is needed. Make sure you are very careful with the bleach, because it's very dangerous to your health. Refill the window with the syringe.

Once again, we are going to test the window. Put the case on a sheet of newspaper. Leave the water window running in the case for 24 hours. After the end of this test, check for leaks. If you don't see any, then drain the window and continue. You must drain the window because it cannot be installed full.

HEADS UP!

Whenever you are dealing with water, it is very *important to test for leaks. As you may have noticed, this mod has now taken three days to complete, although we have only worked on it 20 minutes a day.*

Our aquarium pump is a very small one that we picked up from Wal-Mart for under $10. This unit runs off of household current and includes a handy one-way check valve. We are very glad it includes this separately because it will be easy to see if there is a problem with the water line. We are going to use the one-way check valve between the pump and the window so that we can put the pump below the window if we want to, with no fear of the water siphoning back through the hose to the air pump. If this were to happen, the air pump might be ruined!

Our water window is now installed and complete, as shown in Figure 3-12. Now we just have to worry about friends dropping brine shrimp into it!

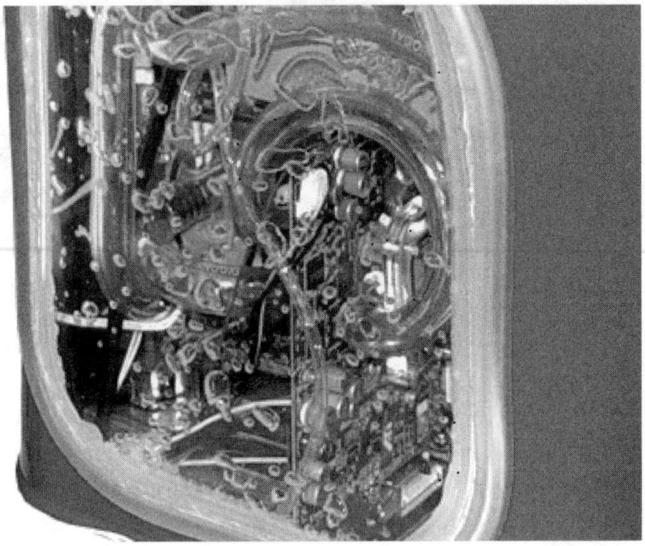

Figure 3-12
The water window in action

TESTING 1-2-3

Here's what you learned in this chapter:

- ❑ How to build a water window
- ❑ Using an existing window as a foundation for the water window
- ❑ Parts, materials, and techniques to build a water window
- ❑ Tools needed to build a water window

Chapter 4

Installing the Water-Cooling System

Tools of the Trade

Screwdriver
Small funnel
Tygon tubing
Hose clamps
Three waterblocks (specially made for our board components)
Hose clamps
Water solution
Thermal paste
Motherboard
Video card

Water-cooled systems are becoming mainstream components, but they are not yet commonly used. Because more people are turning to water as a cooling solution, more and more water-cooling equipment is becoming available as time goes on. We wanted to have the best possible rig, so we went with the best equipment, which was manufactured by Danger Den and provided by Wahoo Computers.

Getting Started

Before we start installing the water-cooling system, the first thing we want to do is make sure that all the parts we need are included. Most manufacturers include a parts list, so we check it to make sure that we don't get halfway done and then realize we are missing something. It's important to read the instructions for your waterblock carefully before you start, because the steps you need to take may be different than the steps we are taking.

We are going to install three waterblocks as part of our mod—one for the main processor, one for the math coprocessor, and one for the video card. Other components that can be water-cooled include your hard drive and power supply. Our power supply will be external, so it would be nearly impossible to water-cool it. Our hard drive is from a laptop and does not generate a significant amount of heat, so it doesn't need to be cooled. Although we will not be water-cooling either of these items, you may choose to cool one or both of them, depending on your project.

We need to test our system for leaks for 24 hours before installing any hardware. We are trying to build a competition-quality mod, and this means taking our time and doing everything right.

Because of the potential hazards of using water to cool our system, our plan for installation and testing has some redundancy in it. We are going to dry-fit every hose in the case to make sure that they are the perfect length. Then we are going to remove the waterblocks from the motherboard (and video card) and test the system for leaks. Lastly, we are going to reinstall the waterblocks, after which the installation will be complete.

Normally, we wouldn't have to be this precise. We could cut the tubes a little longer than needed and save ourselves some time. This isn't a normal case, though, and we don't want to have extra hose in the case that could bind against the walls and make it hard to remove the motherboard tray.

Preparing the Motherboard

To install a waterblock on the chip, it is first necessary to prepare the motherboard. Our Gigabyte motherboard has a black plastic mounting bracket that is used to install a standard heat sink and fan (HSF) on the motherboard. We have to remove this mounting bracket to be able to install the waterblock. The bracket is easy to remove—but first we want to make sure that we are grounded so that we don't shock the board with static electricity. We have an ESD (electrostatic device) table to work on, but you will likely have to find another method of grounding yourself.

The easiest way to ground yourself would be to power down your computer, turn off your power supply, and then touch the frame of your PSU. It may not be sufficient to touch your case frame (which some people do), because this assumes that you have full conductivity from the frame to the PSU. Usually you do, but there are some situations where this may not be sufficient. If your case has a lot of plastic construction (which is very common on many premanufactured systems) or if you are using a clear acrylic case, you may not properly ground yourself just by touching a piece of metal on the frame. It's best to get into the habit of touching the PSU; then, no matter what you do to your case, you will be fine.

Now that the ESD hazard has been abated, it's time to hack apart a perfectly good motherboard. To remove the black plastic bracket, unscrew the four corner screws and remove them. Flip the board over and carefully squeeze the four black threaded inserts so that they will go through the holes in the motherboard. The math coprocessor has a similar mounting method. To remove it, pull up the small rivet at each corner, then squeeze the insert on the other side of the board so you can remove the heat sink. Your motherboard should look similar to the one shown in Figure 4-1.

Figure 4-1 Motherboard with HSF mounting bracket removed

Overclocking the chip isn't included in this project—we're concentrating on the modding of the case. We recommend overclocking your rig so that you can make good use of the water-cooling setup. If you do, and you are planning on using a peltier to further cool your chip, you will want to fill the cavity underneath the chip. The reason you would want to do this is to get all the air out of the cavity, as the air has moisture that the peltier may cause to turn into condensation (water). This water can short your motherboard. You can fill this cavity with a petroleum jelly or a nonconductive thermal compound.

Installing the Waterblocks

You will get either nylon hardware or steel hardware with your water-cooling kit. Nylon hardware has the advantage of being nonconductive, so you are less likely to short out your motherboard. Steel hardware has the advantage of being stronger. We're going to use both kinds of hardware so you can see how they are different.

We're going to install our main processor first, using the metal hardware. Prepare four of the bolts with a nut about 8mm from the end. Put a nylon washer (to prevent chafing and shorting) on top of the nut, and slide the long end of the bolt through the hole. Now put a nylon washer on from the other side, then another nut. Hand-tighten each bolt to the point that nothing moves. The bolts can be further tightened, but if you tighten them too much, the nylon washers may damage them and the surface-mounted parts on your motherboard. The installed bolts are shown in Figure 4-2.

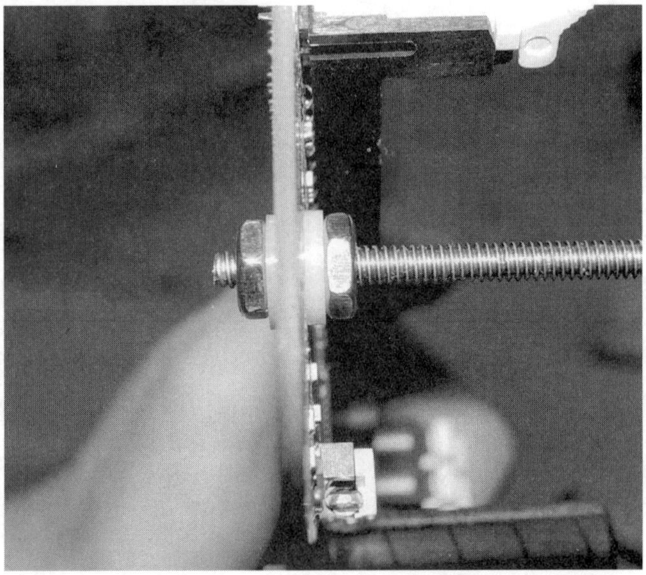

Figure 4-2 Main mounting bolts installed

We have finished prepping the motherboard and we are ready to dry-install the waterblock. We are not going to install the chip until after the leak test is performed. Carefully set the waterblock onto the four bolts. Some waterblocks require a specific orientation to the chip, but ours does not. Slide a washer, a spring, another washer, and a thumbnut onto each steel bolt, as shown in Figure 4-3. Don't tighten them yet; leave them loose. We are just installing the waterblock temporarily while we install our hoses.

Figure 4-3 Waterblock with fasteners started

Repeat this process for the math coprocessor. It doesn't develop as much heat as our main processor and video card, but we are going to water-cool it anyway. We are using metal hardware for this one too, so follow the same procedure. The math coprocessor only has two bolts to keep it in place, and the installation hardware is all much smaller.

Next we have to take apart a perfectly functional video card. Our subject card, which is one of the new ATI models, has a small HSF on it. Before you start to work on the video card, make sure you ground yourself again.

To remove the heat sink, pull up on the black plastic pop rivets so that you can remove the heat sink from the card. You will need to compress the two plastic inserts on the other side of the board to pull off the heat sink, as shown in Figure 4-4 (the fan has been removed so that you can better see the detail).

Figure 4-4
Removing the video card heat sink and fan

When we install the waterblock on the video card, we will be using the nylon hardware. Screw a nylon nut onto the nylon bolt a few millimeters from the end, and push the long end through the board. There is no need for a nylon washer since the nut is not conductive. Gently set the waterblock onto the video processor, then place a washer on top.

This time we are using a washer with a flange that lines it up with the hole in the waterblock. Place a small spring on the washer, then another washer, and then the nut. Install the video card in the AGP slot of your system and screw it down to the PCI bracket. You'll be removing it soon, but you want everything to be installed just as it needs to be so that you can estimate the length of the pipes. The completed video card waterblock installation is shown in Figure 4-5.

Figure 4-5
Video card waterblock, installed

Now that our waterblocks are installed, we need to plan the tubing for our system. We are using professional-grade Tygon tubing, which will resist kinking, and we need to make sure that we make all of our tubing the proper length. We also need to make sure that we leave slack in the hoses going to and from the motherboard so we can slide the motherboard tray partway out of the case for maintenance without having to disassemble the entire system. This means that the hoses have to be long enough that they reach into the case when the motherboard tray has been removed from the bottom of the can.

It's time to start attaching tubing to each device. We want the fresh, cool water to hit the most important chip first, and then go to the smaller chips. Specifically, the water will go to the main processor first, and then the math coprocessor. The water's last stop will be the video card, and then it will go back to the pump to be cooled at the radiator. By routing it this way, the main processor gets the coolest water.

Hold the uncut tubing up to the fitting to determine where to cut it. With our waterblock, the fitting in the center is the inflow, whereas the fitting near the edge is the outflow. Start with the outflow fitting and connect it to the math coprocessor using a short length of hose. We need to make sure we use enough hose without using too much—we can't let the hose bend too much or it may kink and our system will burn up. Push the first end of the hose onto the block's outflow fitting. Next slide two hose clamps onto the hose. Fasten one hose clamp securely onto the outflow fitting. Push the other end of the hose onto the coprocessor inflow, and tighten down the hose clamp.

We are using automotive hose clamps because they tighten with a screwdriver. We want to know that they are as tight as they can be so that we don't have any leaks. There is another kind of hose clamp that you pinch with your fingers to tighten. That kind also works well, but we are a little paranoid about water leaks, so we will use the best available. Repeat this process to connect the math coprocessor waterblock to the video card waterblock, and then to connect the video card waterblock to the water pump intake.

Now that all the waterblocks are attached to each other with tubing, we need three longer tubes. The first will go between the radiator outlet and the main chip. The second will go between the water pump and the radiator inlet. The third will go from the video card block to the water pump inlet. This will complete our circuit. The first and third tubes will have enough slack in them to allow us to move the motherboard for servicing.

Attach a pipe to the water pump outflow and the chip inflow, and push both of these hoses through the metal gas cap that you drilled holes into in Chapter 2. Now you have everything in the case attached to hoses and tightened down with hose clamps, and two hoses sticking out of the top of the case to attach to the radiator, as shown in Figure 4-6.

Figure 4-6
Hoses, dry-fitted

Our radiator is loose on top of the case, but we are going to attach it to the gas cap handles using some tie wraps. We had many ideas on how to attach it, but tie wraps won out. They are inconspicuous, available in a variety of colors, and allow the radiator to be removed in the future. We also considered making a custom bracket that would go between the handles and the radiator, as well as permanently epoxying the radiator to the can, but in the end tie wraps appeared to be the best choice.

Testing the Water-Cooling System

Testing the water-cooling system for leaks before we move on is a critical step. First we remove the waterblocks from the motherboard and video card and move the motherboard tray and the components to a safe location. With the blocks removed, we make sure that all of the hoses are pushed completely onto the fittings and the hose clamps are tight.

Attach the two hoses to the radiator, but leave the hose clamps off of one of them. We are now ready to fill the system. Most water-cooling rigs have a reservoir. Reservoirs make filling and maintaining a water-cooling rig much easier. Regrettably, our system is tight on space. There isn't a place to put a reservoir where it would be easy to fill. As a result, we don't have a reservoir.

TIPS OF THE TRADE

Keep the Valve High

If you find yourself in this situation, the next easiest thing to do is to cut one of your hoses and put in a valve that you can use to bleed off air. Since air rises, the best place for this valve is usually the highest point in the case. We will not be using a valve in our rig, as the highest point is the loop of hose that goes over the top of the case. This would not look nice at all. Instead, we're going to have to be very careful when we connect the tubing.

We are going to fill the system through one of the pipes sticking out of the top of the case. We are using distilled water and the water additive included with our kit. Distilled water is "pure" water without any chemicals or minerals (it's also referred to as "demineralized water," "deionized water," or "battery top-off water"). Minerals could leave deposits on your waterblock, hoses, radiator, or pump, which could reduce the effectiveness or lifespan of your system.

There are many additives available on the market; any additive you use should be a corrosion inhibitor. Some additives also claim to increase cooling power. Realistically, that only happens at higher temperatures than your computer will ever reach, so you will not see much (if any) benefit from them. In addition, some additives are flammable, so make sure you avoid those.

One of the most popular additives glows when exposed to a UV light. This will make your hoses glow in the case, providing a nice effect. Check out all the available additives before you buy one.

When we fill our system, we are careful that we bleed all the air out of it. We do not want any air in our rig because it will make our cooling less efficient. We are using a small funnel to help us fill the water into the system. After the system is mostly full, we push the tube we are using to fill the system onto the radiator and start the pump. This will push any extra air through the system, where we can see it. If any air is pushed out of the system, we will trap it in the top arcing tube, where we can remove it.

We'll remove the last of the air by removing the top arcing hose that we are using to fill the system and capping it with our thumb. Remove what little air there is by adding more water. This is easier to do if you hold the hose straight up so that the air rises to the top. Top off the hose, if necessary, and cover it with your thumb. Now tip the can over slightly and touch the tube, which is full, to the top of the radiator inlet, which is also full. With a deft motion, we push the hose onto the radiator, avoiding getting any air in the line, as shown in Figure 4-7.

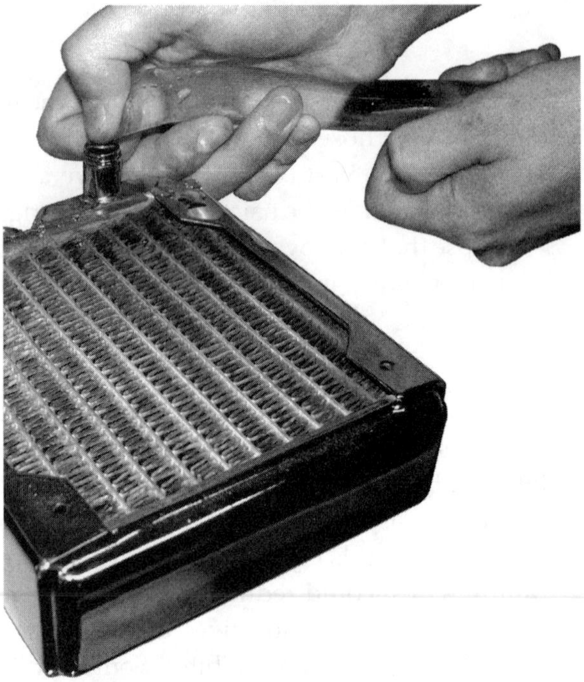

Figure 4-7
Finishing the last pipe connection

This was a very frustrating way to hook up the system, but after several tries, we were able to complete the task with only a small air bubble in the hose. This air bubble rose to the top of the hose and stayed there. We do not think it will adversely affect the system.

Now it is time to wait 48 hours with all the hoses attached and clamped down. Let the system run and look for any drips or leaks. If you find a leak, reseat the connection, reclamp it, or replace the tubing in that section. Happily, we had no leaks.

Finishing the Installation

To finish our installation, we need to install the waterblock on the chip. Be careful when you do this or you may end up crushing the core of the computer chip. This will ruin the chip. We haven't had any problems with this in the past, but you may want to consider getting a copper shim to give your waterblock an additional area to rest on.

TIPS OF THE TRADE

The Shim

A shim is a small piece of metal that provides more surface area for your heat sink to rest on. Shims typically tend to have a hole in them for the processor to stick through so that the processor still touches the heat sink. The shim that is around the processor provides a greater base for the heat sink and helps avoid pressing down on the heat sink too hard.

Now it is time to install the chip and prepare it for the waterblock. To install the chip, we have to lift the metal retaining bar, orient the chip in the proper direction (the pins are keyed), and place it in the holes. Press down on the metal bar to lock the chip in.

To perform a proper installation, thermal compound is necessary. Thermal compound is a putty-like substance that goes between your chip and your heat sink. It fills in extremely small irregularities in the heat sink and allows heat to move between the chip and the waterblock (or heat sink) more easily. Before we do this, we need to explain a little about waterblocks and how they are prepared.

A good waterblock manufacturer tries to keep these irregularities to a minimum, so our waterblock is lapped to a specific grit. The terms "lapping" and "grit" may not be familiar to you, but they are common terms in the world of metalworking. *Lapping* is similar to polishing—it smoothes out the metal. The lapping process smoothes the copper and reduces irregularities. A machine first does this, and when it has lapped the block as much as it can, the block is lapped by hand to 1200 grit. *Grit* is a measurement of particle size used in a process that is similar to sanding. Higher grit represents smaller particles, which give a finer polish.

When your leak testing is done, apply the thermal paste to your computer chip. We use Cooler Master Premium Thermal Compound, which comes with an applicator. Put a small amount of paste on your chip, perhaps an amount equal to half of a dime. Then, using the applicator, spread it evenly over your chip. Repeat this with the math coprocessor and the video card processor.

Add some more thermal paste and spread it evenly over the chip. Cooler Master gives you enough in the syringe to use on several different chips.

After we put all the waterblocks back on their posts, we have to start tightening down the thumbnuts. This part requires patience, because you have to tighten them all evenly. To tighten them evenly, you have to turn each nut only two or three turns before moving on to the next one, all the way down. Work in an X pattern, where the second nut you tighten is diagonally opposite from the first nut. Then tighten the third nut, and tighten the nut diagonally across from it. This should make the waterblock tighten very evenly and reduce the chance of you damaging your chip. Do not tighten the nuts as far as they can go—just get the whole assembly nice and tight. Our main processor and coprocessor are shown in Figure 4-8.

Figure 4-8
Main processor and math coprocessor with waterblocks

We've completed our installation, and are almost done with our system! The next chapter will cover everything else that we need to do to finish off the system so that it will be complete. There is a lot of ground left to cover, and in the end we'll have a great system!

TESTING 1-2-3

In this chapter, you learned the following:

- ❑ How to prepare the motherboard for a water-cooled installation
    - ❑ How to remove the existing heatsinks

- ❑ How to install waterblocks on the main chip, math coprocessor, and videocard
  - ❑ "Dry-fit" the system first for best results
  - ❑ Three ways to fill the system
    - ❑ Use of a reservoir
    - ❑ Use of a valve to remove any excess air
    - ❑ Quick-fitting the connection
- ❑ How to test the water cooling system for leaks before installation

Chapter 5

Completing the Mod

Tools of the Trade

Jigsaw
Drill
Scissors
Soldering iron
Small testing PSU
Screwdriver
Heat gun
Needle-nose pliers
Gloves
Edge molding
A piece of wire
Wire fan grill
Power and reset switch assembly
Masking tape
Black spray paint
Solder
Epoxy
Nuts and bolts of various sizes
Aluminum frame fan (120mm)
1U PSU
Acrylic sheet
Two blue cold cathodes

We are almost finished with our case. As far as overall appearance, this is the most important chapter, because we will finish several things that need to be touched up. In this chapter we'll do several "mini-mods" to finish the case.

The mini-mods that are left include modding the DVD to work with the remote switch that we installed earlier, adding edge molding to all of the sharp edges, modding the power supply, mounting the top fan, and creating a case stand out of clear acrylic.

Edge Molding

Whenever metal is cut, the resulting edges can be dangerously sharp. Therefore, you should always sand down the edges to avoid the potential of someone cutting his or her fingers. A way to make these metal edges even safer is to cover them with edge molding. That's the option we are using. In particular, we are going to cover the DVD-ROM drive slot and the cuts at the bottom of the case.

The DVD-ROM drive slot is more visible than the bottom of the case, so we have to pay more attention to detail when we are putting the edge molding on it. We need four pieces of molding to cover all four sides of the slot. Standard household scissors (sharp) will cut the edge molding very nicely.

TIPS OF THE TRADE

Molding 101

The trick to getting molding to look right is to actually cut it slightly longer than the edge measurements, so that the molding edges press up against each other. In other words, don't try to cut it so that it is perfect; leave it a little big.

You need to cut the ends of the molding for the DVD-ROM drive slot at an angle, but don't make it a sharp angle, as shown in Figure 5-1. We are also going to use edge molding on the bottom of the case, where the motherboard slides into the gas can. When cutting this molding, you should make straight cuts.

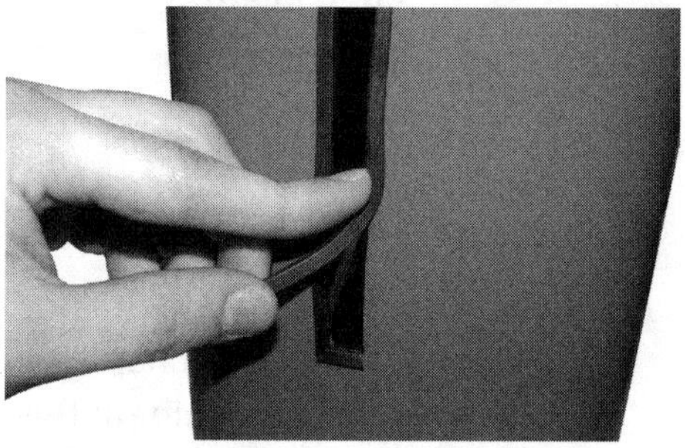

Figure 5-1 Detail of edge molding being placed on DVD slot

One of the nicest things about working with edge molding is that it is cheap and easy to test-fit. As long as you have enough edge molding and patience, you will be able to create perfect seams in all four corners. You don't need to glue it in place, because it won't come off under ordinary circumstances. The edge molding just slips on the metal, no special tools or preparations are needed.

Modding the DVD Switch

While we are working on the DVD slot, we are going to finish the DVD remote eject button. Recall that we aren't going to use the eject button that is on the front of the DVD player. We've mounted a very small rocker switch on the top of the case that will be used to eject the disc.

To wire in the switch, we need a soldering iron, some solder, and a piece of wire. We're going to connect the wire to the switch and solder it so that it's a good, solid connection. Then we'll run the wire down the case to the DVD player.

If you've never used a soldering iron before, here's a tip about technique. The first thing you should do, before you attach anything, is to "tin" the wire with solder. Using the soldering iron and some solder, cover the exposed end of the wire with solder. This "tinning" process will make the wire attach easier to the switch. It's kind of like putting super glue on both sides of something you are gluing.

After you tin the wire, slip it through the hole in the switch post and bend it up. Melt a small ball of solder onto the tip of the soldering iron, and then apply this ball of solder to the joint of the wire and the post, as shown next. Do this with both wire strands, one on each pole. If you want to add more solder to the joint, heat up the connection and melt some more solder onto it. Now you have the first end complete.

TIPS OF THE TRADE

To Crimp or to Solder?

If you want your connection to look and perform better, find some spade lugs and crimp them on the ends of the wires using a crimping tool. Then you can slip the spade lugs over the posts on the switches. This is much more professional, but requires additional tools that we are not using in this mod. Since no one will see the connection, we are just going to solder them on.

Because you are permanently attaching the switch to the case, you need to leave some slack in the wires. This is because the DVD player is mounted on the motherboard tray, which slides in and out of the case. The wire needs to be long enough to allow the DVD and motherboard tray to be completely removed from the case. Take the four screws out of the bottom of the DVD player and remove the bottom cover. In the front of the DVD player, we can see a gray push-button switch with four connections underneath. This is the eject button. We are going to ignore the other buttons.

The next step isn't very easy—there is no place to secure the wires to the connections in the motherboard. Therefore, we have to solder the wires to the existing connections, which is a very precarious way to do it.

The pins that we need to solder the wires onto are the front two posts on the switch. These are small targets, so you need to proceed with extreme care. Using a soldering iron, carefully tin the wire and then get a small ball of solder on the heated tip. You'll have to melt the switch connections before the solder will complete the connection. You can't use too much solder because your target connection is so small. Figure 5-2 shows the final product.

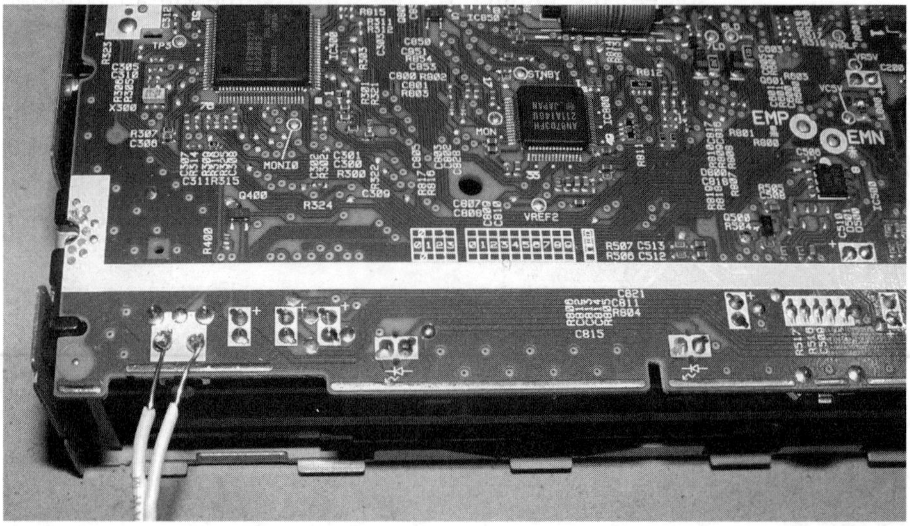

Figure 5-2 Finished DVD switch mod

Now that the connection is complete, screw the bottom cover for the DVD player back on. Your connection is rather fragile, so you need to provide a strain relief of some sort to keep the wires from breaking off of the printed circuit board. A strain relief protects the wires from accidentally pulling off of the board. Decide where to put your strain relief and epoxy the wire in that location. We used a small amount of epoxy—about half the diameter of a dime—on the top of the DVD drive.

TIPS OF THE TRADE

Plug-and-Test

We want to test our handiwork before going further, but we can't test the DVD drive without plugging it in. We use a small NanoPSU from PcMods to test things like this. The NanoPSU plugs into our household wall socket. It converts household current to the 12V current used in computers, and it comes with a four-pin power connector like those used with most computer hardware. It's a quick and effective way to test the unit without having to plug it into the main system.

Before we move on, we need to plug in the audio cable from our DVD player into our motherboard so we can get sound while we are watching movies. There is nothing new here—take the cable supplied with your DVD drive and plug one end into the DVD and one end into the motherboard. This cable is used for the audio signal send by the player to the system. Without it, you would need to watch your movies with subtitles.

Mounting the Top Fan

We mounted the radiator to the top of the case in Chapter 4. Now it is time to add the 120mm fan. We have selected an aluminum-frame fan because it matches the chrome radiator fairly well. Both are silver colored and shiny. We need to make sure that we have the fan pointed the right way—we're going to be pushing air through the radiator and we want it to blow downward.

Whenever you have a fan mounted so that it is on the outside wall of a case, it is a good idea to put a fan grill on it to protect people from accidentally sticking their fingers in it. Sticking your finger in a moving fan shouldn't cause any permanent damage, but it will hurt quite a bit. We have chosen a normal 120mm wire grill for the top of the mod, but there are many different fan grills that you could use. Gold, black, red, and blue wire grills and a host of other options are available if you choose to use a die-stamped or a laser-cut grill.

Screw a fan grill on to the top of the fan. With an aluminum-frame fan, we need bigger fan screws than normal, because the screw holes are much larger. These are self-tapping screws, which means that they cut their own threads in the material they are being screwed into. These screws work great when being used with a plastic material, but they do not cut the aluminum frame of the fan very well. Because of this, we need to make sure our screw stays straight while we screw it in.

To power our fan, we have to run a wire into the case. Fortunately, with the design of our gas can, we can do this without more drilling. We need to fit the fan's power wire through some small places. This means that we will have to remove the white molex plug housing before continuing. By doing this, we will be left with a wire that can be put into some small holes and will be much easier to work with. Take a close look at the molex connector. It is made up of pins that fit in a plastic shell. You can see that there are little flaps of metal keeping the pins in the shell. To remove the pins, take a pair of needle-nose pliers and crimp down on the metal flaps. (You need a thin pair of needle-nose pliers to reach up into the shell to do this.) When you finish, you will have two wires hanging loose with pins on them, and a white plastic molex shell in your hand.

We ran the wire down the radiator and under the handle. There is a small hole under the handle that exits to the gas cap area. If you remove the gas cap, you can see the hole where an air pipe used to be (to prevent air gulps in the can, which cause gas to splash out while it's being poured). Stick the wire through this hole and push the pins back into the molex shell inside the case. They will just snap right back in, and now you will be able to use your fan again. By using this opening, as shown in Figure 5-3, you do not have to put the wire through the threaded part of the gas cap.

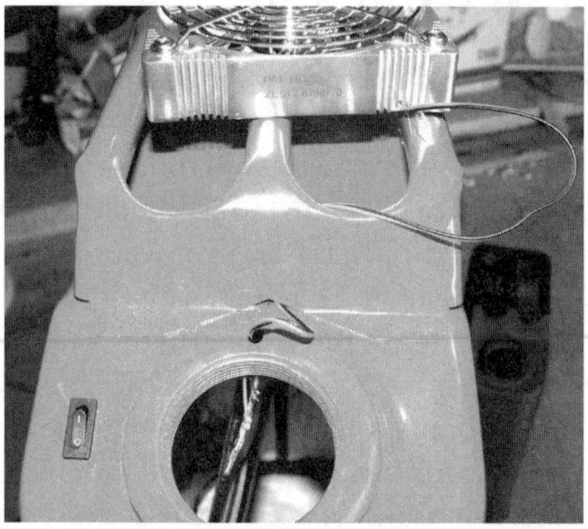

Figure 5-3
Fan power wire

Modding the Power Supply

A power supply won't fit in this case, so we have to do something creative to make the PSU look right. Many laptops have a PSU integrated into the power cord. Specifically, on a laptop PSU, there is a cord leaving the laptop, which goes to a black box, and from there it goes to the wall outlet.

We are going to try to replicate this look with our computer. We start with a 1U PSU, which is only an inch tall. The PSU will still plug into the wall, and all the cabling will go into the case through the bottom.

To replicate the laptop PSU look, we will paint the PSU black using regular spray paint. Before we paint it, we have to mask off the two 40mm fans and any other holes to keep the paint from getting into the power supply and damaging it. Give the PSU about two or three coats on each side, and allow it to dry.

HEADS UP!

Work in a well-ventilated area when you use the spray paint. This will be safer for you, and it will also make the paint dry quicker. Avoid painting outside, if possible, because leaves or bugs could drift into your fresh paint. If you have to paint outside, make sure you put something over the PSU, such as an upside-down colander made out of wire mesh.

The final touch is to cover the wires leaving the PSU and going into the case. Velcro cable mesh is the best solution to cover the bundle of wires going into the case. Velcro cable mesh is easy to use, and removable, but it does require the ends to be heat treated to prevent fraying. Because Velcro goes all the way down each end, we can have wires exit the bundle wherever we want. The finished product is shown in Figure 5-4. We will have to be very careful when we are moving the computer because we don't want to put any strain on the motherboard connections.

Figure 5-4
1U PSU modded to look like a laptop PSU

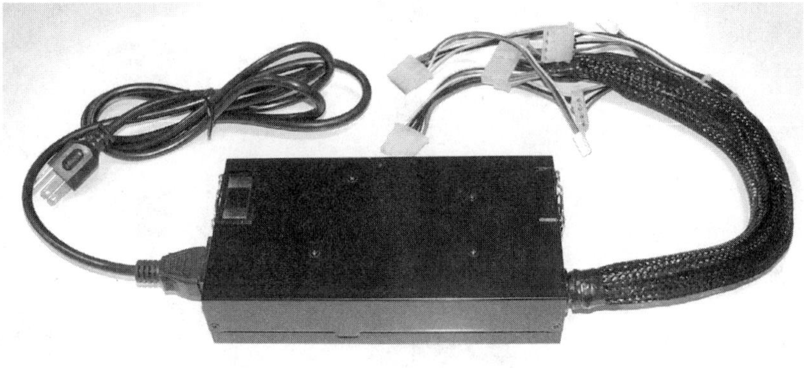

Adding Some Extra Cabling

Our motherboard needs some cabling to make the power switch work. All motherboards have headers for a power switch, and without anything on the header, the computer will not power up. We have two options for the power switch. The first option is to complete the circuit with a jumper—in other words, complete the circuit by putting a jumper on the power switch header. The motherboard will always be on when you flip the switch on the back of the PSU.

The second option is to take the button assembly off of another case. We are going to do this because it makes the mod more professional looking. In addition to the power and reset switch, it includes a piezo speaker as well as the power LED and hard drive LED. Most of the cabling will remain hidden in the case, but we will at least have a power and reset button.

If you've never hooked up a power and reset button, you will need to consult the manual that came with your motherboard; the connections are fairly intuitive. Your motherboard will be labeled with "PLED" for Power LED, "RESET" for reset switch, and similar abbreviations. The manual for your motherboard should have a schematic showing you exactly how to plug everything in.

Other cabling we are adding includes two of the fantastic-looking single-device IDE cables from IOSS (www.IOSS.com.tw). They will be used to connect the DVD drive and the hard drive to the motherboard. They are round cables, unlike the ribbon cables used since the early 1980s. The reason we are using them is that they come in custom lengths and are very flexible, making them easy to use. These cables come in a 20cm length and look very space-age. But the best part is that they actually improve data transmission by up to 15 percent, and we want to have a fast system. All of our cables are shown in Figure 5-5.

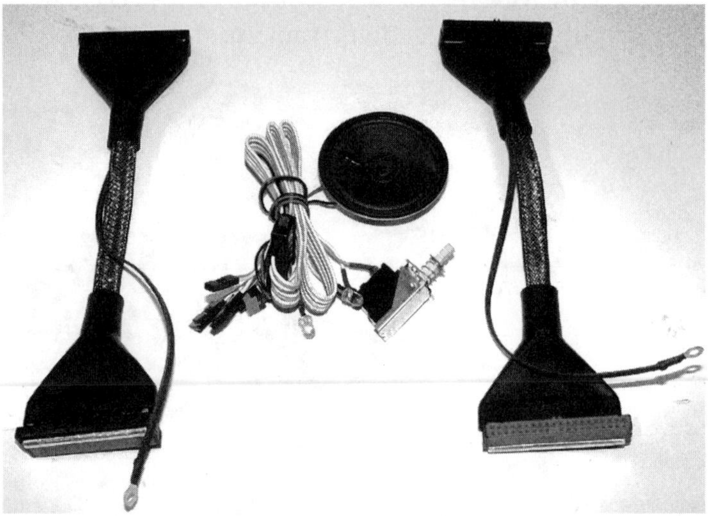

Figure 5-5
Power and reset switch assembly and Gladiator cables

Building a Stand for the Case

All of our cabling comes out of the bottom of the system, so we have to build a stand for the case to sit on. This stand will also include a place to mount our PSU and power switch assembly. We also want to use the stand to provide a broader base for the case to sit on. The gas can is not going to fall over on its own. What worries us is that it seems more top heavy than a standard PC.

We still have a piece of acrylic sheeting left over from our windows, and it is long enough to provide a stable platform for our case. We will heat the acrylic to a very high temperature using a hair dryer and bend it at both ends to create a U-shaped stand, as shown in Figure 5-6. The heat gun works better than a hair dryer and can be found on eBay for around $20. We need to take great care when doing this to make sure we don't snap the acrylic as we try to bend it.

First we need to trace out a hole in the middle of the acrylic for all the cables to go through. The size of the hole roughly approximates the shape of the motherboard tray. We have to use a jigsaw to cut out the hole.

Next, to create the two bends that will create a U shape, we take an extremely large bolt and lay the acrylic over it. Using a hair dryer, we apply heat back and forth over the acrylic. The acrylic is going to get very hot, and, as it starts to heat up, we can start bending it around the bolt, which provides a nice rounded bend point. This has to be done on both sides of the sheet of acrylic to provide a U-shaped stand that we can use. This is an easy procedure to do, and you can easily make the stand any size that you need. Due to the weight of our case, we also epoxied two legs in the center of the stand. These are made from clear acrylic tubing, taken from a broken cold cathode kit.

HEADS UP!

Bigger pieces of acrylic will be harder to bend. You may have to get a professional-quality heat gun or use two hair dryers to keep an even temperature.

Figure 5-6 A U-shaped case stand

We added some cathode lights on each side of our case, and our system is completely built now, as shown in Figure 5-7. You can slide the motherboard tray into the case, if you haven't already.

One job is over, and the next has to begin. The system is ready to be overclocked. It needs a good 5.1 sound card and speaker system, but that isn't in the scope of modding the case, so we aren't going to go into it here.

Figure 5-7
Complete system with LCD screen and lighted keyboard

We have successfully built a super case with a consistent theme. We've used a lot of different products, tools, and techniques to get here. We sincerely hope you have enjoyed reading about it as much as we have enjoyed doing it. And, if you plan to build a case like this for yourself, we wish you the best of luck and hope that we've given you some good pointers that you can use. When you finish it, make sure you post it in some case galleries. You may even want to take it to case mod competitions at local LAN parties. At national competitions, you can even win thousands of dollars for having the best modded case!

TESTING 1-2-3

Here is what you learned in this chapter:

- ❑ How to use edge molding to protect ourselves from sharp edges and make your case look better at the same time
- ❑ How to solder a second DVD eject switch in
- ❑ How to use heat to turn a sheet of acrylic into a U-shaped stand
- ❑ How to use Velcro wrap and paint to make our 1U PSU into a nice-looking external power supply

When you do mod your gas can, camp stove, briefcase, or fishing tackle box, we hope that things go smoothly for you, but we do have one warning: once you start modding, it's hard to stop. It's hard to know when to quit, because there are so many things you can do. You'll find that your project mutates over time and takes on a life of its own. We've already got more ideas for fun things we can do with this mod:

- ❑ Put in components that react to UV light, like rounded cables or glowing water dye.
- ❑ Do something interesting with the power and HDD LEDs somewhere on the outside of the case—perhaps mount them on the acrylic stand.
- ❑ Add two more switches to the top of the case to turn on and reset the system.
- ❑ Mod a speaker system for the case with a similar theme—either with a water motif or a fuel theme.
- ❑ Chrome our case so that it shines like a muscle-car engine.

Project 2

Adding Lights

Chapter 6

Planning the Mod

In this chapter, we'll discuss various ways you can modify your case so that components, such as your video card and motherboard, can be seen clearly from outside the case. But you don't just want to show off components—you want the entire case to look "cool." Combinations of lighting accessories can produce that all-important one-of-a-kind case mod, and modding is all about standing out in the crowd. But while important, lights aren't the only thing you can add. There's windows, of course, plus fans, wheels, and more. There's no limit to how you can modify your case to make it special and unique.

This mod will show off plenty of light, not just from stand-alone lights but with lighted fans and tape. We'll also walk you through the many case cuts for this mod, and how to install controls for operating your lights.

The Early Days of Modding

The original "case mod," in the early days of modding, consisted of only two things: a piece of acrylic that served as a window, and a piece of automotive neon. The window, usually glued directly to the case, was hand-cut from a sheet of clear acrylic. The automotive neon used was purchased from a local auto parts store. To convert it for computer use, the modder had to cut off the cigarette lighter adapter (which was discarded) and put on a four-pin molex plug. By putting on a four-pin molex plug, the neon could be plugged into a standard computer power supply, and was then placed within the computer case. This worked because cars and computers run on 12V power, so the electronics did not need to be changed. What this also means is that nearly anything you might put into your car would also work in your PC!

Overview of Lights and Fans

We've come a long way since the dark ages of case modding. We now have all kinds of case mods that are custom-designed for computers. The major types of mod lighting are cold cathode fluorescent (CCF), neon, electroluminescent (EL) cable and tape, LEDs, and fiber optic (fiber optic typically uses LEDs or CCFs as the source light). The goal of our mod is to use several of these together in the same case so that the whole mod is cooler than the sum of its parts. Our project will demonstrate the latest and greatest lighting techniques of the mod world.

An advantage of many of these lighting types is that they are "cold"—they give off a negligible amount of heat or no heat at all, as opposed to incandescent bulbs, which radiate waste heat. "Cold" lighting is valuable in PC modding, because extra heat inside the case stresses your computer components. It's counterproductive to increase the airflow in your case through the use of additional fans or by using a better heat sink if you are going to put in a lighting unit that generates a lot of heat. Too much heat can damage your computer components, meaning you'll be heading to the computer store instead of enjoying your PC.

The heat problem is why many modders add extra fans to their cases—the cooler the interior temperature of the case, the faster your system can run, and the longer it will last. We'll add fans for this case, but in keeping with our case's lighting theme, instead of using ordinary, nonlighted fans, we'll use fans that are lighted with cold cathode, fiber optic, and LED elements.

When you pick a mod, it's best to choose a theme that involves something that appeals to you. We're going with a NASA-inspired theme for this case, with lots of strategic lighting and a few special effects to make the case look otherworldly. Instead of a few lights, we're going to make this case a cross between a cloud nebula and a supernova!

The primary goal of this mod is to make it as dynamic as possible—meaning that the lights, fans, and controls should interact in such a manner as to be able to change the "look" of the case with a simple turn of a knob. Many mods are static mods with no real moving parts; all they do is sit and glow while their fans spin. We want our mod to be as active as possible, just like the world we live in. The lights and fans are independently controlled and can create varied combinations of illumination, depending on the owner's whim. We have a lot of different lights that we can use, so planning ahead is critical. We're going to make our mod special by using lighted fans with strobe effects, a window on the motherboard side of the case, a color decal for one of the windows, and various ways of wire dressing.

Windows

Naturally, to show off lighting, you need windows. Therefore, part of the plan for this mod is to cut out sections of the case and replace them with windows. Many people like to put one big window in the side of their case. Instead of doing this, we're going to have two windows: a standard, large square window on the main side; and a rectangular window on the rear side, in the door behind the motherboard tray. The square window will have two blowholes for lighted fans, and will be mounted with translucent molding lined with EL wire. The rectangular window will have some indirect lighting with a 12-inch white CCF light. These dual windows will make our case stand out from the rest.

"Motherboard-side" mods are rare, which is a good reason for us to do one. The reason most people don't do a mod on this side is that there isn't much to look at behind the rectangular window, other than the backside of the motherboard. We're going to change that view by doing something we've never seen done before: We're going to download a false-color image from the Jet Propulsion Laboratories web site (www.jpl.nasa.gov), print it out on film, and put it on the window. Painting the back of the motherboard tray white will help the image stand out. This image will dress up the window and will be enhanced by the cold cathode lights.

HEADS UP!

For the purposes of this mod, we've chosen to download the image for the rectangular window from a web site that has public-domain images. If you want to use a copyrighted image, you should get permission from the owner of the image.

Lighted Fans

All the fans we'll install in this case are lighted fans. Lighted fans, including fiber optic fans, LED fans, UV reactive fans, and cold cathode fans, are a relatively new development in the world of case mods. We plan to mount a fiber optic fan in a blowhole in the top of the case; mount two LED fans in blowholes in the square window; replace the fan in the back with a cold cathode lighted fan; and mount a fiber optic intake fan on the bottom of the case. We'll also replace the front intake fans with cold cathode fans.

For the two fiber optic fans, we are going to use separate control circuits to power the fans and the fiber optic lighting effect, enabling us to achieve some cool strobe effects. Regrettably, it will be hard to show a patterned strobe effect in the text of this book, but we'll try to explain it as best as we can. It's a great effect and makes your lighting have more of a texture. In other words, instead of a dull glow, these fans will dance and move with their own tempo, which is another thing you don't see very often in mods. We think of this as a "dynamic" mod as opposed to a "static" mod.

Figure 6-1 shows the three most common fan types: cold cathode, fiber optic, and LED fans. We'll use all three types in our planned mod. The rear exhaust and front intake fans will use cold cathode–lighted fans, the bottom intake and top exhaust fans will be fiber optic, and the two fans mounted in the large square window will use LED fans.

Figure 6-1
Different fans: cold cathode, fiber optic, and LED fans

The intake fan that we will mount in the bottom of the case needs about three inches of clearance beneath the case. To achieve this, we'll add casters to elevate the case bottom. This will have the added benefit of making the case easier to move when it's on the floor. The intake fan's fiber optic circuit card assembly will extend below the bottom of the case, which is why we need the clearance. If we install the fan as-is, the exposed circuit card assembly will be at risk of damage. Also, the scattered light from the LEDs on the circuit card assembly will disrupt the look we are trying to achieve. We can solve both of these problems by installing a shroud that extends close to whatever surface supports the case. We'll cut grooves in the bottom of the case to allow three cold cathode lights to shine through and give the case that "low rider" effect. See Figure 6-2 for the final look for the bottom of the case.

Figure 6-2
Lights, a lighted fan in a shroud, and caster wheels mounted on the case bottom

We will decide whether to keep or replace each fan grill based on its effect on the visibility of the lighted fan. We'll wrap wire bundles with gauze safety tape to neaten the production and add some more special-effect touches.

Controls

We are going to add some control elements for the lights because we want to be able to control each light individually, or in small groups, rather than have them either all on or all off. While we're adding controls, we'll add a second control element to work the fans. These controls will help make our case more dynamic because we will be able to change the mood and aspect of the case very quickly by changing which lights are operational.

Many types of controls are available. Switch-based controls have begun to lose popularity lately because of the difficulty in finding good lighted switch mechanisms at a reasonable price. Rheostat-based controls (which work like a dimmer switch) are becoming more popular because they allow more flexibility in your lighting. Whatever control you choose, make sure you include a control so your lights are not always on. If you sleep in the same room as your PC, you don't want it to light up your room all night. Figure 6-3 shows an example of a switch-based control on the left and an example of a rheostat-based control on the right.

Figure 6-3
A switch-based control and a rheobus

Paint

Paint is an important part of many mods because it's nearly impossible to get all your mod parts in the same color. Often paint is the only way to make the color of your parts match. However, some mods don't require paint; the choice is usually up to the individual modder.

Many modders choose to paint the outside of their case. We won't paint the outside, but there are some places in the interior where paint will help with the overall effect. Since we're adding the rectangular window and transparency on the rear door, we'll use white paint on the back of the motherboard tray to provide a suitable background for our film image. We'll use green opalescent paint for the bottom interior of the case, to help with the glowing effects. The green paint will also be used for some finishing touches on wire bundles and around noncritical components. Finally, we'll daub some brown accent marks here and there on the painted green surfaces, to break up the green and make it look more organic and alien. The exterior of the case will remain the original aluminum, since we have so much lighting activity going on inside.

The Importance of Planning Ahead

This plan involves a number of lights and fans and plenty of equipment. Before you place your orders for parts or make a trip to a modding or computer store, you want to lay out the plans ahead of time, measuring the areas where lights and fans will go, to make sure all this will fit in the case and still leave room for the components. It's nice to have a lighted case, but not so nice if you can't fit your motherboard back in!

HEADS UP!

Because of space limitations, we won't use automotive neon lights. Neon lights can give some nice effects, and are of the "cold" lighting style, but they are very large compared to cold cathode lights, which limits their usefulness.

You want to make sure that you can afford all the parts and tools before you buy them. Each of the next four chapters includes a list of the parts and tools that are required for that chapter's step of the mod. Figure 6-4 shows all the parts that are included in those lists.

Figure 6-4 Full array of parts for this mod

Most of these parts are available either as-is or as kits from modding web sites and companies. Some modding web sites include www.pcmods.com, www.plycon.com, www.directron.com, and www.cyberguys.com; retail stores available in your neighborhood might include CompUSA and Fry's Electronics Store. A search on the Internet will give you many options to choose from.

Ordering and Checking Parts

When it comes time to order your parts, the following question arises: Do you shop around for the best price for each part, or try to buy all the parts from one place? Often it's better to order from one reputable business rather than from several businesses. First, the shipping is usually cheaper if you're ordering everything from one company, unless you're able to buy everything from a local brick-and-mortar store. Second, everything should arrive in only one or two shipments, which makes it much easier to keep track of what has arrived and what hasn't. Third, if you purchase from a reputable supplier, whether online or brick-and-mortar, if any quality issues arise with your parts, you want to deal with someone who will help solve the problem, whether that means refunding your money or replacing a defective part.

Checking the parts is important too. Make sure everything that has arrived is what you ordered—check the same day the parts arrive, if possible. You don't want to be halfway through the mod only to discover that what you thought was a 120mm fan is actually only 80mm! Also, all lights are susceptible to breakage and should be checked upon arrival. Some stores have very short return periods. If the lights you order arrive two weeks before you plan to install them, and you don't discover that they are broken until you attempt to install them, you may not be able to return them for replacements.

Do remember that for many local suppliers, once a part's packaging has been opened, it may no longer be returnable if there is a problem or you decide you don't want or need it anymore. Internet-based businesses tend to be more forgiving about packaging and breakage since their business is strictly mail order. Keep all of your receipts, e-mails, and paperwork for each item until you know you won't be returning that item.

Lastly, wait to order parts or tools until you know you'll have sufficient time to work on your mod. Ordering parts and then waiting a month or more because you have no free time can lead to real problems. If you change your mind about your mod concept or vision, your supplier may say too much time has passed for it to accept return of the purchases.

TESTING 1-2-3

Now that we have planned out our mod, it's time to get started! Here's an overview of this chapter:

- ❑ Early history of modding
- ❑ Overview of lights
- ❑ Overview of fans

- ❑ Planning your mod
  - ❑ Windows
  - ❑ Lighted fans
  - ❑ Controls
  - ❑ Paint
- ❑ Planning ahead
  - ❑ Budget and feasibility
- ❑ Ordering and checking parts
  - ❑ Where to order from
  - ❑ Verifying parts for accuracy

Chapter 7

Preparing the Case

Tools of the Trade

Safety eyewear

*DeWalt router, with at least 20,000 rpm speed**

*Quarter-inch metal cutting bit**

*Templates for 120mm and 92mm fans**

*Guide fence for router**

*Two C-clamps**

Drill

Clear glue, caulk, or RTV adhesive

Bench vacuum cleaner with small orifice tool, plus compressed air, if available

Artist paint brushes

Pop rivet tool (or a screwdriver, if substituting screws and nuts for the pop rivets)

Transparency decals for use in inkjet or laser printers

Square window kit with translucent molding

Rectangular window kit with translucent molding

Lian Li PC-68 case

Caster kit with four casters

Pop rivets (or screws with nuts, if you don't use rivets)

Paint, masking tape, and related supplies, including materials for cleanup; these will vary depending on the paint selected

**Alternate tools: Many modders do not have access to router equipment. The same results can be achieved using a combination of a drill, to make a starter hole, plus a jigsaw, spiral saw, or nibbler. Using these alternates will require more time and a steady hand.*

Before we install any lights or fans, we need to work on the case itself. In this chapter, we will first make several cuts in the case, for windows, for blowholes, and for lighting. Then we will paint the interior of the case, because it will be visible through the window. Next we will mount the caster wheels. Finally, we will create a transparent decal to place in one window.

To make installing the windows easy, we purchased two standard-size window kits from an online mod store, complete with molding. The square window is approximately 12 inches on each side and will be the main window; the rectangular window is approximately 11.25×8.70 inches and will go on the rear door of the case, behind the motherboard tray. We bought both kits with translucent molding, so we can glue EL cable inside it to add an extra glow.

Cutting the Case

Before we cut anything, it's important to take careful measurements of exactly where the cuts will be. Cuts for fan blowholes and for windows have different criteria. Knowing what these criteria are will make your cuts more effective.

Fan Cuts

For fans, the things to keep in mind (in order of importance) are clearance, airflow, and aesthetics. Clearance regards the parts in the case. There aren't many places to put fans in most computer cases. In this case, the manufacturer provided three fans in the case: two in the front and one in the rear. We will remove these and replace them with our own fans. The fans in the top and bottom have different requirements. The fan in the top of the case must be spaced evenly between the sides of the case, to keep from interfering with any parts in the area, and evenly spaced between front and back, to avoid interfering with the power supply in the back or the space in the front. A modder may wish to use the front space to install a CD-ROM or DVD-ROM drive.

Airflow is the main reason for fans in a computer case; the front and rear fans provided by the manufacturer should do an adequate job by themselves. For this mod, though, we want to provide extra cooling power in addition to looking cool. Therefore, the top and bottom fans don't just look good, they help with airflow. The bottom fan pulls cool air into the case, and the top fan expels hot air. The two fans mounted in the blowholes in the large square window are positioned to blow cool air directly onto the motherboard and its components.

Lastly, the aesthetics of the fan locations: different modders will have different ideas about where to make cuts in their cases or windows. We prefer fans to look balanced, hence the centered placement of the top fan and the locations of the window blowholes. Each blowhole is equidistant from the edge of the window and from each other, as shown in Figure 7-1.

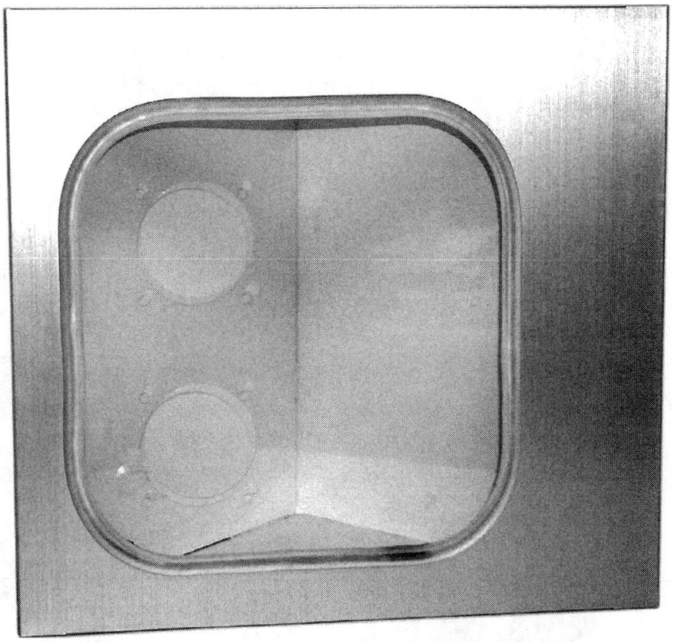

Figure 7-1
Blowhole cuts in the square window. The molding has already been added.

Window Cuts

Window cuts have three criteria as well: they must have clearance on the door, clearance regarding other parts, and aesthetic location just like fans.

The window molding is what impacts clearance for window installation. Whether the molding is translucent, as we're using, or black, it has a profile; it sticks out from the case door. Therefore, when deciding where to place your window cuts, make sure there is enough room for the molding as well, and that the proposed location of the molding will not interfere with the door. Once you make a window cut, you can't change it, and you don't want to discover that your installed window and molding prevent you from putting the door back on the computer.

The molding may also interfere with components inside the computer, although this is less likely than with a fan, due to the molding's lower profile than many fans. It is still something to watch out for. Ideally, you want the molding to be no closer than ¼-inch to any components, to avoid jostling or snagging when the door is removed or installed.

Finally, aesthetics. Again, this is different for different modders. Since most windows are large, there aren't many places you can make a window cut in a door, but nearly all modders use windows to show off what's inside their case. Choose the location that best suits you and your plans, within the strictures of clearance we just stated.

After taking careful measurements, it's time to break out the router (see Figure 7-2). We'll use a router because it generates a very clean and precise cut, and we already have all the templates we'll need. The big consideration for using a router is that it's very hard to do a good cut by freehand, so only use a router if you feel that it's worth it to design and fabricate templates to do your cuts. If you want to, or must, cut freehand, get out the electric drill, plus a jigsaw, a spiral saw, or a nibbler. Using these tools, you can do everything we'll be doing using a router, but you'll have to do it slowly and very carefully.

Figure 7-2 The router after cutting the rectangular window

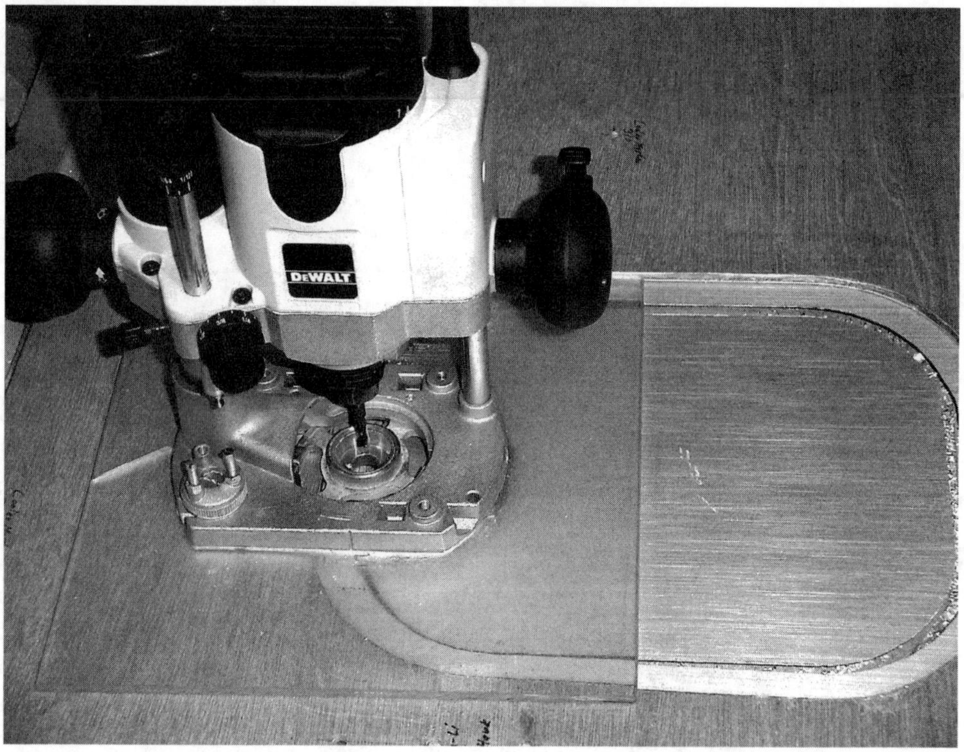

A nibbler removes a tiny rectangle of material per cut. This permits finer control. It also takes a very long time to make a sizable cut. Because the nibbler cuts a rectangle on each stroke, it is very difficult to cut a smooth curve. A nibbled curved cut usually must be smoothed with a file or other abrasive tool.

Electric jigsaws are fast, but you must be very careful to avoid scratching the case when using them.

TIPS OF THE TRADE

Sticky Protection

Apply adhesive paper or tape to the surface that you are cutting. This will provide some protection against incidental damage to the surface. Just be sure to use material that is easy to remove after you are finished.

We cut both windows at the same time. Since each window is in a flat metal panel (the large, removable doors), they are the easiest cuts to make for this mod, as shown in Figures 7-3 and 7-4. Whatever tools you use to cut the windows, take care to do a good job. It's very hard to fix bad cuts afterward.

Regardless of what tools we use, after completing all the cuts, we have to deburr all the cut edges we've generated, even if it looks perfectly smooth. The reason is that we must "break" the corners of the cuts so that they're less likely to cut any of the softer materials. Sharp burrs can cut or scratch the person doing the modding, too, so you don't want to skip this step. To deburr the cut edges, we'll use a deburring tool, shown in Figure 7-5. We can drag the blade of the

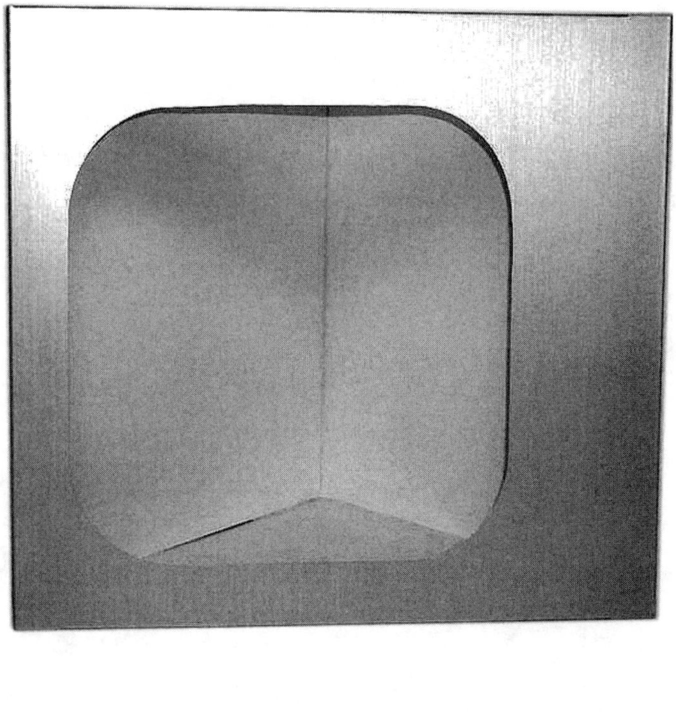

Figure 7-3
The square window cut into the main door, one of the easier cuts

deburring tool along any cut and it will trim away any unwanted aluminum (within reason—you can overdo this if you're not careful). Or you can use a selection of metal files, sandpaper, emery cloth, and more to achieve the same effect, but it will take longer.

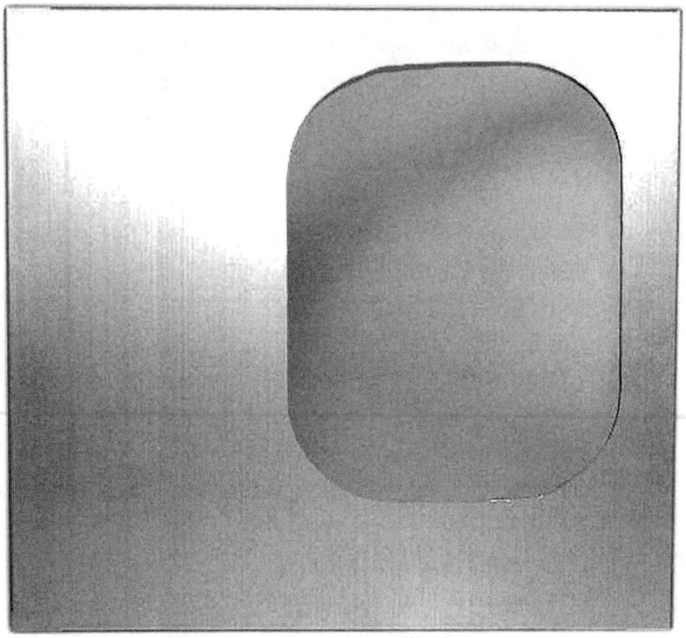

Figure 7-4
The rectangular window cut in the door behind the motherboard tray, which needs deburring on the bottom edge (the lighter areas)

HEADS UP!

Be very careful not to overtrim or deburr any edges. You can cover up some of the cuts with molding or parts, but too much trimming will cause either a lopsided shape or a hole bigger than you intended.

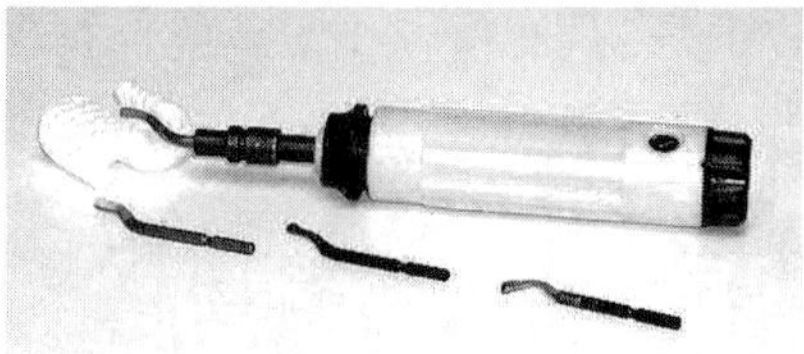

Figure 7-5
Deburring tool

Each window needs further customization. While the rectangular window will get a transparency (discussed at the end of the chapter), the square needs two blowholes cut in it to place two lighted fans. (We'll discuss the fans in Chapter 8.) The blowholes should not be placed too close to the window's edge or each other. Again, the router is put to use after making certain of where the fans will go. (The deburring tool is not necessary on acrylic.)

The bottom of the case requires three slots cut in it, so that the cold cathode lights we'll put there can shine through and give that nice low-rider glow. We'll position one slot, approximately three inches long, at the short end of the case, between the fans at the front of the chassis and the drive bracket, parallel to the front surface of the case. Then we'll position a slot between the side of the case and the motherboard track. There isn't much room here, and we have to dry-fit the cold cathode several times to verify the fit.

HEADS UP!

You can't dry-fit parts too many times. It's better to make sure the parts will fit rather than hope they will!

Once we're satisfied that the slot is where we want it, we mark the centerline on the bottom of the case. The guide track for the motherboard tray is really close to the proposed slot. Also, the pop rivets that hold the track in place prevent us from clamping the template perfectly flat. After we verify that replacement rivets are available, we drill out the rivets and remove the guide track. Now, even if we're a little off on our measurements, we'll still have a functional guide track when we finish cutting.

HEADS UP!

It's usually a good idea to take a picture of the assembly before you remove parts like the guide track. Then you will know what it's supposed to look like when you put it back together.

We clamp a template in place, then "plunge cut" the router at one end and cut straight through to the planned end of the slot. We want the slot to be as long as space allows and still provide support to the two ends of the cold cathode—in this case, 9.5 inches. Lastly, we position a slot opposite the motherboard. There's a little more room here, but for symmetry, we cut this slot the same dimension in from the edge of the case and the same length.

We deburr the three slots at this time; it may not be possible to deburr the edges effectively later. When we're finished deburring, and we're satisfied with the two parallel slots, we reinstall the guide track using fresh rivets. Screws could be substituted for rivets here, but the case will look better with rivets; we've got the rivets, and we have access to an installation tool.

Next we need to cut a hole in the bottom of the case for another blowhole. This one is a 92mm blowhole. All the fans we're using come in kits that include cutting templates. The key here is to place the cut where the fan itself won't interfere with the lights, components, or motherboard, since the bottom fan will be mounted on the inside of the floor.

If you're not sure, dry-fit the fan with all your components installed before you cut. It takes time, but you'll avoid the possible disappointment and frustration of having a perfectly good hole in a perfectly wrong place.

We're going to install a fiber optic lighted fan in this location, so we have two clearance issues. The fan will be inside the case, and the fiber optic light source will be below the case. This way, the fan won't block access to the drive bracket. The bottom of the case will have to be raised to accommodate the light source. If we hadn't dry-fit the parts, we might not have realized this in time to do something about it.

In order to hide the light source from the outside, we'll modify a fan duct, but we'll get into that when we discuss installation of the fans in Chapter 8.

If we were cutting the blowhole freehand (instead of using the router), we'd use the adhesive pattern that came with the kit and carefully drill four screw holes, then drill a starter hole for the fan hole itself and carefully cut to the line on the pattern. When drilling holes for screws, we prefer to use a center punch to locate the holes. Aluminum is a very soft metal, so a light tap will make a serviceable mark. Then we would use a small drill bit, .062 or so, to make a pilot hole, and then finally use a bit sized to the desired finished diameter.

Since we're using the router, we clamp the template onto the case, do four quick plunge cuts for the screws, then plunge into the center hole and complete the circle. Voilà!

The top of the case has another blowhole, this one 120mm, which again we cut with a template: four quick plunge cuts for the screws, then plunge into the center and complete the circle.

Lastly, we modify the fan hole on the back of the case where the factory-installed fan normally is. We're going to install a lighted fan there, so the OEM stuff has to go. The case maker stamped a grill into the chassis and installed an 80mm fan. The grill is efficient, but it'll block the appearance of the lighted fan we want to install there. The new fan will also be 80mm, so we can use the existing mounting screw holes. For the rest, we use a Dremel to cut out the factory grill (while very carefully preserving the arc of the outer diameter of the fan hole). Any lingering roughness is smoothed out using a grinding attachment and a round file, and then we use the deburring tool to complete the job.

Since we'll be installing the rheobuses in the drive bays, no cutting will be needed for those items.

Following all the cuts, we have to deburr the edges so there won't be any sharp bits anywhere. This is something that you should do as you make each cut, but you should certainly do it before you attempt to do anything else after cutting (see Figure 7-6 for cutting ideas). Now we go over the whole case and examine each cut for missed areas. After we deburr any remaining rough spots, we have to clean out the case of any small metal pieces that might cause trouble later.

We clean out the case by shaking it vigorously several times and brushing out all the cracks and crevices. We then vacuum up the pieces that are knocked loose. If you have compressed air, this will help, but the final operation has to be the vacuum cleaning.

HEADS UP!

Make absolutely sure you've removed all loose metal pieces. They will cause nothing but trouble in your case later if you don't clean them out now.

Figure 7-6
Assorted case cuts

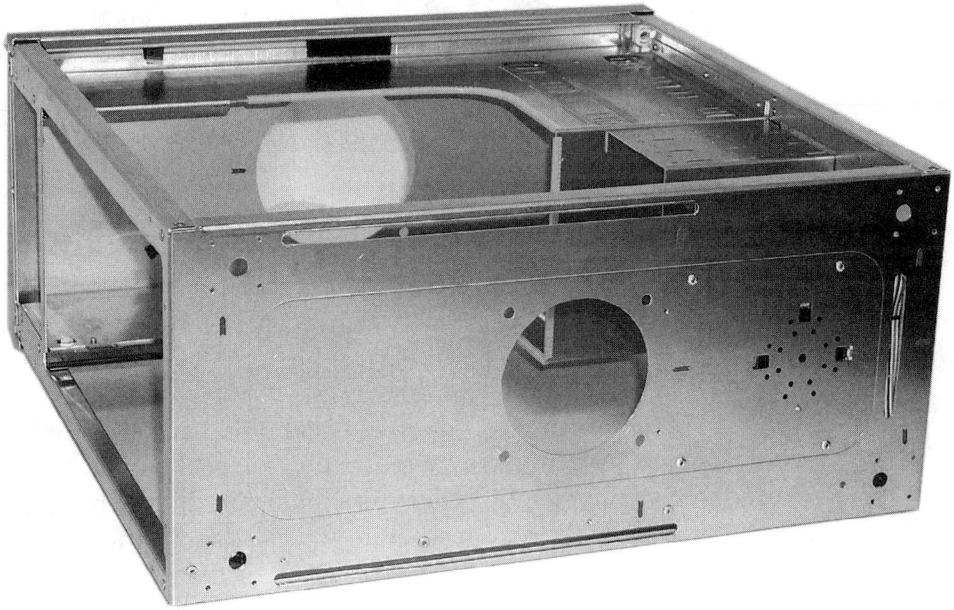

Painting

Time to get painting! The two major areas to paint are the back of the motherboard tray and the interior of the case.

For the back of the tray, we picked "shell white" paint suitable for use on metal. We're using white paint to help the transparency image for the window stand out. On the component side of the tray, we cover the mounting holes with masking tape. We also mask off the edges and motherboard side of the tray, to prevent contamination by overspray. We give the other side two coats of white paint, allowing the paint to dry between coats. Figure 7-7 shows a painted motherboard tray.

After the second coat of paint dries overnight, we remove the masking tape, except for the pieces covering the mounting holes. When we install the motherboard, we'll remove the masking tape from the holes that we'll use, leaving the remaining holes covered. We carefully clean the motherboard tray, removing any unwanted paint and tape-adhesive residue.

We tested different types of paint to get the proper effect, using scraps of metal

Figure 7-7 Motherboard tray, painted on the back side

> **TIPS OF THE TRADE**
>
> **Putty**
>
> For the advanced modder, consider filling in the unused holes with bonding putty. This makes a more cohesive background for the image on the rectangular window. But you should determine which holes you're going to use and fill in the rest before you mask and paint the motherboard tray.

from the case cuts to test colors. Metal paint comes out too dark. We finally decided on fabric paint, available at craft stores: a mix of sparkle green and glow-in-the-dark yellow creates the color we want. Whereas the white paint is applied evenly, the green paint is irregularly daubed on in splotches to the interior case bottom, internal hard drive rack, and other parts of the case interior visible through the window.

HEADS UP!

Don't forget to use masking tape to protect areas you don't want accidental paint on.

We don't need to put paint on the motherboard tray's component side, since the motherboard will cover up most of it, but we do daub some paint along the bottom edge.

Because the floor fan will sit inside the case, we need to use some green paint on the edges of the fan as well, so that it will blend better with the floor. Figure 7-8 shows a painted motherboard interior.

Figure 7-8 The painted interior of the case

Casters

Something to watch out for with wheels on a computer case is that you space the casters evenly on the bottom of the case. If the casters are too close together, the case has a higher possibility of tipping over. A wider wheelbase gives more stability to the case. Therefore, choose carefully where you place your casters. We bought a caster kit from a web-based mod store. This kit comes with self-tapping screws and a drill bit; other kits may vary. We'll use the caster mounting plates for templates.

First we remove the factory-installed feet from the case and discard them. Then we position the mounting plate as close to flush with the corner edges of the case bottom as we can. By turning the caster wheel away from the corner we're working on, we can drill the four holes right through the mounting plate. Next it's a simple matter of screwing the self-tapping screws through the case bottom, four to the caster. Repeat for the other three casters and return the case to an upright position. In this mod, the casters raise the case approximately 2 ¼ inches off the floor, which is plenty of room for the bottom-mounted fan.

However, a quick examination of the penetration of the screws at the rear corners suggests that the points of two screws in each of the rear casters are going to interfere with mounting the cold cathode lights. Sure enough, a dry-fit confirms our suspicions. (This is why it's always important to dry-fit.) There's nothing we can do except grind off the points of the screws until they do not protrude above flush with the inside floor of the case. This is a "cut and fit" process.

It takes us a couple of tries before we determine the right amount to remove from each of the four offending screws. We have to be careful that the cut-down screws will still mesh into the threads we originally formed into the case when we first installed the screws. Figure 7-9 shows the final mounting positions of the casters.

Figure 7-9 The four casters installed on the bottom of the case

Our casters come with locking tabs, which can be toggled to prevent the wheels from turning. This is convenient to keep your case from rolling around, or rolling off a desk or table, once you get it in the location you prefer.

Film

Meanwhile, we want to try a different effect for the window behind the motherboard tray. We don't want a conventional decal or cutout on this window—they're too common and too "controlled." We want a unique look in real color, instead of a white-on-clear decal.

We've picked out an image on the Internet to use for the rectangular window. It's a false-color image of one of the smaller, irregularly shaped bodies in the solar system, with some corona effects from the solar wind. For this mod, we've chosen an image from a web site that has public-domain images. Whenever possible, be sure to either use public-domain images, or secure the permission of the image holder before using the image. The colors in this image are right for the green and blue lighting theme of this mod, and it will scale to fit the space of the window. It requires some tweaking, but that's no big deal with a basic paint or image program.

A pack of transparency decals can be purchased from any office supply store. We printed some practice images on regular paper with different printers to make sure we got the size, alignment, and colors that we wanted, then we printed a decal.

TIPS OF THE TRADE

Check the Printer

Different printers, naturally, give different results, based on laser, inkjet, and printer quality. It's worth checking out how the image will look when printed on different machines; in all likelihood, your friends or family or local copy shop have different printers than you do.

We hold the decal up to a light source, which can be a bright overhead light or a sunlit window, to see if we're getting the effect we want. Once we achieve the right look, we wait to apply the decal until the window is installed in the door.

At this point, all the window and case cuts are complete. The next steps are to install all the cold cathode lights and the lighted fans. We'll discuss these procedures in the next chapter.

TESTING 1-2-3

Let's review the cuts and steps in this chapter:

- ❑ Measure and mark areas for cuts
  - ❑ Measure, mark, and test proposed fan locations
  - ❑ Measure, mark, and test proposed window locations

- ❑ Cut holes in the case
    - ❑ Cut fan holes
    - ❑ Cut window holes
    - ❑ Deburr all holes in metal parts
    - ❑ Clean up all loose cutting debris
- ❑ Painting
    - ❑ Paint the back of the motherboard tray
    - ❑ Paint the interior of the case
- ❑ Casters
    - ❑ Remove factory-installed feet
    - ❑ Add casters
- ❑ Film
    - ❑ Find an acceptable image
    - ❑ Modify image, if necessary
    - ❑ Test-print image
    - ❑ Print image on decal material

Chapter 8

Installing Lights and Lighted Fans

Tools of the Trade

Nibbler tool
Deburring tool or file
Small screwdrivers—Phillips and common (one of each)
Clear glue, caulk, or RTV adhesive
A good laser or inkjet printer
Large wire cutter
Small wire cutter, clippers, or small saw
Sandpaper, emery paper, or other finishing material
Two 80mm green LED fans
Three 80mm green cold cathode fans
One 92mm fiber optic fan
One 120mm fiber optic fan
Two green 10-inch CCF lights
One dual (or two single) white 10-inch CCF light
Two green and two blue 4-inch CCF lights
Paint (left over from Chapter 7)
Supplementary power supply 12VDC (1500 mw)
Two black wire grills—one 80mm and one 120 mm
Black electrical tape, 3/4-inch wide
Clear window decals for printing
One 92mm fan duct
Two or three "Y" splitters (enough to test power connections)

This chapter describes how to install all the lighted elements (but not their controls, the subject of Chapter 9) in the case-lighting mod. It also discusses lighted fans and some of the effects you can create with them.

Installing the Floor Fan and Lights

The first task is to mount the 92mm fiber optic fan on the floor of the case to serve as the intake fan. After you dry-fit the fan (again), install the LED circuit card assembly in the fan duct. Recall that you previously cut the duct to the desired height, cut slots in the duct for the circuit card assembly ends to slip into so they can protrude outside the duct wall and accept the mounting standoffs, and cut "U"-shaped notches in the flange of the duct to clear the same standoffs. Now dry-fit the assembled duct and LED circuit card assembly to the bottom of the case. Hmm. We forgot to provide a hole for the power wires to go through the case!

HEADS UP!

This example shows how important it is to be flexible in your work and to be prepared for anything.

The dry-fit shows where the power wires need to go. Put on your eye protection and break out your trusty nibbling tool. Cut a notch in the case and also in the flange of the fan duct, as shown in Figure 8-1; both notches must be big enough to allow the wires to pass through without chafing on either the duct or the case floor. Next deburr the notch in the case, to minimize anything getting cut (such as your fingers or the wire insulation). Remember to thoroughly clean the case of all chips, dust, and debris that you generated while using the nibbler and deburring tool. Since we dry-fit everything ahead of time, the wires pass through the molded openings as though we had planned it from the very beginning.

Figure 8-1
Case bottom cuts

Now for the tricky part: screwing everything together. First pick a screwdriver that fits through the mounting holes on the fan. Carefully line up the fan on the inside of the case, and the duct/circuit card assembly on the outside. We discover that we have to cut two more notches in the duct flange if we want to put screws in all four corners of the fan. Instead we decide to just use the two screws necessary to screw the fan into the standoffs on the circuit card assembly board (make sure that the LED leads are not pinched before you tighten everything down).

Now hook up the power connector on the fan and bundle the fan leads with the leads from the LED board, so that all the leads exit from the corner of the fan that is nearest both the motherboard tray and the front of the case.

Now it is time to touch up our paint. We break out our bottle of paint and daub a little green on the screw heads and the wires where they are visible so that everything is sickly green and blended in.

HEADS UP!

Don't throw away any paint until you're absolutely done, and don't worry about having leftover paint. If you need to mix more, it's often not a problem, especially with a design like this that does not require an even shade of color.

It's never too early to check out your handiwork, so hook up the rig to a supplementary power supply. Our case seems a little too blue (we started with two blue and two green LEDs), so we are replacing the two blue LEDs with two green LEDs, which looks better. After you are done checking out the performance of the fiber optic fan, disconnect the power so that you can install the CCF lights on the bottom of the case.

We're trying to throw as much light as we can below the case as well as light the interior, but we do not want to mount lights underneath the case because they would be very exposed to possible breakage. We also don't want the green light mounted behind the motherboard tray to shine up into the case. To get these lights as close as possible to the slots in the bottom of the case, we are going to cut off the cubical mounting blocks that came on the CCF lights. If you decide to do the same for your case, use a large wire cutter to ensure that you do not damage the light in any way. Engage the mounting block so that when you close the jaws (see Figure 8-2), the mount splits into two pieces without the wire cutter touching any of the other parts of the light. We do this to two 10-inch green lights and one 4-inch green light (of course, you can choose your own colors).

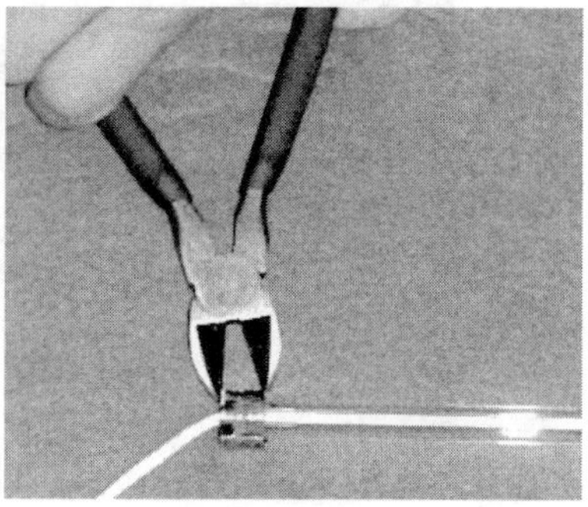

Figure 8-2 How to cut the mounting block properly

HEADS UP!

Be very careful when cutting any part of a lighting component. Make sure all of your parts are safely secured so that you don't waste time and money by breaking a light instead of cutting part of the housing off.

Next take the light destined to be behind the motherboard tray and run a piece of black electrical tape (¾-inch wide) the length of the acrylic tube, making sure that the black tape runs exactly parallel to the long axis of the tube. When you're done, the tape should cover exactly half the circumference of the acrylic tube. This will prevent the light from shining back into the case, and the electrical tape is safe to use on the light.

Place a glob of RTV adhesive where the ends of the black-taped green light will rest on the bottom of the case, taking care to apply enough to form a bed for the tube, but not so much that the excess will migrate into the slot through the case or into the motherboard slide groove. Now seat the light into position, with the lead wires exiting toward the front of the case. Take care to orient the light so that the black tape is opposite the surface of the bottom of the case. Using the same technique, set the other 10-inch light in place with its leads exiting toward the front of the case; then set the 4-inch light in place with its leads exiting toward the motherboard side of the case. With the RTV freshly applied, everything is very unstable, so you must allow all three light installations to cure overnight before you do anything more.

HEADS UP!

You may be eager to keep going with the mod, but you must let the adhesive cure first so that the case looks good and the parts are held securely in place.

The next day, it's time to check what we've wrought. We "daisy-chain" a series of "Y" splitters to provide temporary power to the lights and verify that all systems are up and running. Everything works, as shown in Figure 8-3. Now we'll look at the front and rear of the case.

Figure 8-3
Case bottom with powered lights

Front and Rear Fans and Lights

It's time to replace the two previously removed factory-installed intake fans at the front of the case. Their replacements are two 80mm clear fans with circular green cold cathode elements mounted on their exhaust (inboard) sides.

No special tools are required for this installation—just make sure the power leads exit in the proper location for your desired routing of the bundles. Time for another power-up: Voilà!

By this time, we've accumulated two inverters and several bundles of wire. It would be handy to hide the inverters under the internal drive housing, but there's a factory-installed speaker in the way. We decide to discard the factory speaker, since we're going to install our own speakers anyway. Once we have the speaker out of the way, we dry-fit the inverters in this space. They're a little too high and interfere with the fit of the housing. If we remove the double-sided tape, there's just enough clearance to accommodate three inverters. If we were to flatten or remove the speaker retaining tabs, we could fit up to five inverters in the remaining space. However, we're going to use only three inverters, so we don't have to alter the case in this way. Besides, by using only three inverters, there's some room to hide all the connectors that this setup demands.

Next install the 80mm fiber optic fan in the rear panel of the case, where you previously removed and discarded the factory-installed exhaust fan and removed the stamped grill. We are using a black wire grill to minimize obscuring the light pattern of the fan. We'll continue to use blue and green LEDs for now. Orient the fan so that the leads exit toward the top of the case. Power up the fan to verify that all systems are go.

The Case Top

Install the 120mm fiber optic fan in the top panel of the case, where you already cut the blowhole. As with the 80mm fan, we are using a black wire grill to minimize obscuring the light pattern of the fan. We are installing four LEDs, each a different color: amber, red, green, and blue. Orient the fan so that the leads exit toward the front of the case. Hook up temporary power to the fan and light the circuit card assembly to verify, again, that all systems are go (see Figure 8-4).

Figure 8-4
Case top with powered lights

Now turn the case upside down. Install a 4-inch blue CCF light (or whichever color you prefer) on the inside surface of the power supply bracket. You can locate the light by using the grommet on the edge of the bracket. Orient the light so that the leads exit toward the front of the case.

Now you have a mysterious blue tinge filtering down from somewhere in the upper, unseen reaches of the case.

Behind the Motherboard Tray

It's time to install yet another CCF light. This one is really difficult, because it will backlight the decal on the blank side of the motherboard tray. We want true color here, and as little scatter into the main, green compartment as possible. Our plan is to use a 10-inch light. The only space that seems to meet these requirements is a few inches directly above the taped green CCF light we already installed. But how will we position the light so that it illuminates the way we want?

We dry-fit a white CCF light and power it up. We're not happy with the look. The light is bright enough near the bottom of the motherboard tray, but it fades out about halfway up. This will look terrible with artwork in front of it. The solution: more light.

Instead of one CCF light, we'll install a dual 10-inch CCF light on the motherboard tray, with Velcro so that we can remove the lights easily when the tray must come out of the case. We dry-install the two lights so that they run vertically, one light snug to the front edge of the motherboard tray, and the other light snug to the rear corner of the case. We power up the lights and hold the door against the case to gauge the effect, which looks pretty good, as shown in Figure 8-5.

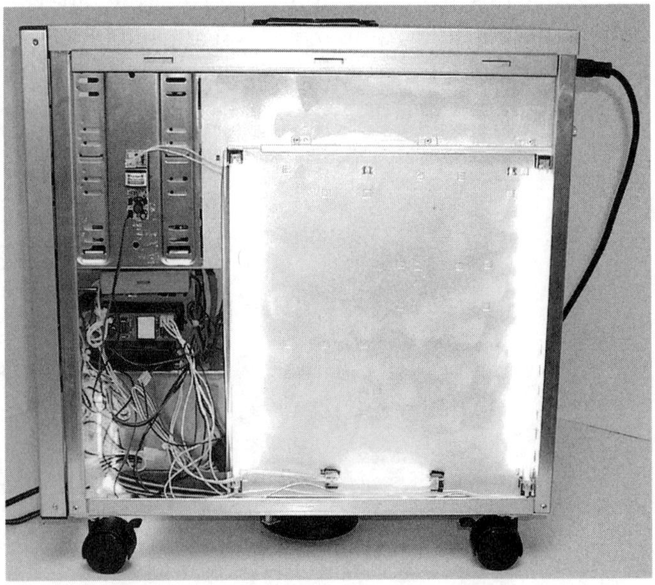

Figure 8-5
Cold cathode lights with white-painted motherboard tray

Next we install the lights using the Velcro patches that come with the kit. We route the leads so that the inverter can be tucked out of sight behind the hard drive bracket. Now we power up the circuit and install the door.

The result is very satisfying, at least to us. The translucent molding picks up the white light and frames the window in a pearly glow around both sides and across the top and bottom, about a half-inch band of light all the way around with a very slight dimming at the middle of the top and bottom of the window. The motherboard has a texture and appearance similar to a movie screen. Although the reflection is bright, there is no glare. It's kind of stark, though, with no image on the window.

After admiring our work, we turn the case so that we're looking from the opposite side. Oops! All that white light is leaking through and washing out our carefully crafted sickly green environment.

We return to the motherboard tray side of the case and remove the door. We carefully disengage the white CCF light from the edge of the motherboard tray, without disconnecting it from the inverter, and lay it on the table just under the case. We get out some ¾-inch-wide electrical tape (black plastic) and cut it to length so that we can stick the tape to the return on the motherboard tray from top to bottom. The tape sticks out about 3/8-inch for the whole length of the motherboard return. We cut another piece of tape the same length and carefully install the second piece on the opposite side of the motherboard return, so that the overhangs of the two tapes seal together.

We've made a crude "sweep seal" that is similar to what you could find on the bottom of doors. This seal has the effect of closing the gap between the motherboard tray and the door, so that much less light leaks into the main case cavity. By using this method, we avoid any actual attachment to the case door. We use black plastic tape because we want the color to be black, green, or white; we want the tape surface to be as slick as possible; and we had black tape on the workbench. See Figure 8-6 for images of the sweep seal.

Figure 8-6 The sweep seal, from two angles

We replace the white lights on their Velcro mounts, then install the door and rotate the case to confirm that very little of the white light is leaking into the main case cavity.

Now it's time to put our chosen image on the rear window. Like everything else, it comes out better if you plan it well beforehand. We are using Hammer-mill-brand "clear window decals," but there are several brands available, and most have easy-to-follow instructions for use.

HEADS UP!

Be sure the decal material is suitable for your printer. Some decals cannot be used with laser printers.

Here's how to coordinate the decal and the window:

1. Select a rectangular window kit instead of a square or other shape because the rectangular kit is almost a perfect fit for the largest commonly available size of decal material—8½×11 inches.
2. This size window will not overlap the edges of your motherboard tray if you positioned the window carefully in the door when you made your cuts.
3. Pick an image that has the right combination of color and subject after you size the image to fit in an 8½×11-inch frame.
4. Manipulate the image so that you can put the film on the interior side of the window and get the look you want. This makes the most sense, because you will rarely disturb the interior side of the window, but you will occasionally clean the external side because of accumulated dust, fingerprints, or pizza oil.
5. After several plain-paper trials, print the decal and then let it dry overnight. This is not always mandatory, but guarantees the ink will be completely dry on the decal and thus will not smudge easily.

Here's how to install the decal:

1. Install the window in the door. Carefully clean the "interior" side, using a soft cloth, and allow the window to dry.
2. Dry-fit the decal to the window. Trim the decal corners and edges to fit very closely to the edge of the molding that retains the window. Do this very carefully so that the decal lies flat on the window, with little or no gap between the edge of the decal and the molding.

HEADS UP!

The decal backing may have gridlines. You can use these to make sure you keep your decal oriented perfectly.

3. Peel off the backing and carefully apply the decal to the window. We found that the best way is to start at one edge and press the middle of the edge down and across the decal, working any trapped air forward and to the sides. Don't get frustrated if you cannot work all the air out and are left with a pattern of bubbles 1mm or smaller in diameter. We discovered after we installed the door that the bubbles "disappear" with or without backlighting. Now your windowed door is ready for installation on the case. Figure 8-7 shows our finished door.

HEADS UP!

The decal is probably removable and reusable. If you think you'll want to do this, save your backing so that you can store the removed decal.

Figure 8-7 Rear window with decal

We install the door. The image looks okay, but without light there is no life. With power to the lights, the image leaps, glowing, from the surface of the window. Because the image is suspended above the mottled reflective surface of the motherboard tray, it seems to shift slightly as your perspective changes.

This is a great way to showcase an image that you're especially fond of. Any image that you can print you can display in true color, thanks to the white backlighting and the blank surface of the motherboard tray.

TIPS OF THE TRADE

Image Is Everything

For this sort of window and lighting mod, you want to pick the right image for your decal. Bright colors with contrast work well. A light-colored or white background is good, because you don't have to use a lot of ink to print it (since white comes out "clear" when printed). You'll also want a well-defined image that is easily recognizable if you do choose a background. A picture of your camouflage-clad space marine shooting gray aliens in a brown hallway isn't going to grab people's attention as easily as your brightly garbed elf wizard standing against the sky.

We install a 4-inch blue CCF light just below the image, but out of sight of the viewer. Like the 10-inch white CCF lights, we mount this 4-inch light on the motherboard tray, using Velcro. This adds a blue sheen to the horizontal middle of the window, fading out in the middle, returning at the very top. We like it, although we probably won't use it to light every image we install.

With all these lights, we need a whole lot of controls. We'll be using all three 3½-inch bays to install rheobuses that have lighted blue knobs. This gives us 12 individual controls. They make a 3×4 pattern of blue rings above the wash of green light emanating from the front intake fans. See Figure 8-8 for a view of the case with lighted rheobus knobs, lighted rear window, and light emanating from the case bottom and fans. How we hook all this up, and where we get the power, is the subject of Chapter 9.

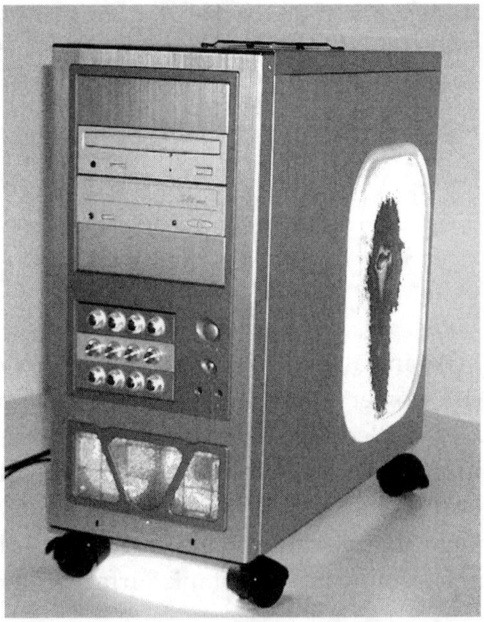

Figure 8-8 Three-quarter case view

The Wide World of Fans

Fans have come a long way in recent years. In the past, only four qualities were used to choose a fan: airflow (in cubic feet per minute, or CFM); loudness (in decibels, or dB(A)); size (larger fans move more air with less noise); and name brand, for people who care about the quality of the components. To a lesser extent, fan construction can also be a factor. Fans have different bearings, the cheapest and noisiest being sleeve bearings. Ball bearings with one or two balls are next on the list, and then Panaflo fans (by Panasonic), which even have bearings that are packed in mineral oil.

Now there are new considerations. There are fans with varying speed depending on the temperature. There are fans with controls directly built in, so that you can adjust the speed manually, without a control device such as a rheobus. But we're most concerned about the last new category of fans—fans that are lighted.

Fiber Optic Fans

Fiber optic fans (two are mounted in the square window) generate different shapes of blurs and swirls of light depending on the fan's speed. As the fan speed is slowed, the lighted portion assumes the appearance of several scimitar-shaped whirling blades, although as you slow the speed of the fan, the intensity of the light also diminishes. This is a great effect, but the fiber optic fan is inherently inefficient because the slower the fan spins, the less light gets trapped by the fiber optic strands, and the darker the effect is.

Fiber optic fans are popular because a variety of visual effects can be achieved with separate light and fan power. However, fiber optic fans cannot be used in every application, because the visual effect can only be observed on the exhaust side of the fan. (Although we do like the cool effect of the light scatter on the intake side of the fan caused by the transmission of the light through the transparent hub and optic fibers.)

If you have a suitable location to utilize its effects, a fiber optic fan can offer several variations of effect: color and combinations of color, pattern, and movement. This makes the fiber optic fan a more dynamic modification effect than any other kind of lighted fan.

Most fiber optic fans transmit light from a stationary light source to an output lens on one or more blades of the fan. The fiber optic fans we are using use high-intensity LEDs mounted on a circuit card assembly in such a way that the individual LEDs can be removed and replaced with others of a different color or intensity, easily and without tools. By using four LEDs of the same color, we can achieve three bands of uniform color. By alternating LEDs of two colors, we can achieve four segments of the circles in the base colors with a gradual blending as it transitions from one color to the next. By picking four colors, the effect can be doubled to provide four segments of different colors in the band. By manipulating the position of the LEDs in their sockets, varying proportions of color can be achieved.

In addition and independent of color variations, varying the speed of the fan will achieve a pattern ranging from a full circle down to a dot slightly larger than the diameter of the optic fiber. These dots will appear to traverse around the circle of the fan blades proportional to the speed setting of the fans. By varying the intensity of the LEDs, this effect can be modified to speed up or slow down the apparent traversal of the dots, even to the point that the dots appear to reverse direction and "moonwalk" (duplicating the well-known effect of the spokes on wagon wheels apparently going backward in movies).

Changing the speed of the fan and the intensity of the LEDs can lead to any of the following and more: full circles of light, short dashes of light that appear to move slowly or not at all around the fan hub, and even strobes or dashes that appear to travel in reverse around the hub.

Cold Cathode Fans

Cold cathode lighted fans provide greater increases in brightness. When the cold cathode bulb is fully powered, it can overwhelm all other visible effects by its brilliance. There are three fans illuminated with CCF lights in the case: the two intake fans visible through filters at the front of the case, and the exhaust fan at the rear of the case next to the power supply. The CCF lights are so bright that in this mod they provide a significant portion of the total light in the case. We prefer to run some of these CCF lights at less than full power to mute the effect of the total amount of light they can put out.

At maximum intensity, it is difficult to see the fan blades other than as a shimmering disc outlined by the brilliant lighted ring of the CCF light. As you reduce power to the CCF light, the fan blades are more visible in the same manner as fan blades illuminated by LEDs, but because of the greater intensity of the CCF light, the fan blades are more visible regardless of their speed than if LEDs were used.

Modifying the Fan Duct

We also need to modify a fan duct to create a shroud for the floor-mounted lighted fan. The lighted fan is so bright that it will outshine the rest of the lights, and we don't want quite that much light out of the bottom. Therefore, we'll use a fan duct to "shroud" some of the light and, coincidentally, protect part of the fan.

The fan sticks up from the floor of the case, but the mounting posts and the printed circuit board with the LED bar hang below the case. Turn the case upside down or on its side so you can work on it more easily.

First you need to drill holes in the "lip" of the fan duct. These holes need to be in the same positions as the fan's mounting posts and the mounting holes you already drilled in the case floor. Because the duct is made of plastic, drilling through it is easy.

Next determine where the fan's LED bar will be in relation to the duct. This bar will be "inside" the duct. You may need to cut holes in the side of the duct to make clearance for the circuit board. This cutting can be done with clippers or wire cutters.

Lastly, most fan ducts come in only one length, and you'll have to cut it down to size. Our duct has ridges on the outside that we can use as a guide to evenly cut and remove the excess. This cutting can be done with clippers, wire cutters, or a small saw. You may want to sand or finish any rough edges after cutting. The finished shroud must have enough clearance off the floor to provide air intake—we recommend no less than half an inch of clearance, more if your case will be on carpet much of the time.

Once this is done, mount the fan in the floor of the case and thread the mounting posts through the case floor and the holes in the lip of the fan duct. Secure the posts with the hardware provided in the fan kit. Secure the LED bar in the duct as well. Figure 8-9 shows how the LED bar, fan, and shroud look from beneath when assembled.

Figure 8-9 Assembled lighted fan and shroud

TESTING 1-2-3

Here's what we've covered in this chapter:

- ❑ The case floor
    - ❑ Mounting fans
    - ❑ Installing lights

  - ❑ Touching up with paint
  - ❑ Testing
  - ❑ Cutting mounting blocks from lights
  - ❑ Gluing parts into the case
- ❑ The case back and front
  - ❑ Dry-fitting parts
  - ❑ Installing the fans
  - ❑ Hooking up the lights
- ❑ The case top
  - ❑ Installing the lighted fan
- ❑ Behind the motherboard tray
  - ❑ Installing lights
  - ❑ Creating and installing sweep seals
- ❑ The rectangular window decal
  - ❑ Making the decal
  - ❑ Applying the decal
- ❑ Types of fans
  - ❑ Fiber optic fans, pro and con
  - ❑ Cold cathode fans, pro and con
- ❑ Modifying the fan duct
  - ❑ Drilling mounting holes
  - ❑ Cutting the fan duct
  - ❑ Mounting the fan in the shroud

Chapter 9

Installing the Controls and Routing the Wires

Tools of the Trade

Clear glue, caulk, or RTV adhesive
Small Phillips and common screwdrivers (one of each)
Wire stripper
Three rheobus units (four control circuits per rheobus)
Gauze safety tape
Electrical tape
Paint (left over from Chapter 7)
Supplementary power supply, 12VDC
Three "Y" power splitters

The lights and fans are installed, but unless you want them to be all on or all off at the same time, you'll need controls. These same controls can help you tailor the effects of the overall mod at any given time. In this chapter, we'll review the types of controls and how to install them.

Introduction to Controls

Your choice of controls is a very important part of your mod. The following are the main types of controls:

- **Switches** These are basic on/off switches. They are the simplest and easiest to wire. When using this type of control, you can buy inexpensive metal or plastic switches at a variety of electronics stores, such as Radio Shack, or you can go for a cool-looking lighted switch.

- **Rheostats** These are controls, such as the dimmer switches, in your house. We are going to use a rheostat device called a *rheobus,* which will enable us to control the brightness of our lights. We will also use a rheobus to control the speed of our fans. This is great for keeping your computer quiet.
- **Sound-activated switches** These are useful for gamers who like to see lights flash in response to what is happening in the game. These switches are fun and heighten the game experience.

Other types of controls are also available, such as temperature-activated controls (used to control fan speed). For our project, we are using only the three rheobus units. However, you can experiment with any of these types of switches to add unique touches to your mod project.

Installation of the Controls

We've installed the lights and the fans, but they won't activate all by themselves. We need to install the controls. We'll be using rheobuses to control the lights and fans. It would be easier to connect all (or most) of the lights into one circuit that we simply switch on and off, but we want to be able to individually control all the lights that we install. If we can control each light, then we should be able to present various "looks" without altering the installation. Since we are using seven lighted fans, we will need to control the fans' speed as well as the light effects on each fan.

The following list breaks down how the 12 rheobus circuits will be used to control the various devices:

- The green LED 80mm blowhole intake fans mounted in the square window will be controlled as a pair, by one rheobus circuit.
- The LEDs of the 80mm blowhole intake fans will be controlled as a pair, by one rheobus circuit. This circuit will also control the electroluminescent (EL) wire embedded in the molding around the square window.
- The green cold cathode 80mm exhaust fan mounted in the rear panel next to the power supply is wired to be "always on." Its green cold cathode light will be controlled separately, with one rheobus circuit.

- The green cold cathode 80mm intake fans mounted at the bottom of the front panel will be controlled by the manual switch that is factory installed on the inner front panel of the case. To be able to vary the intensity of the lights on these fans, the lights will be controlled independent of the fans, using one rheobus circuit to control the pair of lights.
- The fiber optic 92mm intake fan mounted in the floor of the case will require two rheobus circuits, one for the fan and one for the fiber optic system.
- The fiber optic 120mm blowhole fan mounted in the top of the case will also require two rheobus circuits.
- The three green cold cathode lights in the bottom of the case will be controlled as a group by one rheobus circuit.
- The two cold cathode lights that illuminate the painted back of the motherboard tray (so that the reflected light backlights the transparency mounted on the rectangular window) will be controlled as a pair with one rheobus circuit.
- The four-inch blue cold cathode light mounted at the bottom of the motherboard tray will use a separate rheobus circuit, so that varying tints of blue can be introduced into the backlighting.
- The four-inch blue cold cathode light above the square window will use a separate rheobus circuit, so that tints of blue can be introduced into the main case cavity.

Now that we have reviewed how we want to control each of the devices, we will describe the step-by-step process of connecting each device to its control.

Connecting the Exhaust Fan

The factory-installed 80mm exhaust fan was powered directly from the case power supply 12VDC circuit. We will power the green cold cathode 80mm exhaust fan the same way, but we want to be able to tap into the same circuit for other devices. First make sure the computer is turned off and the power plug is not plugged in the wall. Next plug a "Y" splitter cable into the case power-supply receptacle that the 80mm exhaust fan formerly occupied.

The "Y" splitter, shown in Figure 9-1, does just what its name suggests. It splits one circuit into two parallel circuits, or branches. In theory, you could continue adding splitters to branches indefinitely, limited only by the amount of power available from the power supply for the devices attached, and the amount of space available for the devices and splitters. In practice, you will use only as many splitters as you need to power all of your devices.

Figure 9-1
"Y" power splitter

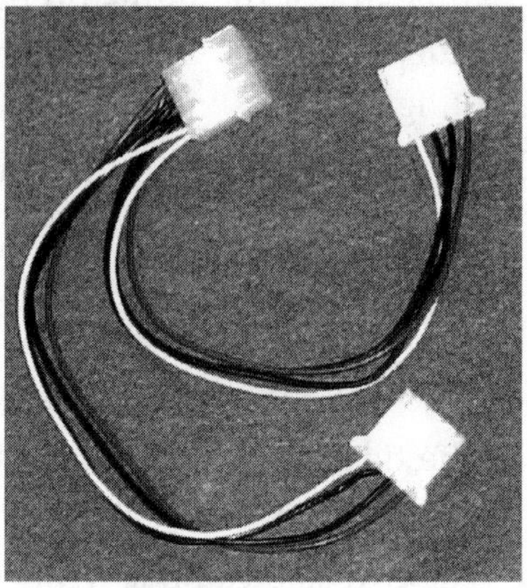

We connect the rear exhaust 80mm fan to one of the splitter branches from the case power supply. Whenever the computer is running, the fan will spin at full speed. Do not connect the green cold cathode light to the splitter. Instead, route the leads for the light across the top and toward the front of the case and down to the 3½-inch drive bay, where you will connect to a rheobus circuit.

Turn on the computer; when you are satisfied the fan is operating properly, turn off the computer.

Connecting the Intake Fans

Next remove the front panel bezel from the case. The connectors for the two green cold cathode 80mm front intake fans are the same as the factory-installed fans we removed. This allows us to plug the new fans' connectors into the factory-installed manual fan-speed control switch that is mounted below the "power on" LED.

HEADS UP!

You must remove the front bezel of the case to operate this switch. The switch may be set for high, medium, or low speed and controls both front intake fans.

Do not connect the green cold cathode wires to the manual speed control switch. Route the cold cathode wires up to the 3½-inch drive bay, where they will be connected to a rheobus.

Turn on the computer and verify that the switch settings vary the speeds of the two fans, as a pair.

Connecting the Rheobuses

We now have four more (lighted) fans and eight lighted devices to control. We can do this with our 12 rheobus circuits. We're going to install the rheobuses in the three 3½-inch drive bays, in three rows of four circuits per row. There is not enough room to install all three rheobuses and then make the desired connections, so we will install one at a time—we will install the bottom row, then the middle row, and finish up with the top row. Figure 9-2 shows how the rheobus units will look when the installations are complete.

Figure 9-2 The three rheobus units as they will be mounted in the case. The difference in knobs is based on style.

For each group, you must route the wiring from the lights or fans to the desired connectors on the rheobus. Then you must install the wiring into the connectors. If the fans and lighting devices that you are installing come from the factory with connectors compatible with the rheobuses, you can simply plug each device's connector into the desired rheobus. If the connectors are not compatible, or if you decide to trim the wires to a shorter length, you will have to use the rheobuses' screw clamp connectors.

First you must prepare each wire. For this you need a wire stripper. After cutting each wire to the desired length, strip one-quarter inch of insulation off the end of the wire, taking care not to nick or cut through any of the strands of copper. Twist the copper strands into a tight bundle, following the natural twist (the wire will resist being twisted the opposite way). Back out the clamp screw of the contact that you want to install the wire into. Insert the wire into the contact, being careful to insert the wire fully, but not so far that the clamp engages the insulation jacket instead of the stripped copper. Holding the wire and connector together, screw down the clamp screw firmly. Gently pull the wire to verify that it will not slip out of the connection. Repeat this for each wire that you connect. For 12 circuits, this process can require several hours' effort.

Fortunately, all of our devices are terminated with connectors that are compatible with the connectors on our rheobuses, so it will take only minutes to plug in all 12 circuits.

We selected four circuits for the bottom row of controls:

- The group of three green cold cathodes that are installed on the floor of the case
- The cold cathodes on the pair of 80mm intake fans at the front of the case
- The LEDs on the fans mounted in the square window, plus the EL wire installed in the molding that frames the window
- The power leads of the two fans mounted in the square window

Route the leads from the fans, LEDs, and EL wire so that the door hides them, except where they must cross the window opening. Stack the inverters (there are four of them) for the fan cold cathode lights behind the front panel, in the empty space next to the 3½-inch drive bays. Continue the routing until you position the connectors next to where the rheobus contacts should be.

The EL wire is easy to hide behind the door. Route the EL leads parallel to the cold cathode leads all the way to the rheobus.

Route the leads from the floor cold cathodes under the internal hard drive bay bracket (remember, you removed the factory-installed speaker earlier), so that the three inverters can reside in this space. Then route the leads from the inverters up to the rheobus.

Next remove the drive bracket from the 3½-inch drive bay by unscrewing the three thumbscrews. Select a rheobus and position it at the bottom of the drive bracket. The drive bracket has a variety of slots and holes to accommodate various devices' mounting screws. Select a position that puts the front face of the rheobus flush with the front panel bezel surface. Dry-fit the bracket/rheobus assembly. When you are satisfied that the rheobus is where you want it to be, remove the bracket/rheobus assembly from the case and tighten the rheobus mounting screws in the bracket.

Route four sets of wires through the rear opening of the bracket and push the plugs into the selected rheobus connectors. Plug a "Y" splitter into the outlet of the supplementary 12VDC power supply. Plug one of the branches into the rheobus power connector—the other branch will power the middle rheobus. Make sure that when you push the rheobus into place it does not pinch any wires or dislodge any of the new, or existing, connections and that all the wires and hardware fit without tumbling into the main case cavity.

Slide the partially loaded bracket back into the case and tighten the thumbscrews. Turn on the supplementary power supply. After you verify that all four controlled devices operate properly, turn off the power supply.

We are going to control the fiber optic fans with the middle bank of controls. We'll control the 92mm floor intake fan with the left pair of controls, and the 120mm top exhaust fan with the right pair of controls. In each pair, the left knob will control the speed and the right knob will control the brightness of the lights.

Route the leads from the 92mm fan behind the internal hard drive bay bracket and up into the 3½-inch drive bay bracket. Similarly, route the leads from the top exhaust fan behind the 5¼-inch drive bay bracket and down into the 3½-inch drive bay bracket.

Next remove the drive bracket from the 3½-inch drive bay. Select a rheobus and position it directly above the bottom rheobus, then tighten the rheobus mounting screws in the bracket.

Route four sets of wires through the rear opening of the bracket and push the plugs into the selected middle rheobus connectors. Plug a "Y" splitter into the open branch from the bottom rheobus splitter. Plug one of the branches into the middle rheobus power connector. The other branch will power the top rheobus. Install the bracket into the drive bay opening in the case.

Make sure that when you push the rheobus into place it does not pinch any wires or dislodge any of the new, or existing, connections and that all the wires and hardware fit without tumbling into the main case cavity. Turn on the supplementary power supply. After you verify that all four middle rheobus-controlled devices operate properly, and that all four bottom rheobus-controlled devices work properly, turn off the power supply.

We're going to use the top bank of controls for our most dramatic effects. These are the lights that have the most effect on the appearance of this case:

- ❑ The green rear exhaust 80mm fan cold cathode light
- ❑ The four-inch blue cold cathode light mounted under the top of the case
- ❑ The portrait effect in the motherboard door (two white cold cathode lights)
- ❑ The accent lighting in the portrait effect (one blue four-inch cold cathode light)

From the rear exhaust 80mm fan cold cathode (remember, the fan itself is already powered), we route the leads up the back wall of the case, across the top, to where we mount the inverter. Most inverters that come in modding kits come with adhesive-backed Velcro tabs so you can mount the inverter anywhere.

We mount the inverter in some free space at the top of the case. From the inverter, we continue routing behind the 5¼-inch drive bay bracket and down into the 3½-inch drive bay bracket.

From the 4-inch blue cold cathode mounted in the top of the case, we route the leads across the opening for a 5¼-inch drive, to where we mount the inverter with the existing cluster behind the front panel. From the inverter, we continue routing down into the 3½-inch drive bay bracket

From the dual white cold cathode mounted on the back of the motherboard tray, we route the leads up to where we mount the inverter with the existing cluster behind the front panel. It's starting to get crowded here. From the inverter, continue routing down into the 3½-inch drive bay bracket. Figure 9-3 shows how much wiring will end up behind the rheobuses.

Figure 9-3
The wiring behind the rheobuses—the wires are undressed and therefore rather messy.

From the four-inch blue cold cathode mounted on the back of the motherboard tray, we route the leads up to the existing cluster of inverters behind the front panel. It is getting really crowded here—too crowded. Using the supplied adhesive hook and loop (Velcro) strip, mount this inverter onto the side of the 5¼-inch drive bay bracket. From the inverter, continue routing down into the 3½-inch drive bay bracket.

As with before, make sure that when you push the rheobus into place it does not pinch any wires or dislodge any of the new, or existing, connections and that all the wires and hardware fit without tumbling into the main case cavity. Remove the drive bracket from the 3½-inch drive bay. Select a rheobus and position it directly above the middle rheobus. Adjust all three rheobuses to be flush, then tighten the rheobus mounting screws in the bracket.

Route four sets of wires through the rear opening of the bracket and push the plugs into the selected top rheobus connectors. Plug the open branch from the middle rheobus splitter into the top rheobus power connector. Install the bracket into the drive bay opening in the case.

Turn on the supplementary power supply and verify that all four middle rheobus-controlled devices operate properly, and that all four bottom rheobus-controlled devices work properly. Then turn off the power supply.

Now that we know all our circuits are functional, it's time to dress our routed wiring.

With all the power splitters and wires looping around, over and under the drive bay brackets, we're never going to get all the bundles hidden from view. Besides, we're trying for a look of out-of-control growth, something that has assumed a life of its own. We wrap the various bundles with gauze safety tape. The result has a kind of woody, vine-like look, looping randomly, draped from the upper recesses of the case. We daub brown splotches here and there, on the system cables as well as the lighting cables. The final effect is shown in Figure 9-4.

TIPS OF THE TRADE

Sticky Gauze

Gauze safety tape sticks to itself without adhesive. For best results and appearance, use a wrapping technique so that a new wrap overlaps the previous wrap by at least 50 percent.

Figure 9-4
Close-up of the green gauze safety tape with brown splotches daubed on

With all the controls and wiring involved, take care at each step to make certain all the controls have been hooked up properly. When it's done, it will make your case truly a thing of beauty.

An interesting side effect in this case is that the lights will never turn completely "off" unless the power source is removed. This has to do with the rheobus units we use to control the lights. Most rheobuses are designed to be used with fans and have a six-to-twelve-volt range of output. Most fans will not turn with less than six volts of power. However, many lights will have some degree of illumination at six or less volts of power. Thus, even when the rheobus controls are at their "off" position, there may be a small amount of illumination coming from the lights. How visible this illumination is will vary depending on each light.

TESTING 1-2-3

Now that you have all of your controls set up, you are ready to "glow." These controls will make your case more dynamic and fun. Here's what this chapter covered:

- ❑ Different kinds of controls
- ❑ How to wire in your fans to your controls
- ❑ Verifying proper operation
- ❑ Wrapping the wires with tape

Chapter 10

Finishing Touches

Tools of the Trade

Hair dryer or heat gun
Pliers
Clippers or scissors
Tie wraps
Electrical tape
Cable clips
White heat-shrink tubing
Supplemental power supply, 12VDC ($15 or less)
A piece of cloth or cardboard

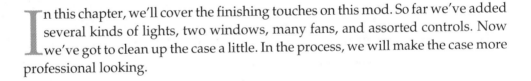

In this chapter, we'll cover the finishing touches on this mod. So far we've added several kinds of lights, two windows, many fans, and assorted controls. Now we've got to clean up the case a little. In the process, we will make the case more professional looking.

Organizing the Wires

On the motherboard side of the case, where the rectangular window is, we need to dress the wires. This is fairly simple. Dressing wires consists of bundling them together for a cleaner look, so you don't have wires all over the place. Bundled wires look more professional and finished. The location of the bundles also contributes to the overall image of the modification.

Dressing wires has become more and more important to case modders everywhere. There are a variety of products you can use to do this. The most accessible are tie wraps or electrical tape. You can also use flex wrap, which comes in both Velcro and non-Velcro versions, available at www.techflex.com. If you use the non-Velcro version, you have to remove all of your plugs from the ends of your wires, install the flex wrap, and replace the plugs on the wires. If you use the Velcro version, black is the only color available. You can also buy wire loom at many automotive stores. Spiral wrap is a good alternative to flex wrap and wire loom, and can be purchased at electronic-parts stores such as Radio Shack, Digi-Key Corporation, and Mouser Electronics. Many of the popular wire-dressing solutions are shown in Figure 10-1.

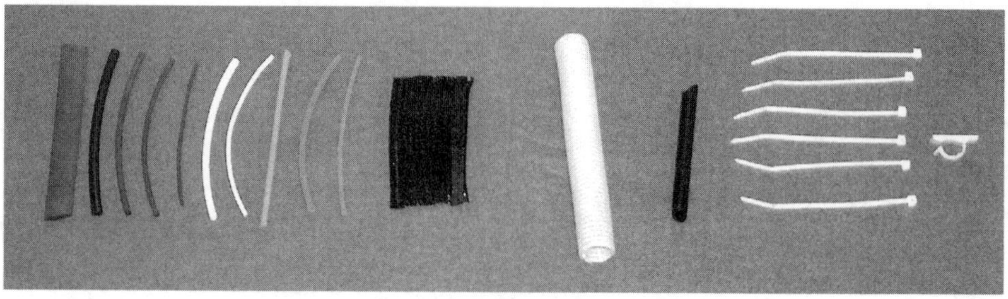

Figure 10-1
Heat-shrink tubing, flex wrap, wire loom, spiral wrap, tie wraps, and cable clamp (tape not shown)

Tape is cheap, readily available, and comes in a variety of colors. If you're going to use tape, you should try to use plastic electrical tape. The appearance of your dressed bundles can be quite attractive in tape; however, it is extremely difficult to work with in confined spaces and complex branching wiring patterns common in computers. For this reason, along with the difficulty of removal, we do not like to use tape. We did, however, make an exception when we dressed part of our wiring by using gauze safety tape, in Chapter 8. The appearance was unique and worth the extra effort.

Many modders like to use plastic tie wraps that have a ratchet-and-pull system for snugging down on the bundle and making a nice, tight bundle. We are going to use tie wraps. They are cheap, easy to use, and come in a variety of colors.

Tie wraps are often a better choice than adhesive tape because they are easier to remove if you need to make changes. After installation, plastic tie wraps must be physically cut off to remove them.

HEADS UP!

Take care not to nick the wires when cutting off a plastic tie wrap. As long as you don't, your wires will remain undamaged.

Tie-wrapping the wires often leaves long "tails" of tie wrap. You can leave these on, but many people clip the tails close to the wire bundle. The long tails are not just unprofessional in appearance, but they can get in the way and may be visible where you don't want them to be. Figure 10-2 shows our case with clean-looking wiring.

Figure 10-2
Wire dressing on the motherboard side of the case

When you dress your wires, don't make them too tight! All wires need some room to flex. If the wires are too tight, they run a higher risk of coming unplugged. Or, even worse, you could disconnect your components by accidentally pulling them out! This could be a real disaster if it happens during a LAN party or a critical online communication. Then you'd have to reattach the wires or parts, and possibly replace them. On the other hand, if the wires are too loose, they look sloppy. Dressing wires is an art, not a science.

TIPS OF THE TRADE

Service Loop

Professionals install a "service loop" whenever space and appearance will permit, somewhere along the bundle. A service loop is essentially an extra loop of wire. If something goes wrong with the plug, the plug can be replaced without having to replace the entire wire. In most cases, you won't have to remove the wire from the bundle.

Now that your wires are all tied together, they should look more like cables. They may be hanging in places you don't want them to be in. You can use self-adhesive cable clips to solve this problem. You can stick these clips onto the inside of your case and then thread or tuck the wires into them. Because the clips are adhesive, make sure you place them appropriately, where the wires will stay out of sight. In this way, they have an advantage over tie wraps, because clips will definitely keep wires close to wherever the clip is. Tie wraps keep the wires bundled together, but the tie wrap does not secure the wires to the case.

Cable clips often have extra "height" to them, compared to tie wraps, so you want to confirm there's room for the clips before you stick them into your case. They can be removed, but you don't want to deal with removing adhesive, particularly in a visible location, so choose your location wisely before installing cable clips. Visible adhesive residue is ugly, and using adhesive-removal solvent inside a computer case may lead to problems.

Dressing Wires that Cannot Be Hidden

Because the square window has two fans installed in it, some wiring is going to be visible. To make these wires look better, we will use heat-shrink tubing to cover the wiring bundle that is visible through the window to achieve the cleanest possible look for the wire bundles. We decided to use white heat-shrink tubing because it should show up better in the primarily green lighting of this mod.

We will cover the wiring bundle by cutting a length of heat-shrink tubing to run the length of the wire from one fan to the next, and shrink that onto the bundle. Then we will cut another length of tubing to bundle the first fan's wires with the wires from the second fan. This second length of heat-shrink tubing has to be long enough to carry the bundle out of sight when someone is looking through the window.

Heat-shrink tubing looks like a flexible hollow tube and comes in many colors—white and black are the most common. You can buy it in reels or cut lengths from many sources, including online mod shops and local electronics stores, such as Radio Shack.

Heat-shrink tubing isn't traditionally used for wire dressing, but to cover connections. When modding, you will frequently use parts in new ways. In fact, the more things you use in an unconventional way, the more people will admire your mod!

The wiring for the electroluminescent cable in the clear molding is tie-wrapped to the heat-shrink bundle (with a service loop) so that only one bundle of wire connects the door to the case circuitry. Figure 10-3 shows the finished product.

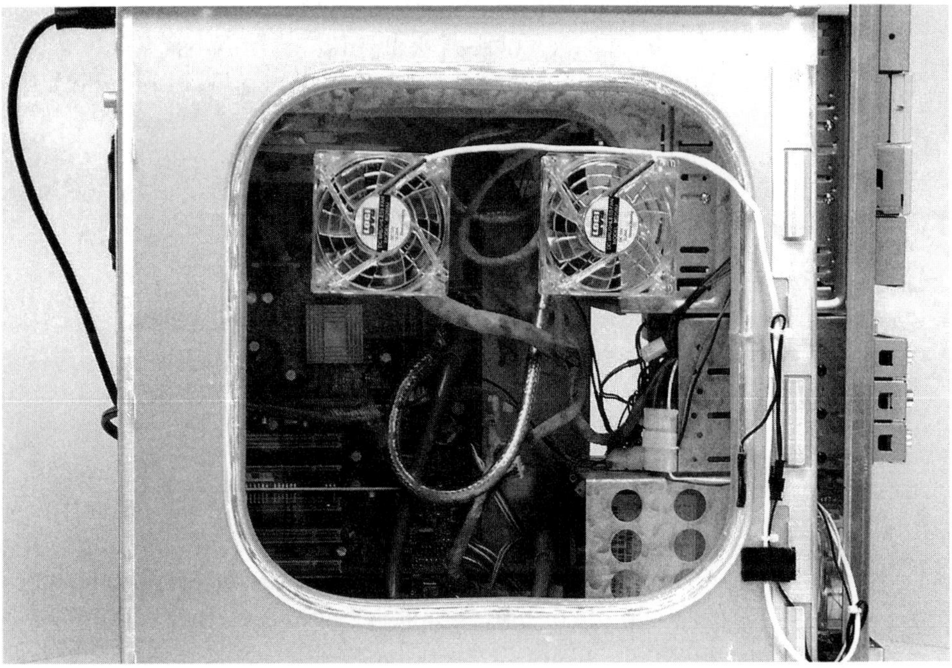

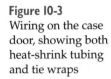

Figure 10-3
Wiring on the case door, showing both heat-shrink tubing and tie wraps

The wires need to be bundled and dressed on the left side of the case as well. Because the wires are more visible on this side, we will spend more time working on them.

Heat-shrink tubing is easy to use. Once the heat-shrink tubing is in place, it should be loose over the wires. This tubing shrinks when heated, and fits snugly around the wire bundle. It's a good idea to practice with a piece of heat-shrink tubing and scrap wires before you try using this on your own wire bundles.

TIPS OF THE TRADE

100% More

Heat-shrink tubing will usually shrink to half the diameter that you buy. To get a snug fit, you need to install tubing slightly less than double the diameter of your wire bundle.

Heat-shrink tubing is harder to remove than other wire dressing, because it is form-fitting to the bundle. If you ever want to remove heat-shrink tubing, you will need a very sharp razor blade—and a very steady hand.

To heat the tubing and cause it to shrink, you can use either a heat gun or a hair dryer set on high. The shrinking happens quickly under high temperature. When it's done, you'll have a nicely bound wire bundle. Usually the wire insulation can handle this level of temperature. However, if you have any doubts, install some of the heat-shrink tubing on a sample of your wire and then take it apart to see whether the insulation is damaged by the heat.

HEADS UP!

To make the heat-shrink tubing get hot enough, you will have to use very hot air. You may want to remove any wiring from the case while you are shrinking it so that you do not heat up (or melt) any soft plastics or components in your case.

We won't use heat-shrink tubing everywhere in this case, just where we think it enhances the appearance. Some of the bundles are still tie-wrapped, especially in places where they won't be visible. As with dressing wires everywhere else in the case, take care that when you heat-shrink your bundles you do not create pinch points or undesirable tension. A picture of some of the finished work is shown in Figure 10-4.

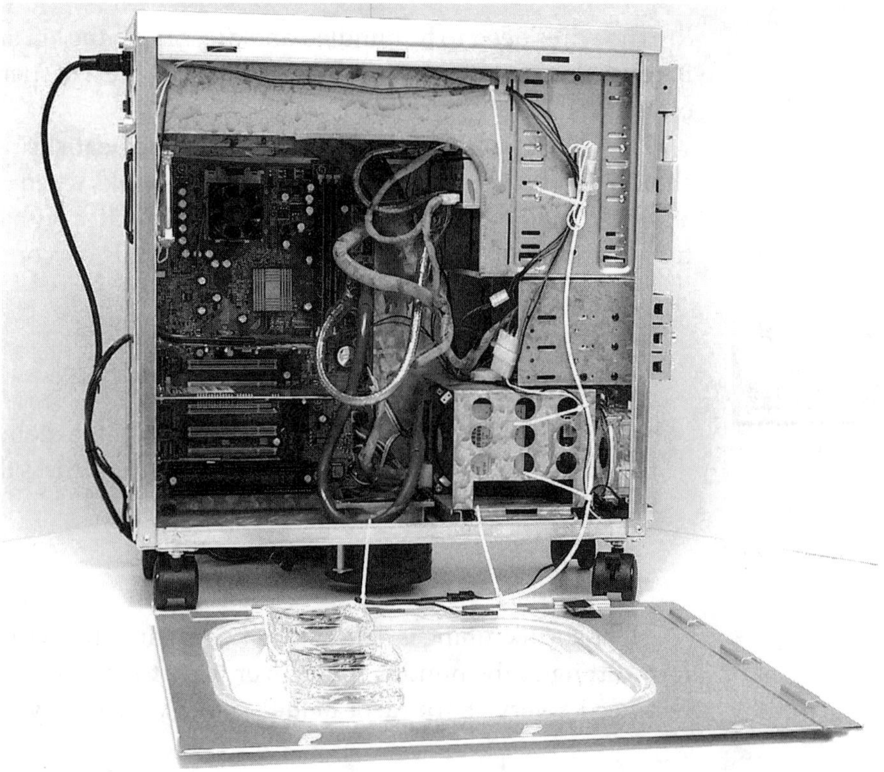

Figure 10-4 Wiring on the main side, showing cable clips, tie wraps, and white heat-shrink tubing

TIPS OF THE TRADE

Another Tubing Use

One other use for heat-shrink tubing is to shrink a short length of it onto a bundle of wire where the bundle is going around a pinch point or sharp corner. This provides protection against abrasion or cutting. You should do this even if that portion of the bundle is not visible to the casual observer.

Powering the Lighting System

Many beginning modders may wonder, "Will my existing power supply handle all of these lights and fans?" This all depends on your system, the size of your PSU, and what kind of a load you have on it before you start modding.

We want our system to be ultra-stable, so we aren't going to power our lights (and the additional fans that we installed) by the main power supply unit at all. We have chosen to add a supplemental power supply so that all of our lights (and additional fans) operate completely independent of the computer power supply. This will help avoid any problems, such as the power spiking when you turn on your case's lights, or the possibility of any bad wiring in the lighting system shorting out your computer.

We are using a very simple installation. One feed powers all of our mods. We could have used switched branches so that any of the subcircuits could be independently controlled, in addition to the existing controls provided by our rheobuses. The combinations are only limited by how much control you desire and the number of PCI plates you are willing to dedicate to manual switching. We prefer to keep it simple, so we are going to use just one circuit.

To provide a clean look coming out the back of the case, tie-wrap the supplemental power supply's cord to the PC's power cord at intervals of every two inches, as shown in Figure 10-5.

The advantage of the supplemental power supply goes beyond providing enough power. The lights and selected fans will work independent of the components, so even if the PC itself is powered down, there are still plenty of lights. The reverse is also true—if you need to use your computer without disturbing anyone with all that light, you can shut down some or all the accessories and still maintain full functionality of your computer. Best yet, the fans will continue to cool the case after the system shuts down, which will provide longevity for your system.

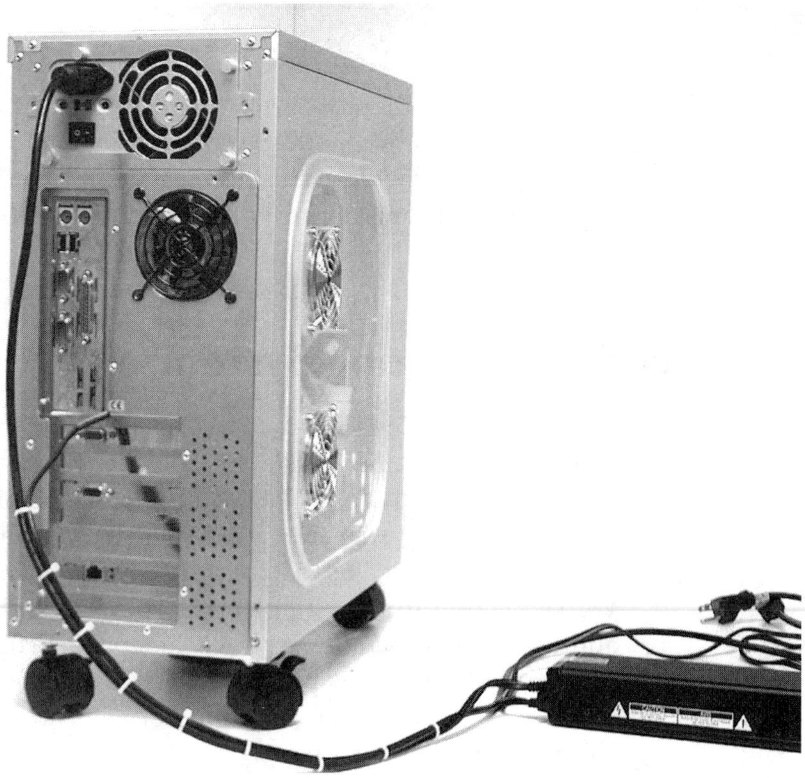

Figure 10-5
The supplemental power supply, tie-wrapped to the main power cord

Fitting On Your Doors

When you are modding your case, it is easy to forget that you need to double-check everything before final installation. In this case, we are talking about your doors. The cold cathode lights mounted on the floor interfere with the retention tabs on the bottom of the doors. By being very careful when placing each door on the case, we determined how much we would have to bend the door tabs so that when the door is put back on it will not break the cold cathode light on the bottom of the case.

TIPS OF THE TRADE

Seeing What You're Doing

When test-fitting a door, remove the motherboard tray, if possible, so that you don't have to work blind. By pulling out the motherboard tray, you will be able to see exactly how much room you have. This only applies if you are mounting components extremely close to the door.

When you are bending metal, use a pair of pliers. If you want to avoid scratching your metal, put a piece of cloth or cardboard on each side of the metal. This will help eliminate scratches that the pliers make as they grip the metal.

Controlling the Fans

Our case is made by Lian Li (www.lian-li.com.tw) and is a very high-quality case. One of the things that this company provides in its cases is a factory-installed fan controller. No other major case manufacturer does this, although some custom case builders will install them for you.

The speeds of factory-installed fans can be adjusted by a control found behind the case's front bezel. These controls are preset at the factory and have three speeds available for the fans. We removed three factory fans so we could install our cold cathode fans. When we installed our cold cathode fans, we connected the cold cathode power leads to our rheobus, and we connected the fan power leads to the original factory controls. One factory-installed switch, found behind the case's front bezel, controls both front intake fans. The exhaust fan in the rear panel is hooked directly to the power supply.

The lighted fans offer various types of effects, depending on the type of lighting technology used, and the combination of the brightness of the lighting and the speed of the fan can create variable visible effects with some fans. All the lights in the mod are controlled independent of any fans by the rheobuses we installed in the front panel, shown in Figure 10-6.

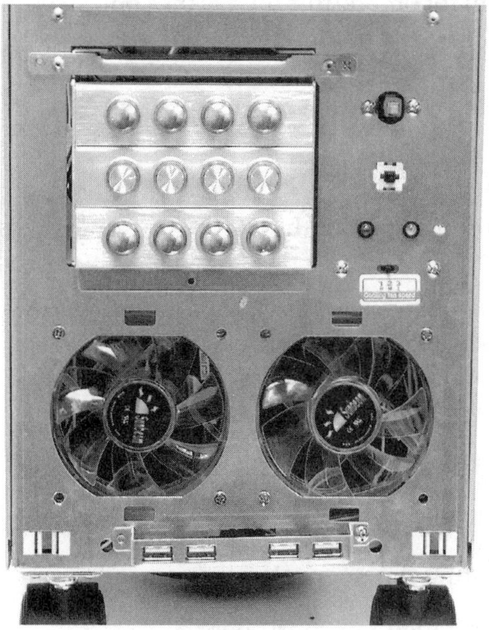

Figure 10-6
Front of the case without the bezel, to show controls

Now that we have finished our wiring and our fans, it's time to power everything up and step back, with the satisfaction of a job well done. The case is unique and attractive (as shown in Figure 10-7).

Figure 10-7
Completed case mod

Most modders will not want to incorporate all of these lighting effects in one case. For most people, only a portion of the effects, or one window, will be plenty. But for others, this mod is the coolest, with enough light at full power to rival Las Vegas. It's definitely the talk of the local LAN party!

TESTING 1-2-3

Here's the summary of all the work done on the case mod in this chapter:

- ❑ Wire dressing
    - ❑ Dressing wires that will be hidden
    - ❑ Dressing wires that can't be hidden
- ❑ Supplementary power
- ❑ Fitting the doors
    - ❑ Adjusting the door tabs
- ❑ Factory-installed fan controllers

Project 3

Morphing the Case

Chapter 11

Planning Your Mod

Tools of the Trade

Rotary tool or jigsaw
Drill with various sized bits
Table saw or router (optional)
Marker
Ruler or straight edge
Masking tape
Scrap- or newspaper
Hobby knife
Screwdriver
Clean-up towel or rag
Sandpaper
Acrylic sheets
Acrylic bonding agent
Plastic polish
80mm LED case fan
80mm fan grill
Fan screws
VIA EPIA 5000 motherboard
Antec 150W microATX power supply
128MB PC133 SDRAM
Fujitsu 18GB 2.5-inch laptop hard drive
2½- to 3½-inch IDE converter
Samsung DVD/CD-RW drive

The previous two projects gave you a taste of what case modification can do for your case. This project takes a different approach to "case modification." Instead of modifying a case, we will attempt to build one from the ground up. This will not be the average steel, beige-colored case normally displayed in every computer shop. We will take a few small pieces of acrylic and bond them together to create one of the smallest mini-sized computer cases you have ever seen.

We are using acrylic mainly because it's cheap and durable. Different sizes and shapes can be cut for various applications. Acrylic is also crystal clear, which provides a great look for your case.

Choosing the Right Parts

Before we begin hacking away at our acrylic, we need to figure out what our needs are. For our project, our goal is to make a complete system, fitted into the smallest acrylic cube case. Because size is a factor, it is crucial that we make measurements down to very small units. For this type of venture, not only does the size of the motherboard matter, so does the size of the power supply and the other components that populate a normal computer case. With this in mind, the basic objects that take up space within a case are the motherboard, optical drive, hard drive, and power supply. A floppy drive is usually not necessary nowadays, but if you need a floppy drive, you can include one.

The largest component is the motherboard, which serves as a good place to start building. There are different sizes, which are more commonly known as *form factors*. These range from full-size ATX form factors to smaller-size microATX varieties. Obviously, a full-size ATX form factor requires more space than a microATX form factor. Depending on what this case and computer will do, your acrylic case will need to be made for it. You will need to decide on whether this will be a file server machine, home theater box, or a gaming system. This simply means a full-size ATX system will not fit into a microATX case—it is physically impossible.

For our project, we are going with an all-in-one type of system utilizing a miniITX-based motherboard. This will not be a powerhouse of a computer but an example of what can be done with this project

The VIA EPIA C3 533 MHz–based miniITX motherboard that we are going to use is definitely under-powered compared to today's gigahertz standards. We chose this model based on pricing alone (see Figure 11-1). We purchased the motherboard for less than $100, but it provides video, audio, LAN, USB, and S-Video out. Included in this price is the integrated VIA 533 MHz C3 processor! There are other models within the EPIA family of boards with faster processors, but, as usual, they have a higher price. The EPIA 5000 will do just fine as a daily-use machine. Memory size is a variable that can be determined now or later. Since this motherboard uses PC100 or PC133 SDRAM, prices for these RAM modules are low. We purchased a 128MB module for less than $20. If you decide to upgrade in the future, the EPIA 5000 has two RAM slots to accomplish this.

With the size limitation of our project in mind, we chose the power supply carefully. The 150W power supply unit from Antec is small (see Figure 11-2), since it is designed for use in a microATX case. It is 5.9 inches long, 3.9 inches wide, and 3.4 inches high. Our system will not consume more than 150 watts of power, so this power supply will be adequate in power output and size. At around $25, it is definitely affordable. Although we chose the microATX power supply for our case, this does not mean that you must also. Smaller units are available, made for server-style cases. These power supplies from 1U cases are smaller, but they are about three times the price of what we paid. The major difference is that 1U units offer higher wattage—usually 300 watts and above. If you can afford such luxury, then by all means go for it. Both solutions will provide the necessary power for your system.

Figure 11-1
VIA miniITX–based motherboard

TIPS OF THE TRADE

Affording the Parts and Tools

Choose your hardware wisely. As most case modders know, price plays a large part in every project. Modders strive to produce something spectacular at an incredibly low price. Make your hardware choices with this goal in mind. Depending on your budget, different combinations of hardware can be mixed and matched. Draw out a plan beforehand. This will help you to avoid spending too much later in the project.

Figure 11-2
Antec power supply

Our hard drive decisions were based on size once again. We chose a 2½-inch laptop hard drive from Fujitsu combined with an IDE converter, as shown in Figure 11-3. This helps reduce the space used by the normal 3½-inch hard drives in most desktop computers. Using a 2½-inch model also lowers the weight of the case overall. The Samsung 32X10X40X12 DVD and CD-RW combo drive is also a space saver. It allows us to use our machine to access DVD discs and to burn CD-R and CD-RW discs.

Figure 11-3 Fujitsu hard drive with converter

One last consideration for our project is the heat variable. The temperature inside this custom acrylic case—and any case, for that matter—can rise to a point where it is detrimental to your components. The EPIA 5000 that we chose uses a passive heat sink to dissipate heat from the processor. This tells us immediately that the processor itself does not put out much heat, since it does not require a fan-equipped heat sink for cooling. Although the 533 MHz processor does not require active cooling, we will place an 80mm fan near it to exhaust some of the heat.

PC Mod Projects
Mod Gallery

"Blue Max"
by Pete Cupial

"Blue Zombie"

by Pete Cupial

"Project Halibut"
by David Williams

"The Black Box"
by Ed Chen

“Merliniplexi”

by Luke Hachmeister

“Hellstorm 2000”

by 3d Cool

"Las Vegas Comet"

"Mini Acrylic"

by Ed Chen

"Epia Sphere"

by Jani "Japala" Ponkko

"Red Tide"

"Retro II"

by Pete Cupial

"Rubber Case"
by PC Mods

We thank the following websites for contributing to the book's Mod Gallery...

www.pcmods.com
www.3dcool.com
www.merliniworks.com
www.gideontech.com
www.metku.co

Modification Overview

This project involves constructing a minisize acrylic case. Before you go to your local plastics shop, you will need to take measurements. Creating your own case is more complex than the actual system integration. You need to determine how much room to give for each component. Certain areas will have parts that rise, such as the CPU and RAM. Other parts, such as the power supply, will need to have a hole cut out of the case.

To get things going, you need to use either a 3-D modeling program or draw things out on paper. Using pencil and paper is probably more realistic for most users. If you don't already own and know how to use a 3-D modeling program, obtaining one and learning how to use it will demand quite a bit of time.

TIPS OF THE TRADE

What About the Tools?

Head over to your local hardware store and conduct a test drive. See which models and brands fit your budget and needs and go from there. Knowing what you are using before buying will save you time and headache down the road. Allocating some money toward tools and accessories early in the game may help you to avoid running out of money in the middle of your project.

We started by measuring our motherboard, since that takes up the most space within a case. The EPIA 5000 measures only about 6½ inches in length and width. This definitely leaves more space for other components. Our case will be in a cube design, so all sides have to be considered. This will affect how you will mount each component onto the acrylic pieces. Measure your other components, too, such as the power supply and optical drive. If you want to include power and reset buttons, you need to dedicate a section of your case for it also. Your acrylic case does not necessarily have to follow ours to the tee.

The same methodology used to design this minisize case can be applied toward a midtower or even a full-size server case. In those instances, since you have already considered a larger-size case, your components could be full size. You may use any old case for its remaining parts, such as motherboard trays, drive cages, and even power and reset buttons. You can use the existing pieces or cobble together something to replace them, using the same dimensions. Our minisize version is a bit harder to construct since nothing available on the market will be anything like it

TIPS OF THE TRADE

Powering Up the Box

Most cases have "power on" buttons. Some motherboards allow for keyboard and LAN power on, in which case you do not have to worry about turning on your system physically. This allows for the system to be turned on by using your keyboard or remotely on a network. If you are having a hard time finding a spare button, check your motherboard manual and see if these "power on" features are available.

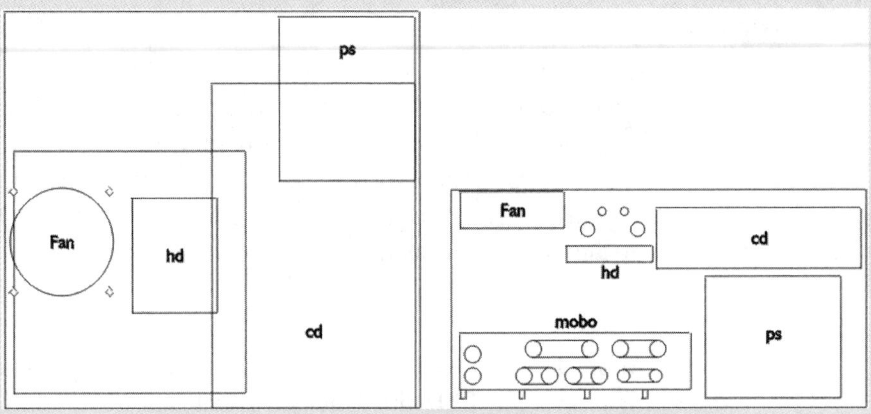

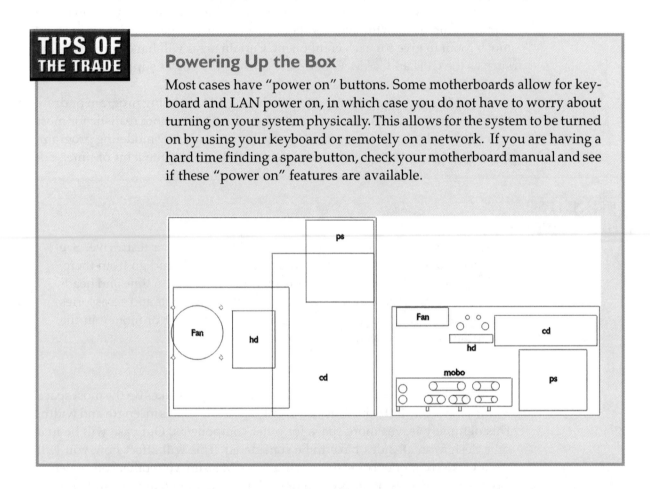

With our minisize case, accessibility is a major concern. We need to address questions such as how RAM and drive upgrades will take place and how accessibility will affect our design. We need to provide some free space within the case to move around. It should not be constructed such that we will need to remove every component just get to our motherboard. We want to try to create a modular type of design that enables us to remove one piece without affecting another piece.

Another consideration when designing is the thickness of the acrylic sheets. The most common sizes are 1/8-inch and 1/4-inch. Thicker sheets increase the weight of your case; they also are harder to drill and cut into. Since the goal of the project is to create a minisize case that is portable and easy to carry, we went with the 1/8-inch variety. See Figure 11-4 for the acrylic sheets we are using.

Figure 11-4
Acrylic sheet used for our project case

HEADS UP!

To determine what size acrylic you need, you can measure precisely or go with a general estimate. Some people opt to bring each component of the computer together and trace out spacing requirements. Others may prefer to just estimate a general size that is needed, purchase a large enough sheet, and cut it down when they get home. Both ways work, and depending on your budget, one may be better than the other for you.

The last factor to consider is how we will put this case together. The most common method is to use acrylic glue to bond your edges. It takes only about 15 minutes for the glue to settle to provide a very strong hold. You may also attach hinges to each sheet, similar in construction to what you would find on a swinging door; you may choose to drill holes and secure each side with long screws. A more advanced method is to use miniature-size acrylic blocks to hold each edge together. Each method has its benefits depending on what you plan to do with the case in the future. If the case will never see an upgrade path, seal it shut and never worry about it. If you plan to replace parts, you may need a hinged or screw version.

For our acrylic cube, we will use a combination of glue and hinges. The top panel of our cube will feature a hinged design, allowing us to open it and add or remove components when needed. The panel will sit flush against the vertical sheet of acrylic on the front. Having an option to upgrade or simply to access the interior of the case is definitely something to look into.

Acquiring Your Parts

You can buy your hardware parts at your local computer shop. Motherboards, memory, optical drives, and power supplies are usually in stock, and can be ordered through the store otherwise. The benefit of buying parts locally is that if anything is wrong with the component, you can return it to the shop immediately.

Remember to factor in the money needed for your tools. This may include rotary tools, jigsaws, a drill, or any other accessory needed for your project. You may not need all of these tools, depending on your plan, but create a budget beforehand.

TIPS OF THE TRADE

What if You Can't Find These Supplies Locally?

Try an online web site for your hardware and project supplies. Take a look at the many sites listed under Pricewatch.com (www.pricewatch.com), which provides a search engine for hardware parts and prices. As always, check out the retailer's site completely before jumping into a purchase. For your acrylic needs, you can order them online through USplastics.com (www.usplastics.com), which offers full-size sheets and other shapes on its web site.

Most of the acrylic pieces will be available at your local plastics shop. Flipping through the yellow pages should yield great results. These shops can cut sheets to your specifications and design; they can provide hole tapping for screws and give your acrylic sheets a finished edge. Finished edges are important in that they provide the best bonding surface when using glue. So, if you plan to bring home a large sheet and cut it down yourself, be prepared to have some type of sanding tool or sandpaper to smooth your edges. Jigsaws or table saws can do the job but can cause the edges to be very rough. You will need to sand afterward if you use one of these types at home. You may need plastic polish to get that professional, clear finish.

TESTING 1-2-3

- ❑ Run through your parts and tools check list one last time to determine whether you missed anything at this point.
- ❑ Try to find your materials at a local plastics shop. Their machinery can cut acrylic far better than what you can do at home. Often their sheets are all machine cut for precision. If you cut your own sheet, you may be able to bring it to the plastics shop to have it finished. Call them beforehand to discuss your project thoroughly.
- ❑ Getting a large sheet is sometimes cheaper than getting a smaller one. If the shop cuts down your sheet for you, do not throw away the excess pieces. You can use them for drive cages and other accessories.

Chapter 12

Cutting the Acrylic

Tools of the Trade

Rotary tool or jigsaw
Drill with various-sized bits
Hole saw(s)
Vise or clamps
Marker
Ruler or straight edge
Masking tape
Scrap- or newspaper
Hobby knife
Screwdriver
Clean-up towel or rag
Sandpaper
Acrylic sheets

After obtaining most of our accessories and parts, we are ready to begin the first part of our project. You should have a few sheets of acrylic cut to your preference. If you purchased a larger sheet, this is the time to figure out exactly how large or how small you want your case to be. Since our project deals with a system based on the miniITX form factor, we will use smaller pieces than normal.

When we ordered our acrylic sheets, we specified the exact dimensions, because we calculated them beforehand. We had the motherboard, power supply, optical drive, and hard drive in possession, so we laid them out on the table and measured the dimensions. Based on the dimensions, we determined that we need two large pieces of acrylic for the top and bottom of the case, and four smaller pieces for the sides. The large piece measures 30½ cm in width and 28 cm in length. The sides of the case will be put together by joining the edges of each piece. Since we are using this method, the sides will not have identical dimensions. The smaller pair of the side pieces measures 15×27 cm. The longer pair of the side pieces measures 15×30½ cm.

HEADS UP!

You may want to get a few extra sheets of acrylic just in case you crack or chip any of the pieces. If you are confident that you can do this project in one try, then save your money.

15 MINUTES

Prepping the Work Area

First you are going to place all the parts on your largest piece of acrylic. This should be the piece that will act as your motherboard tray, because it will secure the motherboard and the other main components. You want to position your motherboard, power supply, optical drive, and hard drive so that you can figure out your spacing issues. You do not want to run out of space after you start cutting and gluing, which can be quite costly. An example layout is shown in Figure 12-1.

Figure 12-1 Component positions on the motherboard tray

For our purposes, we decided to place the motherboard in the lower-left corner. The power supply will go directly above the motherboard; the optical drive will sit vertically to the right. The 2½-inch hard drive will sit in the space between the optical drive and the motherboard. We placed all the pieces on each side to determine whether we have enough room to do what we want. You need at least a half centimeter of empty space at the top and bottom, which gives you enough room to join the pieces together at the edges (see Figure 12-2). After you double-check all the preliminary measurements, you can remove the side pieces of your case.

Figure 12-2
Space check at the edges of the case

90 MINUTES

Marking and Deciding How to Cut Your Acrylic

Now that you have a general idea of what your case will look like, you need to decide where and how you will secure everything into place. You will secure the acrylic pieces by using glue, but what about the motherboard and the other components? You need a way to make these components stay in place without causing any space problems.

TIPS OF THE TRADE

Precise Measuring

Measuring will take longer than the actual cutting process of your project. Keep in mind that acrylic scars easily, so any small mistake will show, even if it is a tiny scratch. Always measure and take precise notes as to where a cut or hole will be. A good rule of thumb is to measure twice and cut once.

For our miniITX motherboard, we will use four small screws to mount it to our tray (see Figure 12-3). To do this, we need to drill our own mounting holes. If you have built systems before, you may know that most trays have brass standoffs that you screw your motherboard into. For our purposes, we will just drill four holes and screw the board down. You may opt to add in brass standoffs; just make sure the holes you create on the acrylic sheet are large enough to accommodate them. To get these motherboard mounting holes to line up correctly, you should place the motherboard on the acrylic sheet and mark off some holes. Use a marker or pencil—you should have something similar to Figure 12-4.

Figure 12-3 Small screws for mounting motherboard

TIPS OF THE TRADE

Nothing Negative Here

Should you be concerned about electromagnetic interference with acrylic and computer components? If someone tells you that computers are meant to be in a metal case, he or she would be right if it were still the '80s, with older equipment. Computers and components in today's market have inherent shielding, preventing them from causing any interference. As far as EMI within an acrylic case, we have not experienced any negative reactions. We also have tested a complete system in a production model of an acrylic case without any negative effects.

Figure 12-4 Motherboard holes

When deciding where to drill your motherboard mounting holes, you have to take into account how you will access the input/output (I/O) ports. This I/O panel is often located at the back of a computer. For our acrylic model, the I/O ports will be located on the left side. Our miniITX model came with its own custom I/O panel predefined with holes already punched out, as shown in Figure 12-5. You can use this as a model to cut your own holes in the side panel, or cut away a chunk and allow the custom I/O panel to show through.

Figure 12-5
I/O panel

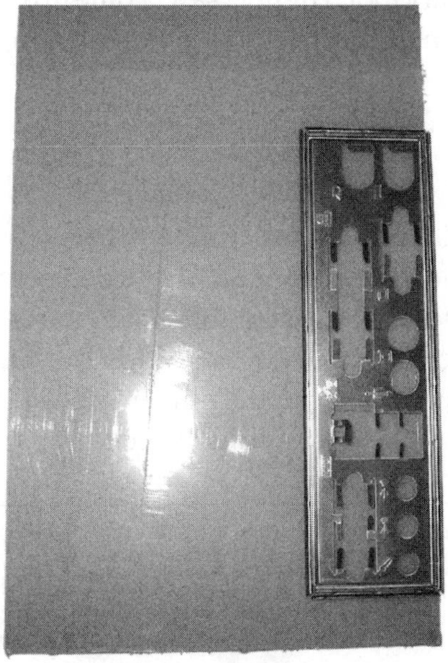

HEADS UP!

Acrylic is usually hard to draw on with a pencil or pen. Use a marker to make your traces through the I/O panel. Your acrylic sheet may come with a plastic or paper covering that you can peel off later. You can also use this layer to draw on.

The power supply needs a few areas cut out to allow user access. The fan exhaust needs to be punched out to allow hot air from the power supply to escape. You also need to allow the three-prong connector for the power cord and the master power switch to show through. The final part of the project to check would be the four screws needed to secure the power supply, which are located on the corners of your power supply.

Start with the exhaust port, because that consumes the largest space. The size of the hole is usually going to be somewhere similar in size to an 80mm fan, because the fans used within power supplies are the same size. To trace the hole for the exhaust port, you can use either of two methods. One method is to trace the hole by placing your acrylic piece over the power supply. Then you would cut the hole out using your rotary tool with a cutting-wheel attachment. This is not a bad way of cutting, but it is time-consuming and usually results in an uneven hole. This also causes the acrylic to melt because of the high speeds of your rotary tool going slowly over the surface. The second method is easier and faster: use a hole saw (see Figure 12-6). This attachment for your drill can cut a perfect hole through acrylic in only a few seconds. The cuts are a lot cleaner when compared to a rotary tool. The hole saws come in different sizes, including convenient sizes that are an exact match for 80mm, 92mm, or 120mm fan-hole sizes.

TIPS OF THE TRADE

Which Hole Saw Is Best?

Most hardware stores will carry hole-saw attachments in various sizes. In the same aisle or area, a nice selection of rotary tools should also be on display. With regard to what is the best one to get, it depends on how much you are willing to spend. For this project, acrylic is easy to cut, so a heavy-duty model is not required. Ask the sales associate for some recommendations on their specific store selections.

Figure 12-6
Hole saws

The power port and master switch will be a tougher cut—they are a lot smaller and are not entirely straight. You can take the easy route and draw the outline of the power connector and switch directly onto the acrylic. But to make it look the best, you will need to break out the ruler and do some calculating. Do not cut the hole to the exact sizes. Make them slightly larger to give yourself some room to maneuver around. For our power-connector hole, we measure it to be about 5½×3 cm. The switch requires a 3×2 cm rectangle. Mark off the coordinates, as shown in Figure 12-7, and your power-supply side-outlet holes should be ready for cutting. The last thing to take care of is the mounting screw holes. Mark off where the holes are on the acrylic with your marker; this part will not be too difficult.

Figure 12-7
Power supply marks

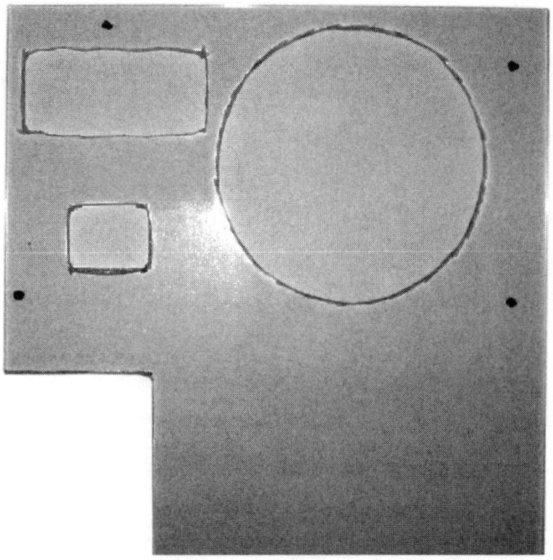

Our Samsung DVD/CD-RW combo drive will have two ways to secure itself within our case. There are screw holes on each side of the unit and on the bottom. Since we are placing our drive vertically, the bottom mounting method will be used. Before marking the acrylic for the four holes, we need to take into account how the front tray will eject. For our purposes, we remove a rectangular piece the size of the front face plate of our drive. We use the measurement 14½×4 cm. After you determine where the optical drive will be mounted, you can mark off the four bottom screw hole spots on the acrylic, similar to the marks shown in Figure 12-8.

Figure 12-8
Optical drive marks

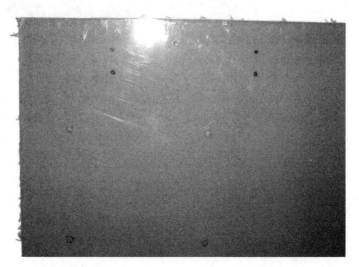

HEADS UP!

Try not to cut too much away for your optical drive's face plate. The spacing around the edges of the front face of the optical drive should be minimal. Try for a smaller cut. If that does not work, sand down the edges a bit, to even things up.

The last component we need to address is the hard drive. Just like the optical drive, the 2½-inch hard drive can be mounted either from the bottom or on the sides. We will drill four holes through the motherboard tray to secure it down using the holes on the bottom of the drive, which will lay the hard drive horizontally. Since our hard drive is so small, it fits perfectly between our optical drive and motherboard. Mark off each hole using a marker, as shown in Figure 12-9.

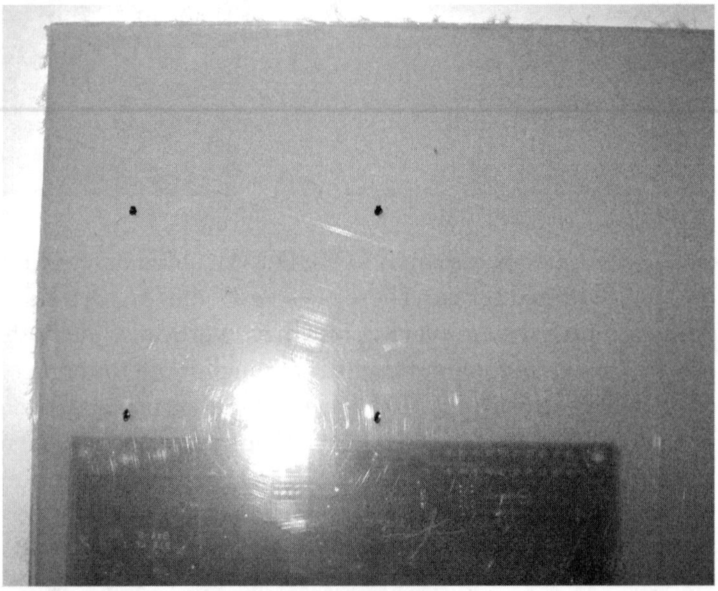

Figure 12-9
Hard drive markings

60 MINUTES

Cutting Your Acrylic

Before you attempt the cutting process, prepare your work area. Clean off any surface residue that can possibly scratch your acrylic sheets. If you have a work bench set up for woodworking, try to secure a vise or a set of clamps—they can help hold down the sheets while you work on them. For the areas where you have marked off for cutting, place an outline of masking tape around the outside, as shown in Figure 12-10. In case you make a sudden movement, you have a small area to cushion the slip.

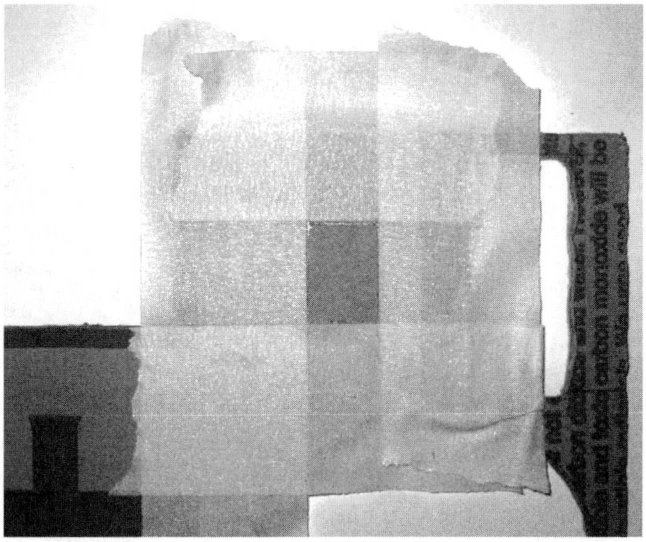

Figure 12-10
Masked-off outline

In our project, there are a few straight edges. Normally, scoring the acrylic and then snapping it off is easier than cutting the pieces out with a power tool. For our example, it may prove to be a wiser choice to do everything the hard way. There will be certain smaller pieces that will stick out after you cut away some of the major parts. Snapping it off with your hands will cause the whole sheet of acrylic to fracture or break apart.

HEADS UP!

For your rotary tool, try to keep it at the lowest setting—somewhere in the 15,000 RPM range will suffice. You do not want to go any faster; doing so will cause melting to occur. This can alter the flatness of your sheet and emit unpleasant odors. Work on this project in a well-ventilated workspace.

Your first cut will be the I/O panel for the motherboard (see Figure 12-11). Move the rotary tool slowly over the marked outline; work your way around it once. Instead of going deep and cutting through the acrylic, you want to go layer by layer. Once you have finished the initial cut, use a sanding-tool attachment on your rotary tool, or traditional sandpaper, to smooth out the edges. Line up your side piece to the motherboard and check to see if it matches up. If you have areas where it does not align correctly, try to sand it down to fit. Sometimes this will be enough to make the perfect fit; other times you will need to start over on another piece. Do not overdo it on the first try if you are not sure—you can always sand down a piece of acrylic, but you cannot add acrylic back after you cut it off.

Figure 12-11
I/O panel cut

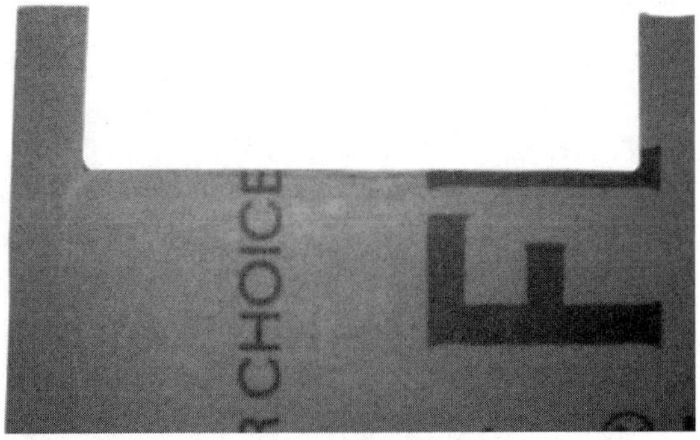

After you cut out the I/O panel, line up the motherboard on the tray to see if it still lines up with the mounting holes you drew earlier. If it does not, recalculate the spacing and mark off the holes again in the new position. Since we are using a smaller screw to mount the motherboard, we will be using a $\frac{7}{64}$-inch drill bit to make our holes. You may need to use a different bit size for your own project; adjust your specifications accordingly. For this part of the project, you do not want to drill through completely to the other side. Drill down about three-quarters of the way through and stop. After each successfully drilled hole, take your screw or brass stand off and try it. If the hole is too small, try a larger drill bit and expand it. The holes you create should be similar to Figure 12-12.

HEADS UP!

If you smell burning plastic at this point, stop cutting and let the acrylic cool before continuing. Since the rotary tool is operating at very high speeds, the heat can cause your acrylic sheet to change shape. If that happens, there is nothing else you can do except to use another piece. Cut slowly and you will save yourself time and money!

Figure 12-12
Motherboard holes

Cut the power supply exhaust hole (see Figure 12-13) using an 80mm hole-saw attachment to your power drill. Drill through in slow spurts; going too fast will crack your acrylic very quickly. The process should only take about 30 to 60 seconds to complete.

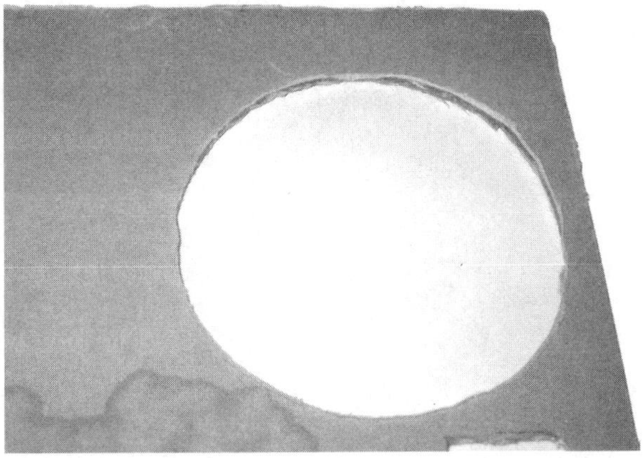

Figure 12-13
Power supply exhaust hole

Switch to your rotary tool to cut the holes for the power connector and switch (see Figure 12-14). Slowly touch the surface of the acrylic and cut in layers. Do not cut all the way through. Try to keep melting of the acrylic to a minimum. After you have cut all the sides of your rectangle, push the small piece of acrylic out (it should pop right out).

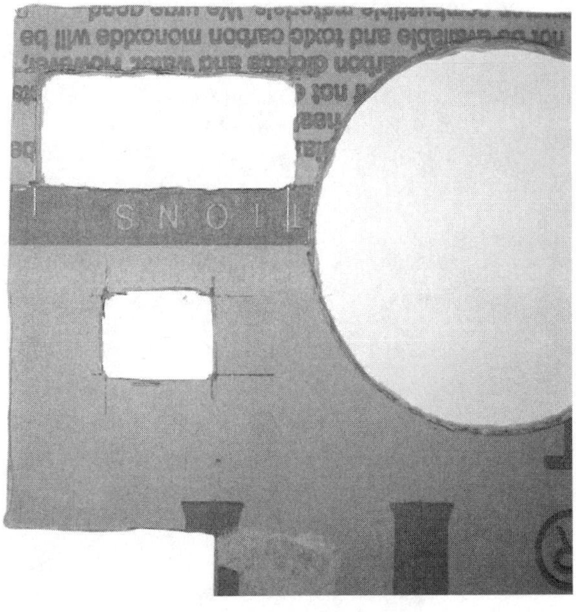

Figure 12-14
Power connector and switch holes

The next portion of the cutting process involves the cuts for the optical drive. The optical drive is very similar to the I/O panel for the motherboard. It is rectangular in shape (see Figure 12-15), which should pose no problem for your rotary tool. Mask off the area if you wish, and cut through in layers. Check the fitment; if it matches correctly, move on to the next step in marking off the mounting holes.

Figure 12-15
Face plate of the optical drive

Using a marker, follow the same routine as before and put a dot where the screws will go through. Since we are securing the optical drive using the bottom holes, we need to drill the hole completely through the sheet. The screws are the same size as the motherboard screws we used earlier. Operate your drill slowly and you should have an evenly drilled hole in seconds.

The hard drive will also use the same size screws as the motherboard and optical drive. This makes it easier because you do not need to change drill bits; use the same size of 7/64-inch bit. The screw will now go completely through the acrylic sheet, so carefully drill through in short spurts. With each hole drilled, check your hard drive and see if everything is aligned correctly. After you complete all four holes, you are done with the hard drive installation (see Figure 12-16).

Figure 12-16
Hard drive mounting holes

TESTING 1-2-3

- ❑ Sanding down the edges that were cut can greatly improve the appearance. Use the sanding attachment on your rotary tool or use sandpaper to smooth things out for a crystal-clear look.
- ❑ After you have completed all the cutting, quickly check the edges and holes to make sure they match up to your components. This is the time to fix anything, before you start putting your case together.

Chapter 13

Piecing It Together

Tools of the Trade

Rotary tool or jigsaw
Drill with various-sized bits
Marker
Ruler or straight edge
Masking tape
Scrap- or newspaper
Hobby knife
Clean-up towel or rag
Acrylic sheets
Acrylic hinges
Acrylic glue
Glass-needle glue applicator
Hole saw(s) (optional)
Vise or clamps (optional)
Needle files (optional)

In Chapter 12, we prepared most of our acrylic pieces by cutting them to fit the components. This chapter discusses the next step, which is to join the acrylic pieces together to form the case. To do this, you have a few options available, depending on the thickness of your acrylic material. For thicker acrylic, corner block screws or locking hinges can be used. For our thinner acrylic, we will use acrylic glue to secure each piece. We will also use acrylic hinges to secure the top panel so that it can be opened.

The general shape of our case when completed will be square. It will have a larger piece on the top that will be attached by a hinge in the back. This top sheet of acrylic will flip upwards, enabling us to access the inside of the case if we need to make changes. The input and output ports will be accessible on the left side of the case, which is where the power supply will be oriented.

30–60 MINUTES

Accessibility of Internal Components

One thing should be noted before joining all the pieces together: You need to provide a way to power up your computer. Nearly every consumer case on the market today has a power-on button or switch, which is usually a large button on the front of the case, in the same vicinity of the power and hard drive LED indicators. Some may find this an unnecessary addition to a case. You may opt to just have the power-on button or switch tucked away inside the case. When you need to power on the unit, just lift the top panel, turn on the power, and then close the panel. That may be a solution, but we decided to mount our own power-on button on the front of the case. We are also adding LED indicators, which are shown along with the power-on button in Figure 13-1.

Figure 13-1
Power-on button and LED indicators

TIPS OF THE TRADE

Spare Parts

You can remove the power-on, reset, or LED indicators from an old case and use them in your project. If you do not have any extra accessories of this type available, head over to a local computer store and ask for some. They should have an abundance of them available for a low price or, in some cases, free of charge.

On our project case, we want to mount the power-on button and LEDs on the front panel. You can place them anywhere on your case, but for easy accessibility, the front area is the best choice. We opted to leave out the reset button, because in past experiences, we have rarely used it. Less clutter in this area and less wire clutter inside the case will make it easier to handle later on. The power and hard drive LEDs will be situated directly above the power-on button, as shown in Figure 13-2. Our choice for the positioning of the power button and LEDs may not be what you need for your project. You may wish to hide it on the side or on the back, giving the case a much cleaner look.

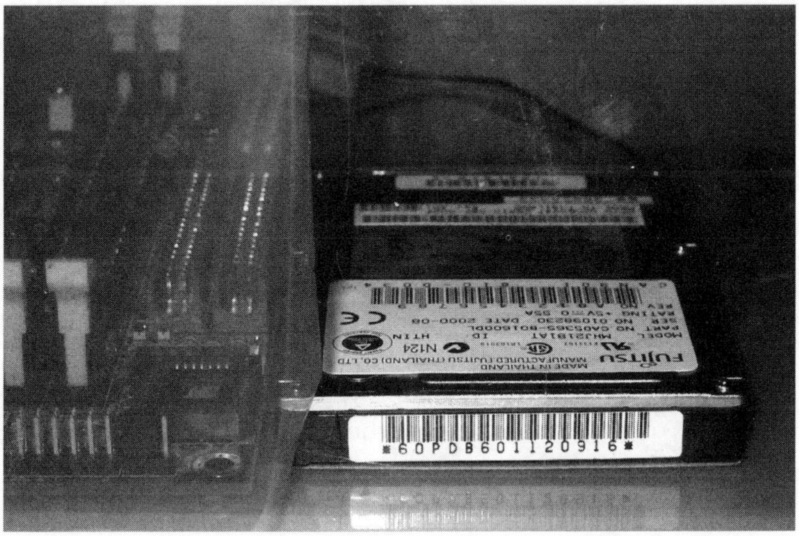

Figure 13-2 Power and LED area on front panel

When you buy your LED indicators, make sure to pick up some corresponding holders (see Figure 13-3). If you are lucky enough to have an extra case, you may already have some of these holders. Remove them from the old case and transplant them over to the new case. We will use 5mm LED indicators for our application. (The other common size is the 3mm variety.) Make sure to acquire the appropriate size for your application. The holders are important not just for aesthetic reasons, but it also keeps the LEDs in place. Without them, the bulbs will slide in and out whenever you tilt the case.

Figure 13-3 LED holders

TIPS OF THE TRADE

New or Used LED

If you cannot find LED holders on an old case, you can purchase them from any electronics shop, such as Radio Shack. They are usually black, with about five to ten in a pack. Make sure to purchase the correct size holder for your LEDs; otherwise you will have a hard time keeping them in place.

The next step is to figure out how much space on the front panel you need for your LED indicators and power-on button. Our LEDs will take less than a centimeter of space, while our power-on button is only about 2 cm in height. Since the button and indicator lights will be in the same area as our hard drive, we need to clear some space to prevent any space issues in that area. You do not want to squeeze the LEDs into the same area that the hard drive is occupying. Doing so will make it difficult to swap out the hard drive in the future. We measured about 6 cm from the base to where we want to mount our LEDs. Right below them will be the power-on button, giving ample room for the hard drive to sit on the bottom. Before you drill, measure where you want the LEDs to come through. Having them off-center can make your whole case look awkward. Take a ruler and measure the width and height and draw lines horizontally and vertically. Use a marker to put a dot where the two lines meet; this is the spot where you want to drill. You should have marked something similar to Figure 13-4.

For our 5mm LEDs and holders, a 7/32-inch drill bit will be the ideal size to create the hole. Be sure to proceed with caution while drilling through the sheet. Take your time on this one; you are just about done with this part of the project. Follow the same method for the hard drive LED hole.

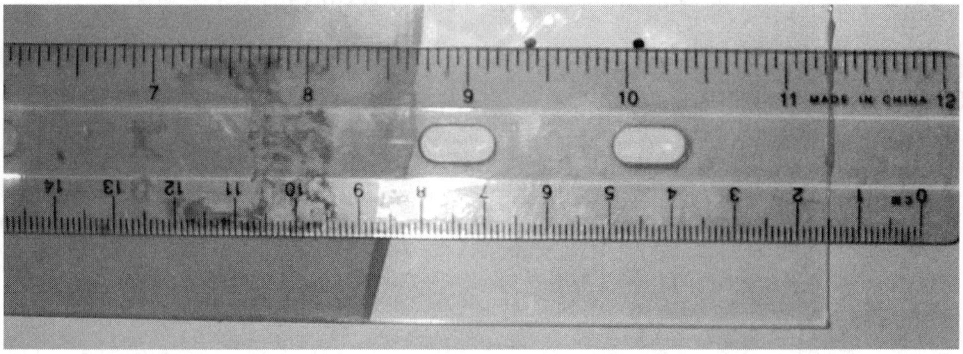

Figure 13-4 Drill hole and ruler lines

HEADS UP!

Use slow drill bursts while creating the holes. Drilling through the sheet too quickly can cause it to crack or break. The last thing you want to do is go out and purchase another sheet because of a drilling mistake. Take your time and measure everything twice, then proceed to cutting or drilling.

Using your drill, you should be able to produce a smooth-finished hole in a few seconds. After you drill the hole, push the LED holder through and see if it stays in place. If you find that the hole is not large enough, grab a larger bit and expand the hole. With the holder in its hole, take your LED and push it through the holder. It should lock in place with a tight fit. Follow the same installation method for the hard drive LED and its holder. The result is shown in Figure 13-5.

Figure 13-5
LEDs installed

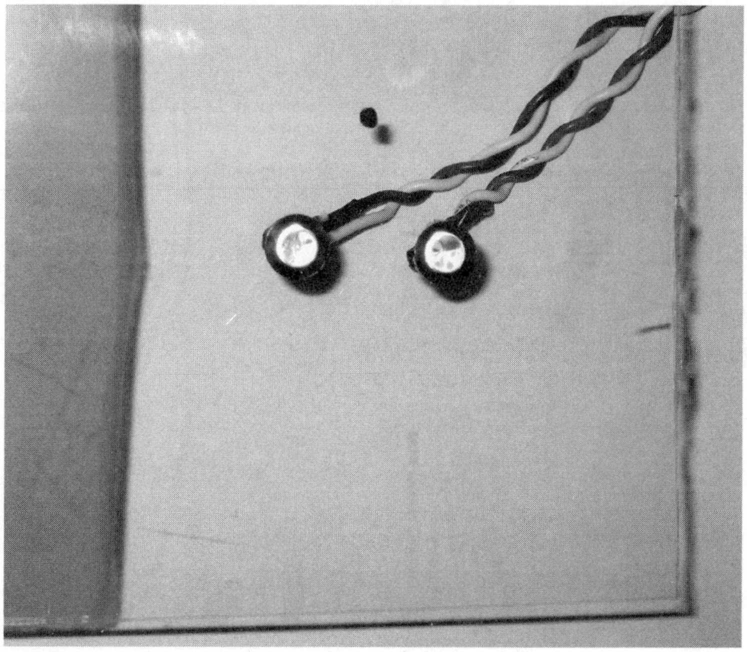

The power-on button hole requires a much larger drill bit. The downside to using a larger drill bit is that it poses a higher risk of cracking the acrylic sheet. If you want to avoid this risk, you can use the 7/32-inch drill bit to drill the hole and then use a needle file to sand the edges to enlarge it according to your specifications. Although our power-on button is triangular in shape, the rear of the button is circular. It has a locking washer that will keep it from coming loose, as shown in Figure 13-6.

Figure 13-6 Power-on button installed

TIPS OF THE TRADE

Needling Around

A needle file is very handy in situations where the size of the hole needed is slightly too large to make using a standard drill bit. You can sand away a small portion without much effort. The next time you are at the hardware store, you may want to pick up a needle file just in case.

30–60 MINUTES

Cutting the Exhaust Fan Hole

To combat the heat generated by the computer, we will install an exhaust hole in the top panel. This is the same panel that will flip open to allow access to the computer's internals. The exhaust hole will be situated in the middle of the panel, sized to fit an 80mm fan. Since we have an all-acrylic case, we decided to use an 80mm LED fan (shown in Figure 13-7). The lit fan should give the case a nice colored effect.

Figure 13-7
80mm LED fan

> **TIPS OF THE TRADE**
>
> ### Exhaustion
>
> You may not need an exhaust fan in your setup, but because our processor uses a passive cooler, a fanless heat sink, an exhaust fan is definitely a good idea. If you feel you need to use a larger fan, they range from 80mm all the way up to 120mm.

Measure the top panel's width and length. If you are positioning this fan in the middle, then draw some horizontal and vertical lines to line up your fan. To make it easier, you can obtain an 80mm fan grill to use as an outline. Also remember to draw the four fan screw holes necessary to keep the fan in place, as shown in Figure 13-8; the fan grill is also a good outline for this.

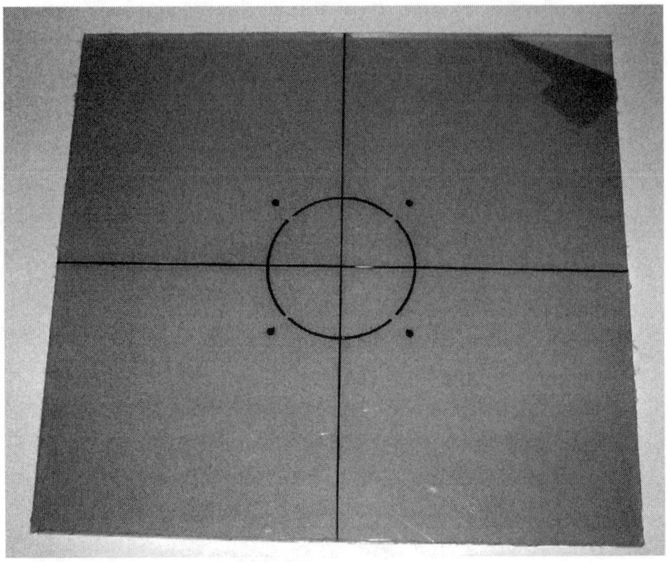

Figure 13-8
Fan-grill tracing

Use a rotary tool or a hole saw to create your exhaust hole. For either method, proceed with caution and cut slowly. For added cutting protection, mask off the area around your outline with masking tape. Use a 3/16-inch drill bit to create your fan screw holes. After you drill each successive fan screw hole, line up the fan to check if it indeed lines up correctly. After you cut all four fan screw holes and the exhaust fan hole, take your fan and grill and screw them down with the appropriate screws (see Figure 13-9).

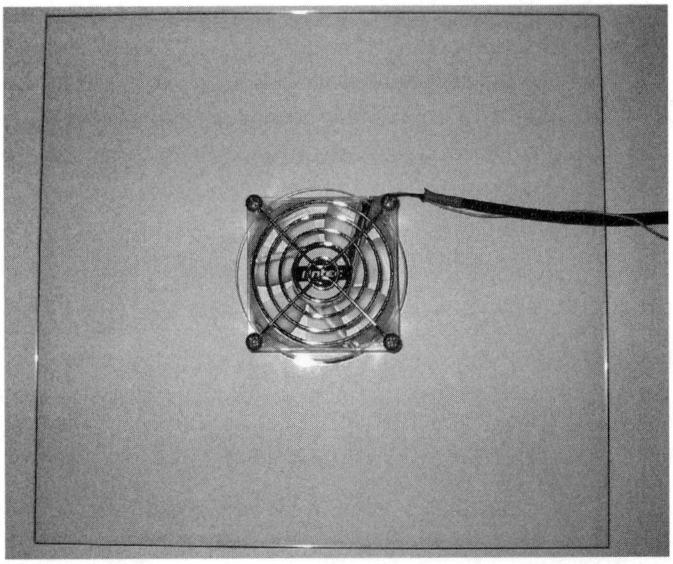

Figure 13-9
Fan and grill installed

Now that we have installed the power-on button, indicator lights, and the exhaust fan, it is time to join the edges together. Clean up the work area for any scraps and acrylic scrapings that you may have created earlier. While using the acrylic glue, you want a clean area to work in.

60–90 MINUTES

Gluing the Case Together

The acrylic glue we are using is highly evaporative, which means that if you leave it open for a while, the amount of glue you have will diminish over time. So you want to purchase this when you are absolutely ready to put the pieces together. Once you purchase it, keep it in a cool place away from sunlight. You may also want to put some masking tape around the edges of the bottle to slow down evaporation, as shown in Figure 13-10.

Figure 13-10
Acrylic glue bottle

TIPS OF THE TRADE

Glue Recommendations

A common brand of acrylic glue is called Comstik. Most acrylic and plastics shops in your local area should carry these acrylic glues. Some come in tubes while others come in bottles. Ask the local salesperson for glue recommendations for your acrylic project.

The acrylic glue is fast-drying, so you need to work quickly and efficiently to make sure it doesn't dry before you secure the acrylic pieces together. Because the glue dries so fast, you cannot simply apply a layer onto the surface of the pieces and then join them together. You need to use a glass-needle glue applicator, which you can purchase from a local hobby shop. (The most common use for these is to glue together small model parts.)

We will start by attaching our side pieces onto the base of our case. To use the needle applicator on your acrylic pieces, position the two edges of two pieces together. By dropping a thin line of glue on the side where the edges join, the glue will seep into the two pieces and bond it immediately. This method works similar to the way a paper towel soaks up water. Press down tight for a couple of minutes until you feel the edge hold onto the other piece by itself.

Repeat the same step for the other side pieces; you should have something that looks like Figure 13-11. After you have joined together the side panels, you will want to concentrate on the top panel. However, before you start working on it, give the side panels about a day to fully dry and bond. For a more even bond, purchase a set of clamps to apply pressure during the curing process of the acrylic (see Figure 13-12).

Figure 13-11 Four side panels joined

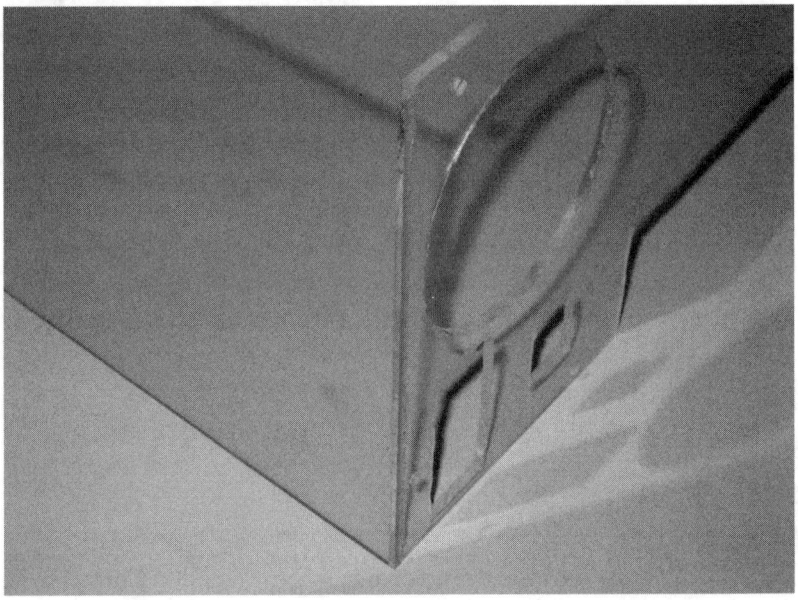

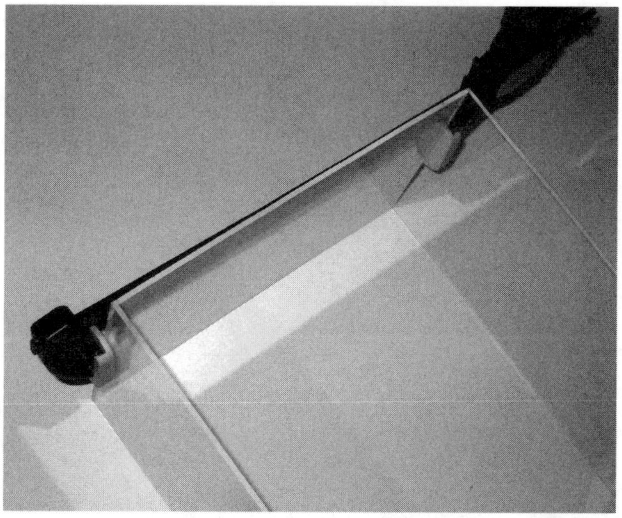

Figure 13-12
Clamps

We will use acrylic hinges for our top panel, shown in Figure 13-13. You can purchase these at the same place where you purchased your plastic goods. Our top panel is not large, by any means, so having two hinges to support it should be sufficient. You may decide to seal this box shut or use screws for your own application. We find that hinges allow for easy access to our computer innards.

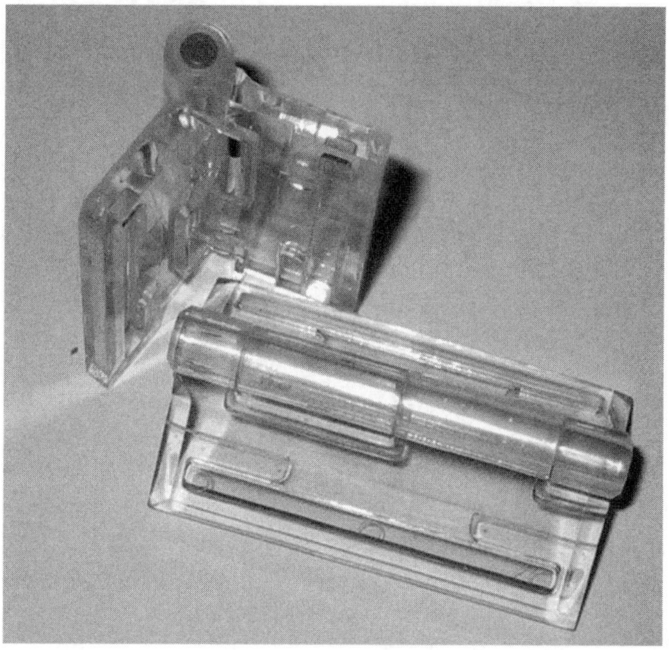

Figure 13-13
Acrylic hinges

The hinges have a flat side, which is the side that will attach to the top panel and the rear panel's surface. Think of it as a storage chest with a top lid that opens upward by the use of two hinges at the back. Measure the two spots that you want to attach the hinges to. Our hinges will be located closer to the outer edges of the top panel. We measured about one inch on each side and put a line there with our marker, as shown in Figure 13-14.

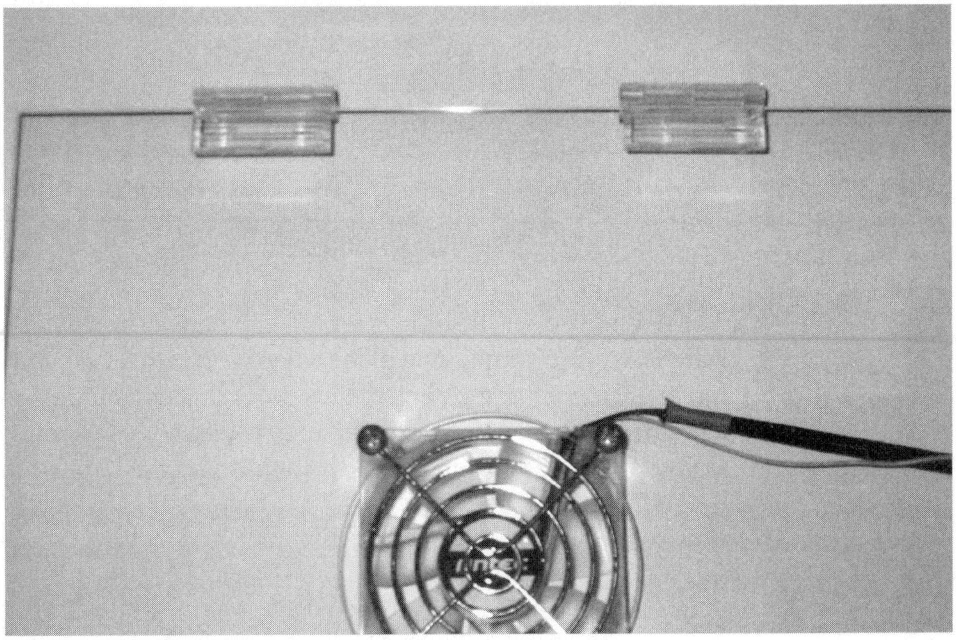

Figure 13-14
Hinge marks

Apply some glue on one hinge and press it down onto the top panel first. Repeat this step for the second hinge on the other side. Give them a few minutes to bond before you proceed. Move the top panel onto the four perpendicular side panels and line up the hinges and see if the hinges can be operated. If you have enough room and the alignment is correct, then remove the top panel. Take two hand-gripping clamps and position them over the hinges. This will put some pressure on the glue while it fully cures. Give this 12–24 hours to bond fully before proceeding.

After a day, remove the clamps and check to see if the alignment is still correct. The last step of our project is to attach the other ends of the hinges to the rear panel. Follow the same procedure. Apply a bit of glue on the secondary part of the hinge and drop it down over the rear panel. After a few minutes, apply the clamp over the hinge while it is bonding. Give it about half a day to a day to fully cure; you should have something similar to Figure 13-15.

Figure 13-15 Hinges attached

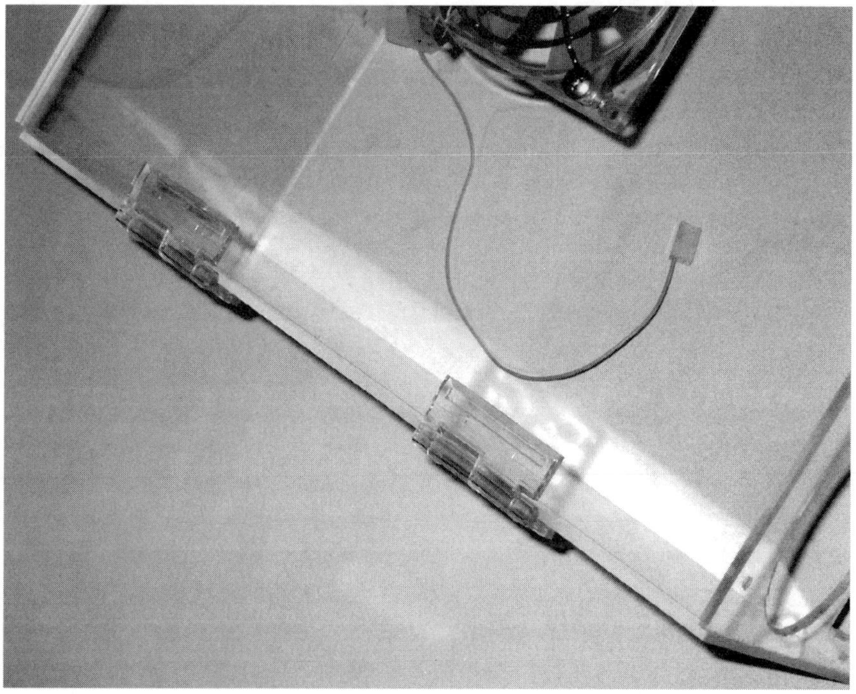

- After you have glued all the edges together, put all your components in and run a quick check for any spacing problems. If all measurements were precise, everything should fit right into place.
- The next section will deal with accessorizing your case, so clean up your work area and prepare for a bit of electronics work!

Chapter 14

Adding Components and Accessories

Tools of the Trade

Four-inch CCFL light
Neon tape
Neon string
Mountable LEDs
Electric tape or heat-shrink tubing
Zip ties
Wire tires
Rubber bands
Scissors
Hobby knife
Wire stripper
Phillips screwdriver

With all the acrylic pieces glued together, it is now time to get to the fun part: accessories. The first thing we need to do is install all of our components and make sure they fit. If there are any problems with fitment, this will be the time to fix them. Adding accessories—which can vary from lights, to extra fans, to any other enhancements that you can think of—is the icing on the cake of most case modifications. For our acrylic case project, we thought the best way to showcase the material would be to use different lights.

Before you set off to hunt down every light you can think of, you need to make sure you have enough room to accommodate the lights you choose. For example, if you decide on a 12-inch neon tube or a CCFL (cold cathode fluorescent light) tube, you have to measure your own case dimensions first. Our case is just a bit over 12 inches on one side; the tube might fit, but it may be too close for comfort. We need to keep in mind the case's size limitations, so all the lights we have chosen are smaller and more manageable.

60 MINUTES

Installing your Components

After your case has been clamped together for a least one day, remove the clamps and examine each edge. You should have a sturdy case that resists bending. If your case seems shaky or loose, check the edges to see whether you missed any areas to glue. Also check whether the lid opens and closes without obstruction. At the end of Chapter 13, you should have run a quick check of whether your computer components fit inside the case. If everything seems all right space-wise, you are ready to secure the hardware with your screws.

HEADS UP!

If you have any loose edges or areas, do not continue until you fix them. You do not want to install all of your components only to have them drop out from the bottom when you lift up your case.

The first component to install is the motherboard. Place it over the holes that you created earlier and drop down all the screws through the board. Tighten the ones in the corner first and work inward. For our motherboard, there are only four screws to tend to, so we just work in a clockwise direction. After you have tightened down the last screw, check the I/O area of the motherboard (see Figure 14-1) to see if all the ports are still accessible.

Figure 14-1
Input/output of the motherboard

TIPS OF THE TRADE

Trim to Fit

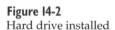

If your motherboard ports are blocked slightly by the acrylic, you can still make this work. Remove your motherboard and any other components from the case. Take a flat needle file and work it along the edge that is blocking the motherboard. Clean up any debris in the area inside the case and try positioning your motherboard again. Repeat the process if necessary until you are able to fit the board to your liking.

The next item to install is the hard drive. For our case, we are mounting it from the bottom of the base using four screws. Before you proceed, double-check that all the holes line up correctly. This is the time to fix the problem if they do not line up. Run your screw through the hole first to see if it fits. If you are feeling resistance, remove the screw immediately. Proceeding any further can strip the head of the screw and leave it wedged in the hole. Remove all the components from the case; it should just be your motherboard at this point. Take a drill bit one size larger and run it through the hole. Remove the bit and run the same screw through it again. There should be a lot less resistance than before. (Also check your optical drive mounting holes at this point. If they have to be fixed, you need to do it before you secure the hard drive.) With all the holes lined up correctly, you can proceed to secure each screw down into the hard drive (see Figure 14-2).

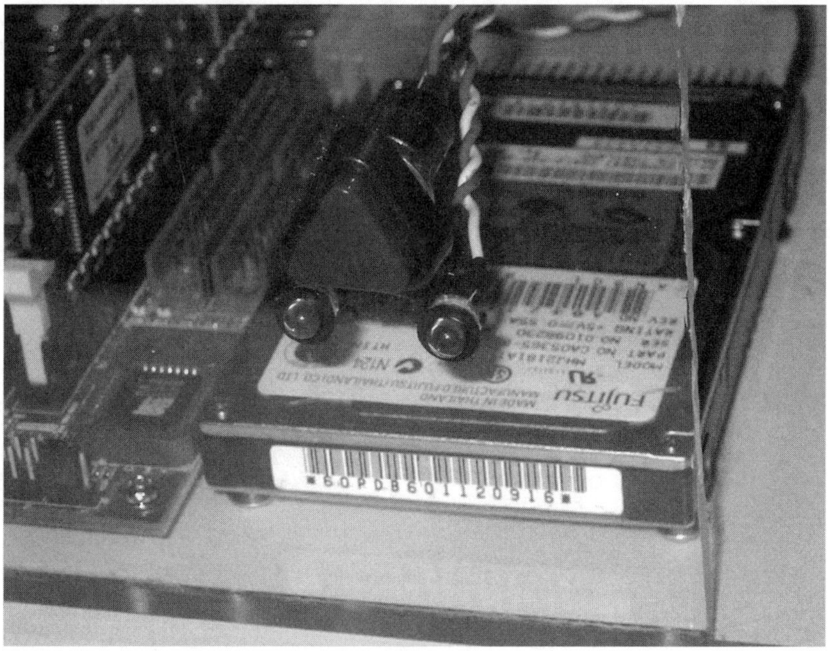

Figure 14-2
Hard drive installed

To secure our optical drive, we are going to use the same type of screws that we used for our hard drive. For our purposes, it was easier to turn the case around and position it on the edge of a table. The mounting holes should now be facing upward while allowing you to hold the optical drive upright underneath with your hand. Take four screws and secure the drive (see Figure 14-3).

Figure 14-3 Optical drive installed

HEADS UP!

Do not overtighten the screws! You run the risk of stripping the screw or the threads within the drive. Avoid using a motorized screwdriver. They are usually too fast for this type of application. Using a conventional screwdriver will give you a lot more control over speed so that you don't strip the screw heads or threads.

After you install the motherboard, hard drive, and optical drive, check the front and sides of the case for any bulging or other problem areas. If you notice any bulging or bending, you may have tightened the screws too much. You should have something similar to Figure 14-4.

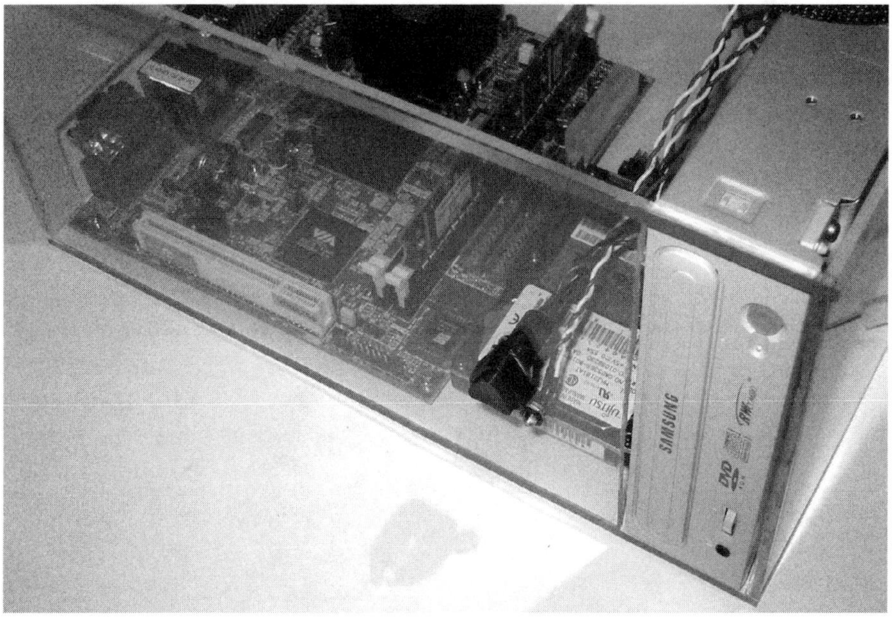

Figure 14-4
Components installed

The last piece of the puzzle is the power supply, as shown in Figure 14-5. Before you tighten the screw down to secure the power supply, check the spacing to make sure it clears the motherboard and is not touching it. If all holes match up, install the power supply by slowly tightening each screw in an X pattern. As with your hard drive installation, if the holes are too small, take a larger drill bit and enlarge them slightly if you need to.

Figure 14-5
Power supply

With the construction of our case, we actually have extra room next to the power supply, as shown in Figure 14-6. This area can be used to hold most of the wire clutter that will accumulate when everything is connected. We also have room to install a much larger power supply if we need to in the future. In future projects, if you want to ensure that you have sufficient room to upgrade components, you can plan for that in the design stages. For the purposes of this project, that isn't necessary.

Figure 14-6
Extra space

The last step of the installation is to connect the power connectors and IDE cable for the hard drive and optical drive. You can tidy up the wires with some zip ties, wire ties, or rubber bands. The IDE cable can be replaced with a rounded variety if you are limited in space. Since we had enough operating room, we don't need to change from the stock flat-ribbon design. We also had extra space near the hard drive and optical drive, as shown in Figure 14-7. There is enough room there to place a small CCFL tube, neon wire, or LED.

Figure 14-7
Extra space between the drives

After you link all the connectors and cable, you have finished the last part of the main project. The next step is to add some spice to the mix with lighting. Close the lid and check if your fan will hit any of the wires inside. Since our fan is in the middle, there is a wide-open space free from any cables (see Figure 14-8).

Figure 14-8
Lid closed

30 MINUTES EACH

Lighting

The first light we are going to install is the widely available CCFL tube. CCFL tubes are similar to neon tubes in function, but vary greatly in design and light output. These tubes are called *cold cathodes* because they lack a filament. This type of light is great for case modders, because without a filament, the tube produces a lot less heat, which may mean fewer fans are needed—which means less fan noise. CCFLs are used widely in scanners and backlighting for LCDs (liquid crystal displays). You can substitute CCFL tubes with neon tubes, but neon tubes have a substantially lower light intensity than CCFL tubes. For our project, we went ahead with a smaller CCFL tube, measuring only four inches (see Figure 14-9). If your case is larger, you can go up to a full 12 inches.

TIPS OF THE TRADE

Online Shopping

If you have trouble finding these neon or CCFL kits or any modding accessories in your local area, head to an online retailer. Major retailers carry a full line of lighting equipment at fairly competitive prices. Make sure you e-mail a retailer beforehand if you have any specific requests or questions about your project needs.

Figure 14-9
Four-inch CCFL

If you want a more even glow, line up a few of these 4-inch tubes in a row, or purchase a longer 12-inch sample. A 4-inch tube by itself does not give off that much light, but it is great for spotlight or accent lighting.

When you purchase these tubes, they can come unassembled, which means that there are no molex or power switches connected. You can buy complete kits with everything connected. Depending on your ability to connect wires and plugs, choose whichever one is easiest for you. If you get the unassembled variety, just remember that there is a 12-volt wire and a ground wire. The easiest way to wire up the CCFL tube is to splice into a molex connector (see Figure 14-10). As long as these two wires are connected to the correct power leads from your power supply through the molex connector, the light should be functional.

Figure 14-10
CCFL installed

TIPS OF THE TRADE

Wrapping Securely

If you purchased an unassembled kit, make sure all the wires are securely wrapped. Heat-shrink tubing is recommended, but electrical tape can be used as a substitute. Do this to prevent your system and power supply from shorting out.

We also picked up a package of neon string, shown in Figure 14-11. This is similar to a neon tube but in the form of a thin string. This design lets you bend the neon and position it anywhere you want. Although the string gives only a fraction of the light of a normal neon tube, it creates a different effect in your case. Most neon string kits come with an inverter, which can power up to two strings at once. These kits are always preassembled with wires wrapped and molex plugs already connected.

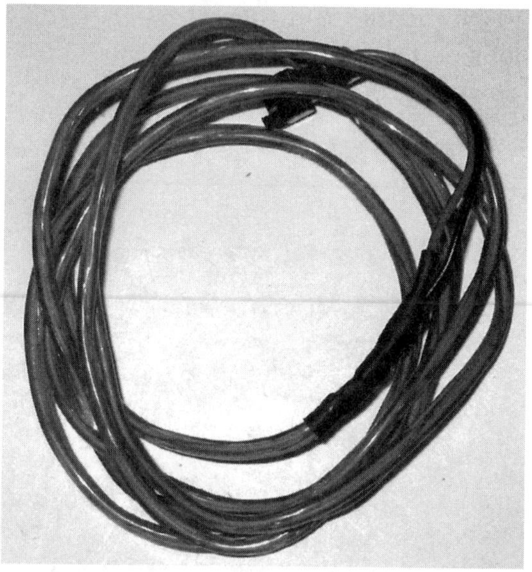

Figure 14-11
Neon string

The neon string works best in total darkness; it will not shine as bright as a CCFL tube when there is ample lighting in the room. The string varies in color— for our application, we opted for the blue version to match our fan (see Figure 14-12). Installation for the string is straight very straightforward: Plug the power connector from the string into one of the molex connectors on your power supply. If there is a On switch on the inverter for the string, turn that on and power on the system.

Figure 14-12
Neon string installed

A variation of neon string is neon tape, otherwise known as EL (electroluminescent) tape, shown in Figure 14-13. Instead of the round string, the tape is flat and harder to bend. This causes problems if you want to go around corners and edges of your case. Most EL tape kits come preassembled like the string, so this should be easy to install. The kit also uses an inverter to power the entire length of tape. One advantage tape has over string is that it has a peel-away adhesive backing that allows the tape to stick to surfaces. This works great on flat surfaces but is cumbersome to use around corners.

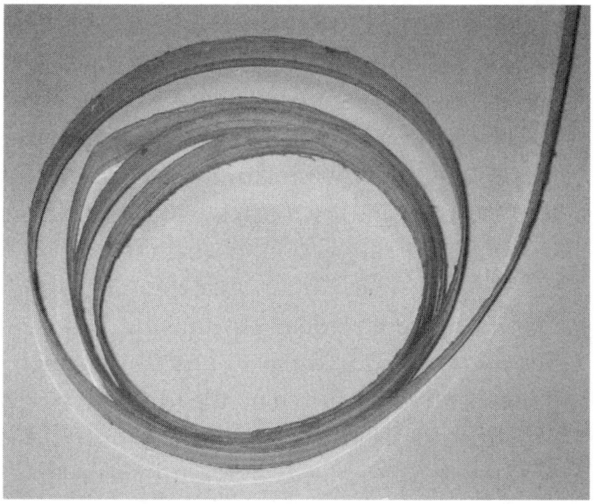

Figure 14-13
EL tape

Since space is not abundant in our project case, we laid the tape down on the bottom and throughout the rear of the case (see Figure 14-14). We tried not to bend it because that can break the tape. The packaging for the tape mentions that you can cut away a piece and power it separately. If you wish to do this, you need an extra inverter and a way to bond the tape to the wires from the inverter.

Figure 14-14
EL tape installed

HEADS UP!

If you do plan to alter the tape you purchased, read through the warranty information. Once the product has been altered, the warranty may be voided or changed. Contact the manufacturer if you are unsure or have any further questions.

The last piece of lighting we picked up is a Flexiglow Lazer Beam Kit (see Figure 14-15), which includes three 5mm LEDs encased in translucent housings that can be mounted in various spots of your case. The kit includes a central control box that allows you to turn the unit on, make it flash, or turn it completely off. The kits come in an assortment of colors, so matching them to your case should not be hard. Each housing has a peel-away adhesive backing, which allows us to stick them to any flat surface. This can be vertically on the side panels or upside-down on the top lid. The translucent housing can be moved up to 180 degrees. Once they are placed on a surface, the lights can be moved around to highlight different areas of your case.

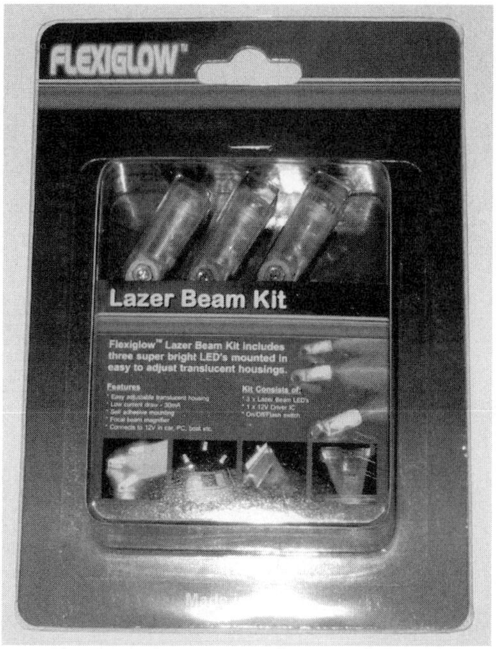

Figure 14-15
Flexiglow Lazer Beam Kit

In our case, we attached one LED directly over the top of the motherboard. Another one is located in the front, shining to the left panel. And the last one is located on the top lid, shining downward. The positioning of the LEDs is shown in Figure 14-16. We can change the positioning later if needed.

Figure 14-16
Lazer LEDs installed

All these lights can be used individually or together. We recommend using no more than three of these at one time, because anything more will result in conflicting color themes. Each kit comes with its own inverter or control box. This allows you to turn off each one and use some of the other features that the lights come with like flashing or sound activation. For our project, we want the lights to be on whenever we turn the computer on. We just adjusted the light setting to the on position for each of them (see Figure 14-17).

Figure 14-17 Neon string and CCFL

TESTING 1-2-3

- ❏ If you connected your own wires for an unassembled kit, double-check everything to make sure they are secure. This is especially true for any bare wires or connectors. Prevent them from shorting out your system.
- ❏ You are just about done, so clean up your work area. We will discuss some future modifications you can do for your clear acrylic case in Chapter 15!

Chapter 15
Finishing Touches

Tools of the Trade

Acrylic sheets
Window tint spray, vinyl dye, or plastic paint
Window tint film (optional)
Rotary tool
Pointed grinding-wheel attachment for rotary tool
Clamps
Goggles
Clean-up towel

Now that you have completed your case and installed all the components, it is time to add some finishing touches. If you have decided that all you want is to have a clear acrylic computer, then you can stop here. On the other hand, if you want to expand a bit on the project, this chapter is for you. We will discuss two simple additional miniprojects you can accomplish that should add some uniqueness to your case.

The first project describes the use of paint to tint the acrylic a different color. Since clear acrylic cases are becoming quite popular, creating a case with a different color can set your case apart. Our second miniproject involves etching. The process of etching involves using your rotary tool to engrave a design into the acrylic. This is a permanent mark, unlike stickers and other adhesives. Etching is not uncommon; there are probably numerous plastic products in your house or office that have been branded by using this method. We will take that idea and adapt it to our project case.

1–2 HOURS

Changing the Color

The first thing people will notice when they see a clear acrylic case is the clarity; seeing a computer encased in what appears to be an invisible box is always intriguing. The alternative is to combine this invisible box idea with a bit of color.

On most new automobiles, there is an option to purchase tinted windows. This is a factory process done on the glass to give it a darker look. On the outside, it may appear that the glass is dark or even black. Unless you stand up really close to the glass or light is shining behind it, you will not see what is inside.

If you have a car that does not have tinted windows, you can still get them tinted. Take your car to a window shop and they will be able to apply a window-tint film. This film works the same way as the factory glass, but over time it does fade and lose color. You can also purchase at specialty stores window tint sprays that mimic factory-tinted glass or plastic. For our project, we will use the widely available and affordable vinyl dye. We will also show you a newer paint product specifically made for plastics. Both types of sprays come in a variety of colors. You can choose whichever is most complementary to your lighting within the case.

> **TIPS OF THE TRADE**
>
> ### Color Acrylic
>
> If you know that you want to color your acrylic before you begin building a case, you can ask the plastics shop whether it carries any color acrylic sheets. Some places do have these in stock. If not, they can order it for you.

Vinyl dye was created for use mainly on vinyl-covered seats. Instead of coating the surface with layers of color, vinyl dye seeps into the material and stains it. Because of this staining, there is no need to prime or clear-coat this process. It also dries a lot faster than conventional spray paint.

We also picked up a new spray from Krylon, created specifically for plastics. It boasts similar drying capabilities—only 15–20 minutes. There is also no need for a primer or clear-coat layer when using the plastic spray. Both the vinyl dye and paint are available at your local auto parts store or hardware store; the cans shown in Figure 15-1 are good examples.

Figure 15-1
Spray cans

> **TIPS OF THE TRADE**
>
> ### Always Test First
>
> Before you start spraying colors on your case, conduct a test. Try to find any leftover pieces of acrylic to test the spray on. Sometimes you cannot tell what the color will be until you apply it onto the surface. Instead of ruining the finished case, you can decide on a test piece whether a particular color is really what you want.

If you are going ahead and coloring your case, remember to first remove all the components that are inside. Depending on which piece of acrylic you want to paint, you may or may not need to remove all your components. Take a clean towel or cloth and wipe the surface clean also—you can get professional plastic cleaner from the plastics shop or hardware store. You want to get rid of any dust or fingerprints that may have been left on the acrylic. Practice on a small piece of acrylic first; make sure to peel off the protective plastic or paper that may be covering it (see Figure 15-2).

Figure 15-2
Acrylic sheet with protective paper

Find a place outdoors or a place that is well ventilated. If you have a garage or a workshop, that will work even better. Clean up the area to eliminate any dust particles from settling onto the surface while painting. Put on a filtering mask for painting if you are sensitive to the fumes. We'll start off with the plastic paint from Krylon. We were not sure what color would look best—blue was a bit overused—so we thought we would give red a shot. We are going to apply two layers of it to give the acrylic sheet an even distribution of color. Spray from the left or the right side in a back-and-forth motion. The first layer will not completely cover all areas in color, as shown in Figure 15-3, but do not worry, because you are going to apply a second layer.

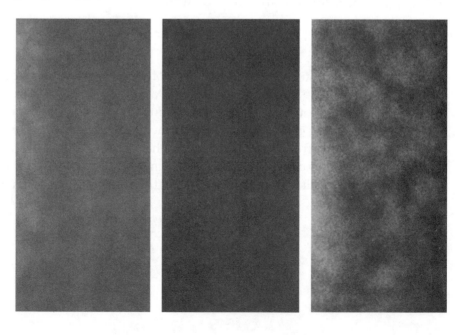

Figure 15-3
First red layer applied (left), a second layer (middle), and the smokier Plasti-Kote finish (right)

Wait about 15–20 minutes before handling the sheet. You do not need to sand this piece as you would normally on wood or metal. If the surface seems dry enough after 20 minutes, place it down and apply the second layer as you did with the first. Wait another 15–20 minutes and then check the surface again. You should have a clean and evenly distributed red color throughout, as shown in Figure 15-3.

We also tried the conventional black color using vinyl dye. Our dye is made by Plasti-Kote; you may need to get a different brand, depending on availability at your auto parts store or hardware store. The results are not as bright and colorful as the red plastic paint; instead it creates a smokier finish. Apply the vinyl dye in the same manner as the plastic paint. Start with one layer and give it about 15–20 minutes to dry before handling. Figure 15-3 shows the result after one layer of dye.

Keep in mind that priming and sanding are not necessary. Vinyl dye is meant to seep into the plastic and stain it, as opposed to covering it with layers of color. Apply a second layer of dye to complete the process (see Figure 15-4). If you want it to be darker, apply an additional layer. It may make it too dark, so be wary of how much you spray on. After the test piece of acrylic has been given enough time to dry, we place it on our case. Using the green four-inch CCFL behind it, we are able to see through the case without any problems. Notice that the area over the power supply is completely black. This is normal, because any area that is not lit behind it will appear to be a lot darker.

Figure 15-4 Finished vinyl-dyed piece

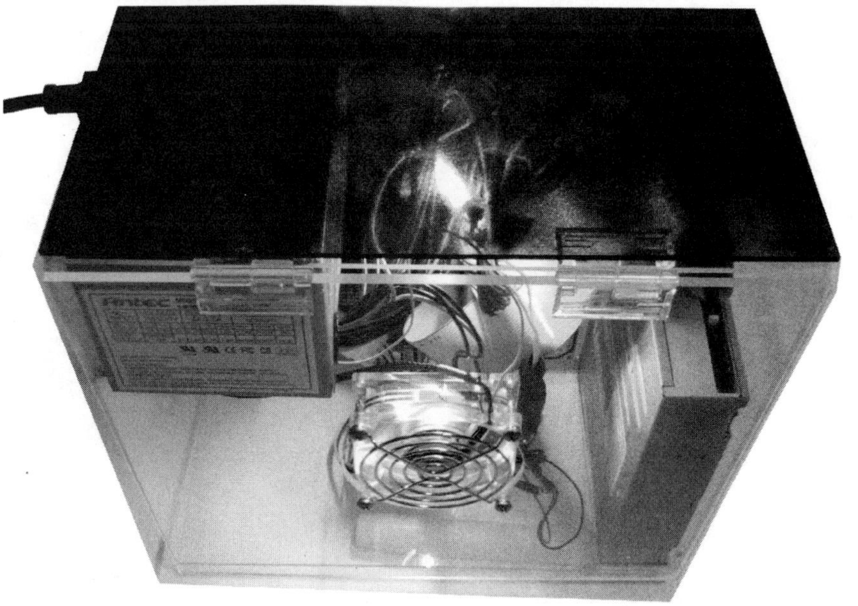

HEADS UP!

If at this point you decide that this is not the effect you want, you can stop. Since we used an extra piece of acrylic, there is no harm done. You can always go back and try this again later if you get tired of the crystal-clear look of your case.

30–60 MINUTES

Creating an Etching

Etching the acrylic can bring a whole new level of design to any acrylic surface. To create an etching, you would just have to carve or scrape the surface of the acrylic in the form of a design. This is meant as a replacement for a sticker or a decal; you can create pictures or words without ruining the overall appearance. An etching can really stand out as a centerpiece of your case if lighting is directed on it correctly. There are many online retailers who currently offer pre-etched windows, but for a totally customized look and feel, you will have to make your own design.

For this extra part of the project, you are going to have to find a sturdy work table. The edge of this table should stick out a bit so that you can use clamps to hold down the acrylic while you work. The other major tool you need is the rotary tool along with the pointed grinding-stone attachment. We are using a Dremel rotary tool, which includes the grinding stone in the set (see Figure 15-5). If you do not have this attachment, you can ask for it at your local hardware store. The part number for our grinding stone is #953.

Figure 15-5 Dremel with grinding-stone attachment

The basic process of creating an etching is to just scar the surface of the acrylic. Using the grinding wheel makes it really easy; just touching the surface slightly creates this effect. Depending on how strong a design you want, you can etch deeper into the acrylic. At this point, find yourself a clamp to secure your acrylic, similar to the one shown here:

HEADS UP!

Start at a slower speed of about 10,000 RPM on the rotary tool with the grinding-stone attachment. If you are confident, you can increase the speed for a faster or deeper etching. As always, protect yourself by using goggles—the fast-speed rotary tool can send hot pieces of acrylic into the air!

After you have prepared your rotary tool and clamp, it is time to decide on a design. Some people may wish to add their name to their case, or maybe a small picture of their favorite logo. Whatever you decide, try to keep it simple. A complex picture or letter combination can be very difficult to etch. For our project, we went with a picture of a small dragon, as shown in Figure 15-6.

Figure 15-6 Dragon picture (left) and acrylic sheet over design (right)

We had to resize the picture on the computer first before we printed it. Resize your own picture if necessary; your project case may not be as large as ours. The dragon itself is just one single color, which will make the process a lot easier. Once you have your design printed or drawn out, place it on the table and put the piece of acrylic over it, as shown in Figure 15-6. If you are using a sheet that has a protective plastic or paper layer, peel it off first.

Take the clamps and place them on the corners of the sheet to secure it. Two clamps will usually do the trick; use more if you have to. Turn on your rotary tool and run it over the larger solid color of the design first. You may want to create an outline first and then fill it in. Whichever way you choose, just etch slowly and you will not have any problems. Start off in a larger area to test out the process of etching with your rotary tool. Work your way outward from there, which should give you a good starting point for your etch, as shown in Figure 15-7.

Figure 15-7
Etching completed

Once you are finished, take a clean towel or cloth and wipe away the excess acrylic shavings. Bring the acrylic up to a light and see if you missed any areas. If you did miss any, just clamp it back down and finish off any spots you may have missed.

The easiest way to showcase an etching is by attaching a light to the edge of the acrylic sheet. Shining a light directly through the sheet perpendicularly sends the light directly through. Think of it as a fiber optic cable; shining a light parallel through the plastic sends the light throughout the sheet. We used our green four-inch CCFL tube to accent our etching (see Figure 15-8). You may also use an LED—both methods work fine.

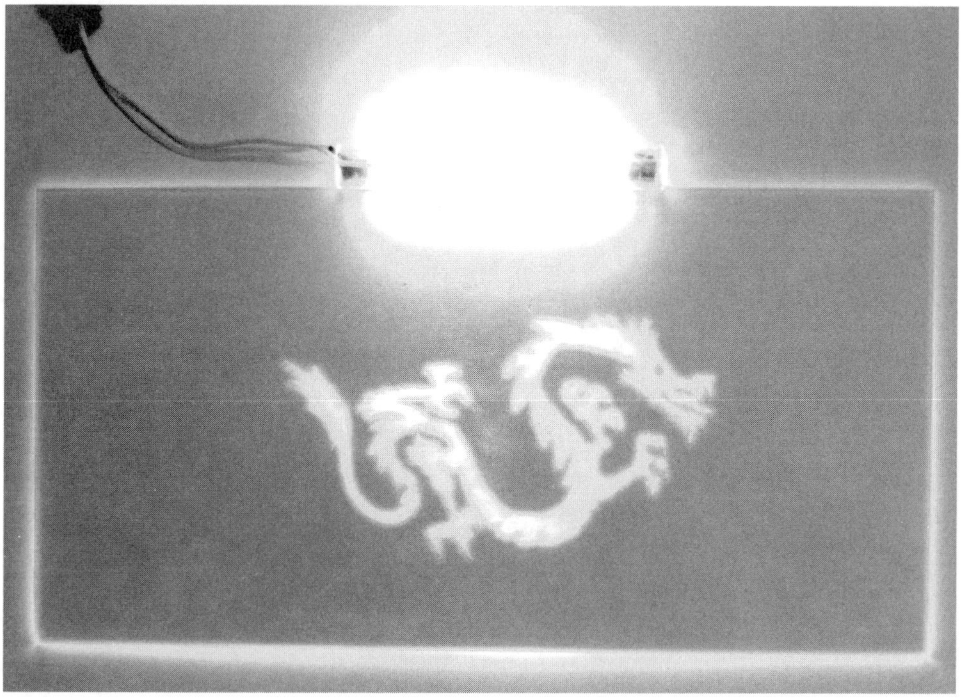

Figure 15-8 Dragon etching lit with a CCFL

Is That It?

The two extra modifications we have explained are just the tip of the iceberg. If you feel that the coloring and etching are mods you want to do, then apply these two extra projects to your case. If you are still unsure, test it some more on any extra acrylic pieces you have lying around. There are other variations to the theme you can apply to your clear project case. Mix up the coloring and etching to create a unique combination. Whatever you do, just remember that this is your case project. There are no cases or modifications that will be the same, especially since this project is one of a kind. Let your imagination run wild and your case mod will turn heads at any event.

TESTING 1-2-3

- ❑ After coloring your case, give it about 24 hours before you put everything back together. This should give it enough time to dry completely.
- ❑ The etching is a permanent design, so decide carefully what you want. As always, test it first on an extra piece of acrylic if you are unsure.

Project 4

Epiphany in Blue

Chapter 16

Planning the Mod

The mods in the following chapters are geared toward creating not only a great-looking case, but a functional one as well. With the addition of some windows, lights, and extra peripherals, your PC case can be turned into something that not only looks great, but has a purpose too.

By integrating a TFT screen into the case, the system can be used without having to be connected up to a monitor. When a monitor is connected, the TFT screen could be used for playing a movie while working on the main screen, or for storing extra windows and toolbars in a graphics application.

An external LCD screen will allow you to view system information, news reports, and song information when listening to music. The custom keypad that you are going to build for it will launch various applications, so you won't need to clutter up the desktop with dozens of shortcuts.

The final look of the case is also important. If you are planning a specific look, you may want to use a certain color scheme. It's important to have this sorted out early so that you can buy the relevant parts (lighting, paint, components). If you leave this until the last minute and can't obtain the colors and parts you require, it's possible that you may not be able to achieve your desired effect. Don't forget that your keyboard, mouse, monitor, and speakers can also be modded to fit into your design. You could either buy colored parts that fit with your scheme or dismantle your existing ones and give them a coat of paint.

Planning the Mod

Before you get started on this project, you need to have a proper plan, which should detail all the parts needed, tools required, and the desired outcome. By spending some time on this at the start, you should be able to avoid problems further down the line. So take some time out to detail exactly what it is you are trying to achieve and how you are going do it.

Our planned mods are as follows:

- Side window, top window, and lighting in the case
- Window and lighting in the CD drive
- UV-reactive colors on the motherboard
- Internal TFT screen
- External LCD screen

When making your plan, allow for contingencies. You never know when things might go astray. For example, the TFT screen that we are mounting inside the case will be sitting behind the front bezel. The case must have 3×3½-inch drive bays because that's where the screen will sit. In addition to this, we need to have sufficient space around the drive bays to mount the screen.

If the case isn't suitable for mounting the screen where you want, don't despair. By making allowances for this at the planning stages, you may find that it will sit in the 5¼-inch drive bays. The screen used in the mod will occupy 3×5¼-inch bays. If your case has a limited number of drive bays, you could make it an external screen instead.

It's also important to order the jobs properly. We are not painting our case, but if we were, we would do the cutting first to avoid damaging the painted surface. By ordering things correctly, you save yourself the headache of possibly going back and doing a job again.

Parts

Now that we know what we're doing, it's time to go shopping for parts. The list of components is as follows:

- Lian Li PC60 mid-tower case
- Four Akasa Nebula Arctic Blue 80mm LED fans
- Akasa 824Cu-Blue CPU Cooler
- Two 45cm UV reactive IDE cables
- Two 30cm UV cold cathodes with invertors
- Matrix Orbital LK204-25-WB-V LCD screen
- Five-inch portable games console TFT Screen

As you can see, this list really only includes the parts for the case and the mods. Case modding is probably one of the few aspects of computing where the specification of the PC is secondary to the look!

HEADS UP!

We will be voiding the warranty on most of the components. If the warranty is important to you, plan mods that can easily be reversed. It's a bit tricky to send back a CD drive once you've cut a great big hole in the top of it!

Tools

The next step is to determine which tools you need. There is a wide range of tools on the market, and choosing the right tool for the job can make a big difference. The following tools will be needed for the mods in this project:

- ❑ Drill
- ❑ Dremmel or jigsaw
- ❑ Needle Files and medium grit wet and dry paper
- ❑ Heat gun
- ❑ Glue gun
- ❑ Soldering iron

When it comes to choosing power tools, you will have several options, the biggest of which is whether to choose power tools or cordless tools. Cordless tools have an advantage if you need to work in areas where there are no electrical outlets. But other than that, power tools are a better choice. They generally have larger motors, are capable of running at higher speeds, and you don't need to worry about the batteries running out halfway through a job.

After getting the tools sorted, it's time to look at the accessories for the tools—such as drill bits, saw blades, and so on. The choice of bits and blades can be quite daunting. You should use HSS drill bits and saw blades designed for working with metal. These are made from high speed steel, and are more than capable of drilling and cutting through computer cases. A fine- toothed saw blade will give you a smoother cut, and it can also be used for cutting acrylic. As you can see in Figure 16-1, the teeth on the HSS blade we will be using are very fine compared to the standard jigsaw blade shown below it.

Figure 16-1
Sharp teeth (top) versus the jigsaw blade (bottom)

If you are using a multi-tool, then the fiberglass-reinforced cutting discs are the best choice for cutting metal. They are more expensive than the other types of cutting disc, but they last longer and have less chance of breaking during use. It's also worth getting some deburring stones for the tool. These help clean up any sharp edges after cutting. But you could always do this by hand with some fine files.

HEADS UP!

When shopping for tools, don't forget the safety equipment! If you slip and scratch your case, it's easy enough to replace. Fingers and eyes are not so easily replaced, so make sure you have safety glasses and gloves.

It also helps to have a workbench and a few clamps to keep things in place when you're cutting them. Metal panels have a habit of vibrating when they're being cut, so being able to hold them steady with clamps will make the job much easier. A long ruler or spirit level is also handy to have. It keep your lines straight when measuring, and you can also clamp it to your panels and use it as an edge to keep your tools heading in the right direction.

HEADS UP!

It can get expensive to buy all of the tools you need, so ask your friends and family whether they have them. It's quite possible that they will be able to lend you most (if not all) of the tools needed. It's also possible to rent tools, if you can't buy or borrow everything you need.

Accessories

As always, you will need a few items that don't fit into a neat category. They're not strictly tools, and really aren't parts; they're just the extra accessories you'll need to complete the mods that will be covered in the next chapters. The following items should be available from an electronics store:

- ❑ Nine solderless LED holders
- ❑ Three T3-sized plastic project boxes
- ❑ Five male and two female molex connectors
- ❑ One 1000mcd 5mm blue LED and a 470 Ohm resistor
- ❑ 2.5mm DC power lead and socket
- ❑ Silver-conductive paint and silver-loaded epoxy
- ❑ Yellow, black, and red wire—around 12 inches of each
- ❑ Self-adhesive cable clips, cable ties, and self-adhesive pads

The silver-conductive paint and silver-loaded epoxy are pretty much as their names imply. They have a high silver content, which enables them to conduct electricity. This will be extremely useful when it comes to building the keypad for the external LCD screen.

HEADS UP!

The silver paint and epoxy give off fumes, so make sure you use them in well-ventilated areas. Because they conduct electricity, be sure not to use them near your PC. If you get some on your components, it could cause a short circuit and damage your PC.

Because they have a high quantity of silver, these products can be very expensive.

HEADS UP!

Many car accessory stores sell kits to repair heated rear windows. These include a substance very similar to silver-conductive paint and should work just as well.

We will also need some parts from a hardware store:

- ❑ Acrylic sheet
- ❑ Double-sided tape, masking tape, insulation tape, and super glue
- ❑ Four self-adhesive rubber feet

- ❏ Black spray paint
- ❏ Thin paintbrush

The last few items should be easily obtainable, and you may have some of them in the house already:

- ❏ Two overhead transparency sheets
- ❏ UV reactive marker pens
- ❏ Nail varnish remover and cotton balls
- ❏ Food container with a 4-to-4½-inch diameter rim
- ❏ DVD case

Most highlighting pens are UV reactive, so you may already have some of these. Some colors are more reactive than others, so it would be worth checking this in advance.

Practice Makes Perfect

It can be a daunting task to use power tools on your case. To save your case from becoming a rather expensive guinea pig, take some time to learn how your tools work, and the best way to use them with various materials. If you are unfamiliar with cutting metal and acrylic, try to gather some pieces that you can sacrifice as you learn the tools. You might be able to get hold of some off cuts from a metal or plastics workshop, or maybe even buy a cheap PC case to perform your first mods on.

Knowing that it doesn't matter too much if you make a mistake will help boost your confidence as you start work. If you do make a mistake, just throw away the test piece and try again.

If you know someone who is familiar with using the tools, ask him or her for advice. Take your time as well. You're not trying to mod your case in the fastest time possible. You want to create something that is personal and unique to you. This will require planning and patience.

Where to Mod

With all the parts gathered, and the tools ready to go, it's now time to find a suitable place to work.

Ideally you need somewhere that has plenty of space, light, and power. A garage or workshop is the best choice, followed by working outside (where you may be limited by the weather), or you could work in the house.

Cutting case panels creates lots of metal dust and filings. Trying to clean these up from a carpeted floor is going to be difficult at best.

You also need somewhere with good ventilation when using spray paint. The fumes can be nasty, so when using the paint, it might be best to do it outside. You can then take the parts inside to dry.

When working, keep the floor space around your work area clear. You don't want to be tripping over cables or items sitting on the floor.

The Finished Article

After you work through this mod project in the following chapters, you will have a customized case with windows, lights, an integral TFT screen, and an external LCD screen. To give you an idea of what it might look like, Figure 16-2 shows our results with the room lights off and the PC running.

Figure 16-2
A finished PC Mod

Now that you know what you're aiming for, get to work!

Chapter 17

Power Tool Frenzy

Tools of the Trade

Power drill with 3mm and 8mm HSS metal drill bits
Jigsaw with fine-toothed metal cutting blade
Multi-tool with reinforced cutting discs
Craft knife, needle files, and screwdriver
Workbench and clamps
Medium-grit wet and dry paper
Safety goggles and gloves
Masking tape, double-sided tape, sticky pads, and super glue
Ruler and pencil
Food container with a 4- to 4½-inch rim
Acrylic sheet
Nail varnish remover and cotton balls
Overhead transparency sheet
DVD-style case

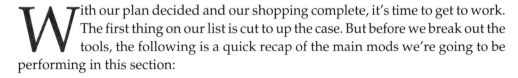

With our plan decided and our shopping complete, it's time to get to work. The first thing on our list is cut to up the case. But before we break out the tools, the following is a quick recap of the main mods we're going to be performing in this section:

- ❏ Insert side window in the case

- ❑ Insert top window in the case
- ❑ Insert window in the CD drive

There are also a couple of other cuts we can make to improve the case. Many cases come with spaces in them for additional fans to be fitted—there is often a metal grill in place, though. While these grills may reduce the chance of you sticking your fingers into the fan blades, they reduce the airflow considerably. They also tend to look unsightly. The PC-60 case has one of these grills on the removable motherboard tray, and another on the top of the case.

We are going to remove the rear grill, not the top one. If we were to cut out the top grill, we would have a square hole on the top of the case. Square fan covers are hard to find, so we will leave the grill in place. The design of the grill on the top should also contrast nicely with the planned shape of the windows.

We can also perform a "stealth mod" on the CD drive, which involves hiding the drive behind one of the drive bay covers. Then, when you look at the case, there are no ugly beige drives to spoil the effect. The drive tray can be ejected either from inside your operating system or by pressing the corner of the drive bay to activate the eject button.

The Case

This is the Lian Li PC-60 case that we are going to be using:

This is a great case to work on for several reasons. It's made from aluminum, so the case itself is light, looks good, and is fairly easy to cut. Everything is held in place using thumbscrews or push pins, so dismantling the case is practically a toolless job…and dismantling the case is exactly what we are going to do next.

Completely dismantling the case is a very important step. When drilling or cutting metal, you can generate a significant amount of metal dust. If this dust comes into contact with your system components, it could short them out and cause damage. By removing as many parts of the case as possible, you can cut and drill away from the main chassis of the case, which limits the possibly of causing damage.

There is one minor fly in the ointment, though—the top of the case is not removable. If you look closely at the next illustration, you will see two rivets at the top of the case. On the back are another pair. These rivets hold the lid on.

Removing the lid is simply a matter of drilling through these rivets. With a 3mm bit, drill through the center of each.

Drilling through each rivet might require a reasonable amount of force, but try to control the drill. If you are pushing too hard when you break through the rivet, the drill will rush forward, possibly scratching the case.

Believe it or not, that's your very first mod! It might not seem that impressive on the surface, but it's a mod nevertheless.

15 MINUTES

Removing the Fan Grill

The first thing to do is to remove the fan grill from the motherboard tray. Before cutting, it's a good idea to mask around the area you will be working on. If you have any minor slips while cutting, the masking tape should help save your case. Once the area is masked, we're ready to cut the grill. It's a fairly tight working area, and you may struggle to maneuver a jigsaw, so a multi-tool makes the job a bit easier.

HEADS UP!

You're not in a race to complete these mods. Take your time, and remember the old adage: measure twice, cut once. It's very difficult to stick bits of metal back into your case if you make a mistake!

TIPS OF THE TRADE

Cutting Slowly

When cutting through the grill, keep in mind that you don't have to go through it in one go. You can slowly score your way across it, using two or three cuts to finally get through. This method will put less stress on your tool and help your cutting discs to last longer.

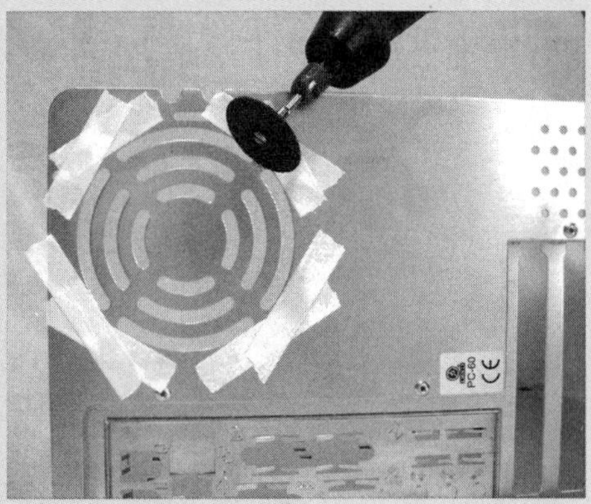

Once you have removed the grill, you'll probably need to clean up the edges a bit. You can do this with a deburring stone on the multi-tool, or by hand with some needle files.

60 MINUTES

Cutting the Side Panel and Inserting the Window

Cutting up your beautifully finished case panels can be a daunting task, but with the proper precautions, there's nothing to worry about.

Start by covering the entire outside of the panel with masking tape. This will prevent scratches when the panel is resting on the workbench. We're going to be doing all of our marking and cutting on the inside of the panel. By doing it this way, any marks on the panel will be out of sight

HEADS UP!

When marking out for your window, take notice of how your side panel fits onto the case. If the panel has to slide, make sure you allow for this. Putting the window too close to the edge of the panel will cause you problems when you refit it.

We have decided on a fairly square window, but with two of the corners curved to help it stand out a bit more. The window is also fairly offset on the side panel.

The window is placed in such a position that you can't see all the ugly drive bays at the font of the case. They aren't that exciting to look at, so we might as well not show them. It does allow us a large view of the motherboard and other components in the system.

After marking up, we mask the inside of the panel as well. Although it's on the inside and won't be seen, we don't want to scratch the panel if we can help it.

HEADS UP!

Before starting work, make sure the panel is securely clamped in place. It will vibrate a lot during cutting. The panel will also get very hot around the area you are cutting, so take care if you handle the panel soon after cutting.

If you are going to cut the panel with a multi-tool, you can start cutting at this stage. We are going to use a jigsaw, so first we need to drill a hole to fit the jigsaw blade into.

With an 8mm metal drill bit, we drill a hole on the inside of the window marking, but reasonably close to the lines.

Our jigsaw has a metal base plate, which will severely scratch the inside of the panel, so before we start cutting, we are going to mask the jigsaw as well.

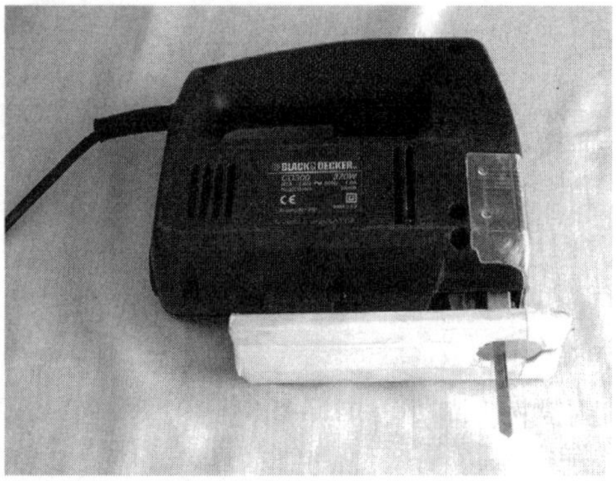

We're now ready to start cutting the panel. Lower the jigsaw blade through the drill hole and start following the lines you have marked on the side panel. Because our window has a couple of right-angled corners in it, we need to cut the window in two stages. The second stage will be a repeat of the first. Here you can see the panel after we have cut half of the window:

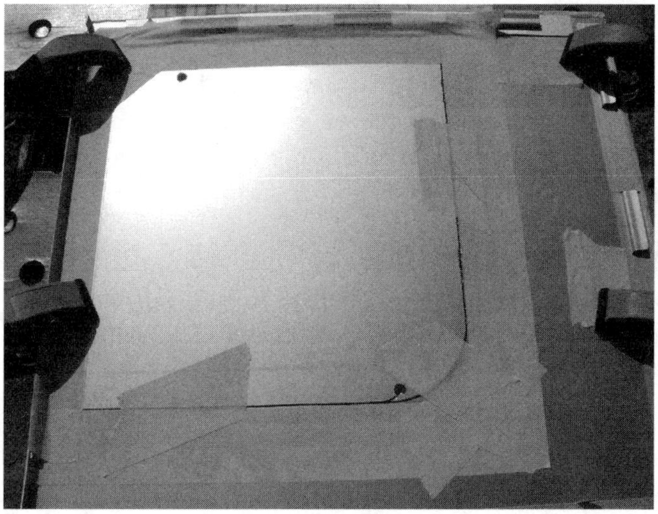

After following the line halfway around, we stopped and drilled another hole on the other side of the window. We also removed and replaced the masking tape on the bottom of the jigsaw. It can collect a lot of metal shavings, which get in the way and will possibly scratch the panel. You may also notice in the above illustration that there is some masking tape over the cut. This helps hold the panel together so that, when we cut the last little bit, the inside won't just fall out and possibly spoil the cut.

Once the window has been cut all the way around, we have something that looks like this:

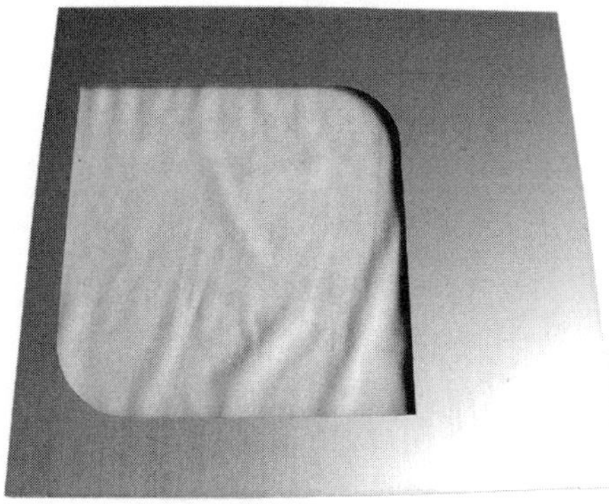

TIPS OF THE TRADE

Any Cut Will Do

If your cuts aren't too neat, don't despair. There is a wide range of edging available that you can fit over your cutout. This will hide any rough edges on the cut. You can then stick the acrylic window to the inside of the edging to complete your window.

It's still a little rough around the edges from cutting, so the edges need tidying up with some needle files. If you have a steady hand, you could use a multi-tool with a deburring stone instead.

HEADS UP!

Don't throw away the part of the panel that's been cut out. We may be using it in another mod later.

With the edges cleaned up, we can now fit the window itself. I'm using a sheet of 2mm acrylic as the "glass." We measured the acrylic so it is about one inch larger than the cut we made in the panel. Cutting the acrylic is very straightforward—you can use the same metal blade in the jigsaw as you used when cutting the panel—just remember to remove the masking tape from the bottom of the jigsaw first! Leave the protective covering on the acrylic while you're cutting it. This will be sufficient to stop it from getting scratched.

HEADS UP!

We don't recommend using a multi-tool for cutting the acrylic. The cutting discs tend to melt their way through the acrylic rather than making a clean cut.

We placed double-sided tape around the edge of the window on the inside of the panel. After removing the protective covering from the acrylic, we lowered it down onto the tape and pressed.

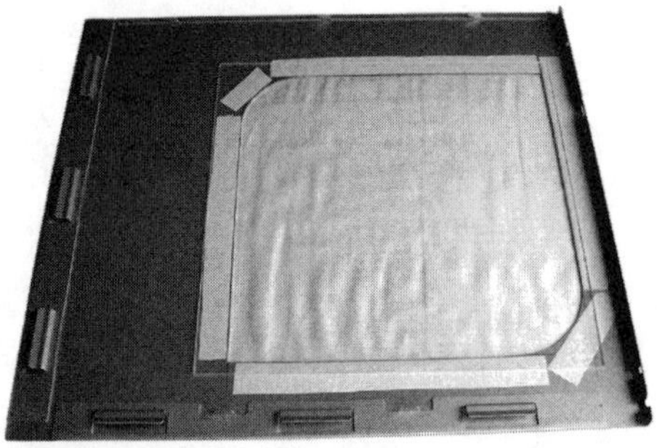

The side panel is now done, and we can move onto the top panel, for which we will follow a very similar series of steps.

45 MINUTES

Cutting the Top Panel and Inserting the Window

The top panel is next onto the workbench, but there a couple of things you need to be aware of first. The panel sits on the chassis of the case. If you put acrylic to the edge of the top panel, the acrylic will sit on the chassis instead of the panel. If this happens, the panel won't fit properly, and because the side panels interlock with the top, the panels won't fit properly either.

With the top panel placed back on the chassis, we traced out the inside dimensions of the case onto the inside of the top panel. We can now see how much room we have to play with:

The pencil lines show us the absolute maximum size that our window can be However, we need to be able to fix the acrylic onto the top panel, so our actual cutting lines need to be a bit farther in.

After bringing the lines in, we marked up a similar pattern to the one we used on the side panel window—two curved corners and two right-angle corners.

As previously mentioned, we are leaving the top fan grill alone, because there is little benefit in cutting it out. Taking the window that far back won't give much more of a view, and the style of the grill should contrast nicely with the window. With the marks made, it's time to mask everything up again and get ready for cutting.

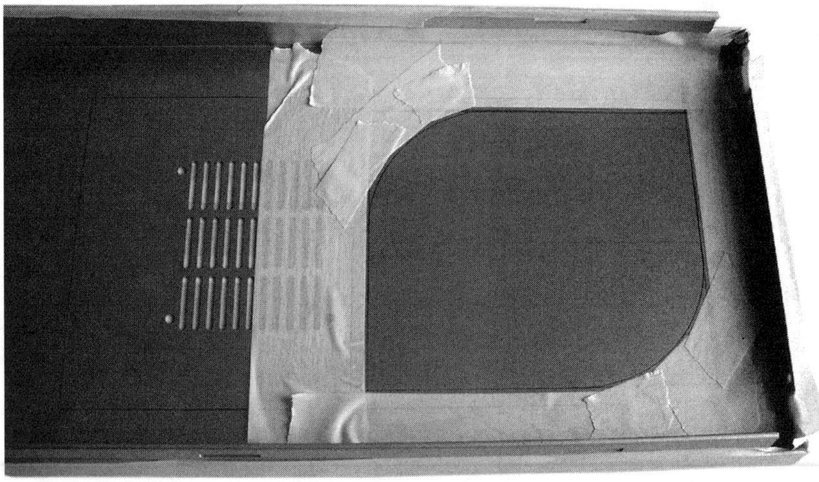

We start off in a similar way to the previous cut, by drilling a hole for the jigsaw blade to fit into. Because the space inside the case lid is tight, we removed the base from the jigsaw to make it easier to maneuver. Once the first half was cut, we drilled another hole, then cut the second half. We end up with a top panel that looks like this:

Again, we need to cut some acrylic for the window. Because of our space constraints, we can't be as generous with the overlap this time. We cut the acrylic a half-inch wider than the hole and about one inch longer. We use double-sided tape to hold the acrylic in place.

After all that hard work, it's time for a little indulgence. Putting the panels back on the chassis, we can see that the case is coming along nicely so far:

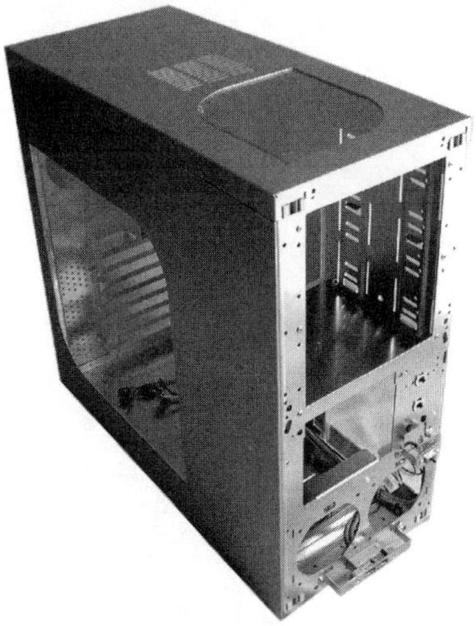

45 MINUTES

Cutting the CD Drive and Inserting the Window

Now that we have a window in the top of case, we need something inside the case to view through the window. Because the CD drive tends to sit at the top of the case, we can put a window in that as well. The window should give us a good view of the CD spinning inside the drive.

We need to grab the screwdriver again so we can dismantle the CD-ROM drive. The drive should come apart fairly easily. If you stick a straightened paperclip into the emergency eject hole, the tray should pop open. Slide it all the way out. The front of the tray should come off if you bend the middle toward you a bit and then slide it up.

With that out of the way, turn the drive over and remove the screws from the bottom. The outer casing should come off. The front bezel may have some little plastic tabs that hold it on. If you push them in, the bezel should slide forward over the CD tray. Once dismantled, it will look like this:

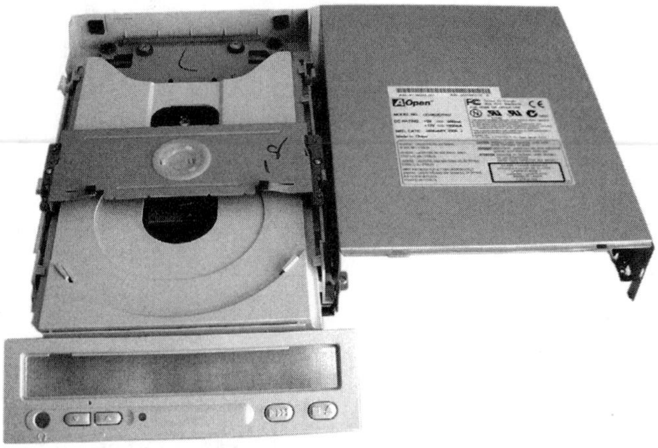

Using a craft knife, slowly (and carefully) remove the label from the top of the drive.

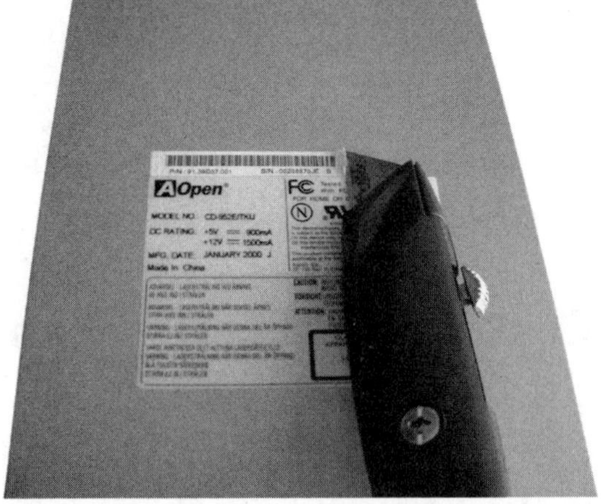

After you remove the labels, you may have some of the glue left on the top of the case. You can remove this by rubbing the top of the case with cotton balls soaked with nail varnish remover.

Cutting a perfectly round hole in the top of the drive is going to be tricky. To make things easier, we're going to use a rim to hide the rough edges of the cuts. Because the top of the drive is so close to the innards, it's going to be very difficult to use something like window edging—it would protrude into the drive too far, and could interfere with the operation of the drive. Time to look for alternatives.

This coffee container fits our needs perfectly. The container itself is made from cardboard, so it is easy to cut, and the rim has a nice, shiny finish. This container is about 4 inches across, but anything up to 4½ inches should be fine for this purpose.

With the top of the case cleaned and the rim prepared, it's time to measure where to cut the hole. Measure the top of the case to find the middle of the width, and draw a line. Line up the top casing with the drive itself, and find the center of the drive where the CD sits.

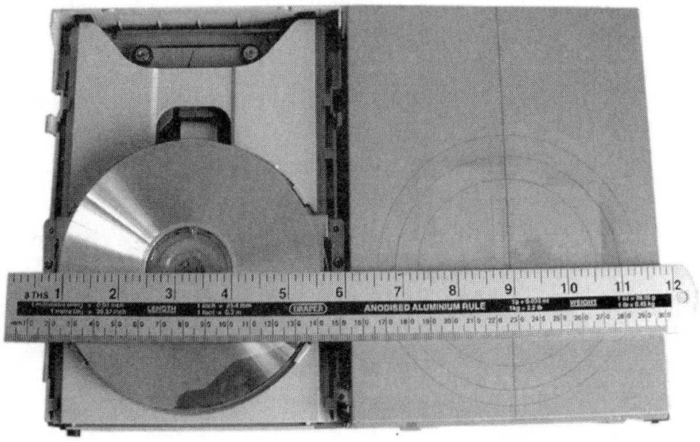

Position a CD on the top of the case, center it on the marks you have drawn, and draw around it. Then position the rim on the casing, center it, and trace around both the inside and outside.

To cut a hole for the window, we just need to cut roughly the point between the two inner circles. We mask the drive casing, and cut through it with a multi-tool.

After cutting, we have a very rough hole that looks like this:

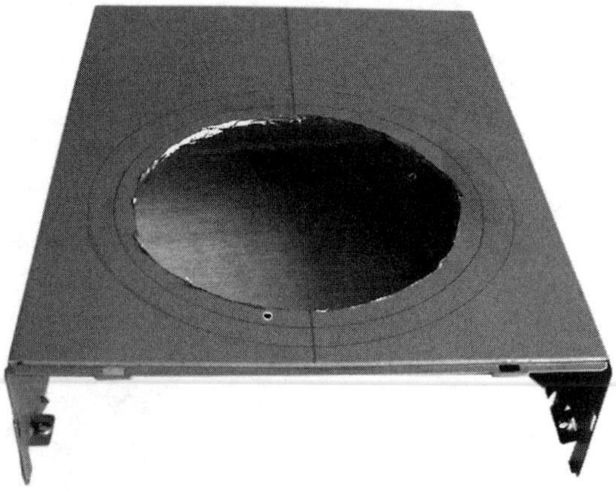

A few minutes with the needle files (or a multi-tool with a deburring stone) should be enough to remove the sharp edges and generally smooth it out.

Before we stick the window in place, we need to pretty the drive up a bit. The casing is a rather dull-gray color, but we can fix this with some medium-grade wet and dry paper. There's no magic to using wet and dry paper—it's pretty much the same as using normal sanding paper. The only difference is that you work with the paper while it is wet. Just remember to rinse the paper and the drive case under the tap every few minutes to keep things clean.

TIPS OF THE TRADE

Careful Sanding Action

When sanding, keep your movements along the same plane. If you start off by moving up and down the case, stick to that motion. Switching to a different angle will leave you with a "grain" that runs in all different directions.

After a short time, you should see the metal start to come through.

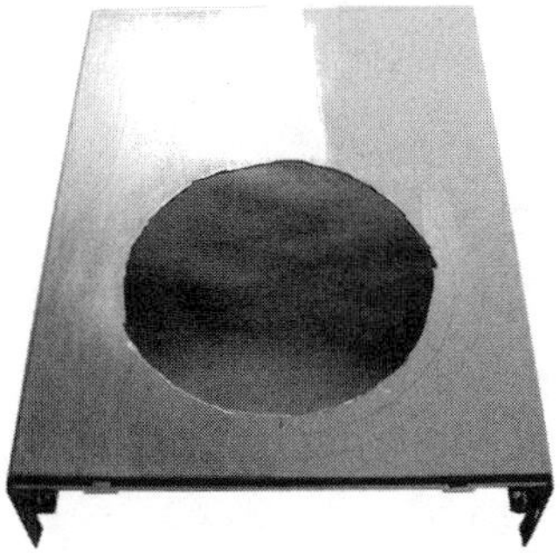

As you can see, the shiny metal underneath is much better looking than the ugly gray coating that was present before. It also matches the finish on the PC-60 case.

We can also remove the cross bar that supports the CD in the drive and give that a rubbing as well. Once everything is sanded, dry it thoroughly, step back, and admire your handiwork.

Now we can start on the process of actually sticking the window in place. As mentioned earlier, the top of the drive sits very close to the internals. This means we can't use the acrylic sheet that we used on the case windows. We need a thinner alternative. We are using a transparent sheet that is used with overhead projectors, which we cut to size, and then glue it in place.

HEADS UP!

Keep the glue away from the edge of the window so it will have space to spread out when you press the plastic into place. This will stop if from oozing onto the visible part of the window.

Put glue all around the bottom of the rim, line it up so the rim is centered, and press it into place. Again, be careful that the glue doesn't seep out onto your window.

Placing the top of the drive back onto the internals, we can see how the final drive looks:

HEADS UP!

The CD drive needs to sit in the second bay down due to the height of the rim used on the top of the drive. You could always trim back parts of the chassis if you want to fit it in the top slot.

The drive now needs to be partly reassembled in order to perform the next mod. Put the covers back on it and reattach the front of the tray. Do not put the bezel back on the drive.

15 MINUTES

CD Drive Stealth Mod

The stealth mod is one of the easiest and quickest mods to carry out, and it can dramatically improve the look of your case. By hiding the CD-ROM drive behind one of the case's drive bay covers, it blends right in.

The first thing we need to do is cut the legs from one of the drive bay covers. With a multi-tool, remove the legs so that the edges are flush to the drive bay cover.

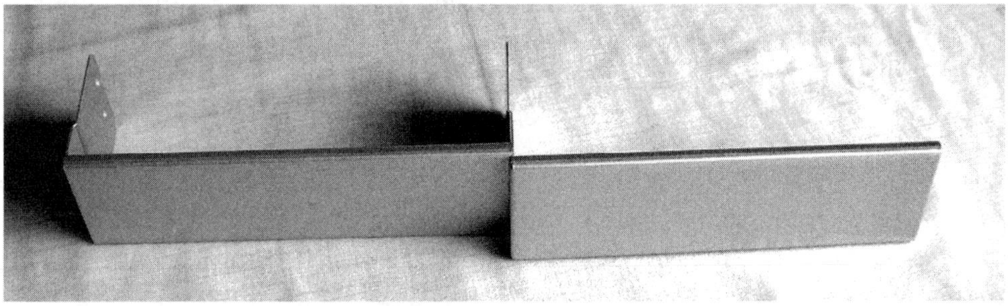

We then need a DVD-style plastic case. These cases have handy little plastic clips in them that normally hold booklets in place. We're going to use one to activate the eject button on the CD drive.

Remove the clip from the case with a pair of wire cutters. Carefully line up the clip so that it will contact the eject button when you press the corner of the drive bay cover, then stick it to the inside of the bay cover with sticky pads.

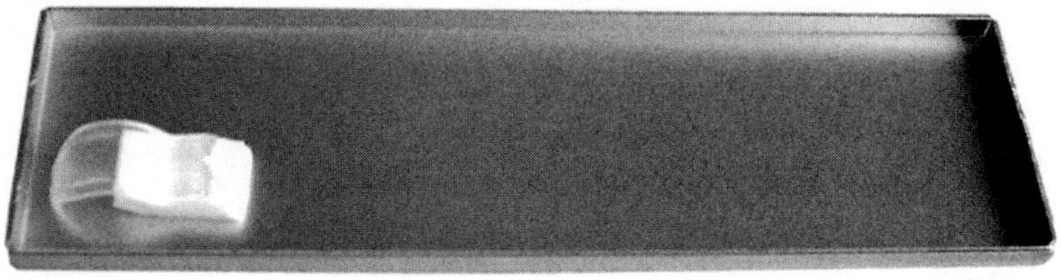

Put a couple of the sticky pads on the front of the CD tray, then mount the CD drive in the case.

It can help to put a drive bay cover each side of the CD drive so that you can check that the stealth cover will be lined up properly with the others.

Remove the covers on the sticky pads and press the drive bay cover onto the CD tray. Once it's pushed into place, make any final adjustments to the positioning of the CD drive so that it seamlessly blends into the case.

That looks much better than having the nice lines of the aluminum case spoiled by a beige CD-ROM drive.

TESTING 1-2-3

In this chapter, we've covered quite a bit of ground, but we are now well on the way to creating a personalized PC case. We've removed the fan grill from the motherboard tray, put in a side window, top window, and CD window, and stealthed the CD drive.

The following quickly recaps the steps needed to carry out these mods:

- ❑ Remove fan grill from motherboard tray
  - ❑ Mask around area
  - ❑ Cut out grill
  - ❑ Smooth off rough edges
- ❑ Side window
  - ❑ Mask the panel
  - ❑ Mark out the window shape
  - ❑ Cut the side panel
  - ❑ Smooth off rough edges
  - ❑ Cut acrylic larger than the window hole
  - ❑ Stick acrylic to the inside of the side panel
- ❑ Top window
  - ❑ Mask the panel
  - ❑ Mark out the window shape
  - ❑ Cut the panel
  - ❑ Smooth off rough edges
  - ❑ Cut acrylic larger than the window hole
  - ❑ Stick acrylic to the inside of the top panel
- ❑ CD window
  - ❑ Remove top cover from CD drive
  - ❑ Remove labels from cover
  - ❑ Mask the cover
  - ❑ Mark out the window shape

- ❑ Cut the cover
- ❑ Smooth off rough edges
- ❑ Lightly sand the cover
- ❑ Remove CD supporting bar
- ❑ Lightly sand the supporting bar
- ❑ Fit supporting bar
- ❑ Cut transparent sheet larger than the window hole
- ❑ Stick transparent sheet to the inside of the cover
- ❑ Cut rim from coffee tin
- ❑ Stick rim to the outside of the cover
- ❑ Reassemble CD drive without the front bezel

❑ Stealth CD

- ❑ Cut legs from a drive bay cover
- ❑ Smooth off rough edges
- ❑ Cut clip from DVD case
- ❑ Stick clip inside bay cover so it will contact the CD eject button
- ❑ Mount CD drive in case
- ❑ Stick drive bay cover to front of CD tray

Chapter 18

Let There Be Light

Tools of the Trade

Screwdriver
Pliers
Wire cutters
Soldering iron
Hot glue gun
Four Akasa Nebula Arctic Blue 80mm LED fans
Two ultraviolet cold cathodes and inverters
Two T3-sized plastic project boxes
Sticky pads
Three LED holders
Three male molex connectors and one female molex connector
Self-adhesive cable clips
Fluorescent marker pens
470 ohm resistor
1000 mcd 5mm blue LED
Heat-shrink tubing or insulation tape
Lengths of yellow, black, and red wire

With some windows cut into the case, we need to add some lights so that we can properly see the components. There is a vast array of different lighting products on the market, and choosing which ones to use can be a bit of a nightmare. The products you choose will be dictated by your budget and needs, as well as other constraints such as the amount of room in the case.

If your plan is solid, you should already have a good idea of the color scheme, so you just need to pick lights that match. You can of course mix and match colors, with one color at the top of your case and a different color at the bottom. The final effect will depend entirely on the look you want to achieve.

Lighting Options

Before you can decide which type of lighting you need, you should take a look at the various types of available products.

Neon and Cold Cathode Lighting

One way to light your case is to use neon or cold cathode tubes, which are available in a wide variety of colors and sizes, and tend to be the most common form of lighting.

Neon tubes are often a little thicker than cold cathode tubes, and they also put out less light. Because of this, cold cathodes are becoming the norm when lighting the whole case.

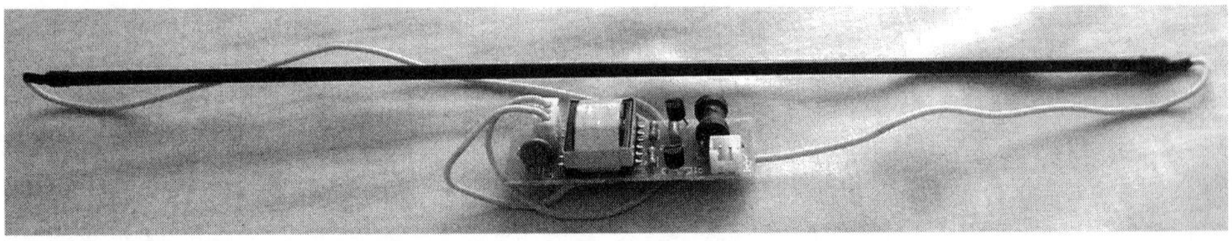

Don't be fooled by their name, though; cold cathodes are not cold. When running, they do get warm to the touch, but they shouldn't cause any heat-related problems in your PC. Temperatures may rise by a couple of degrees, but that's all.

HEADS UP!

Neon and cold cathode tubes are fragile. They can smash easily if dropped or have something heavy placed on them, so take care.

LEDs

LEDs are another way of lighting your case. It's now possible to buy some extremely bright LEDs, and these can work very well in certain areas. Generally, the brighter the LED, the narrower its field of light is.

Due to the narrow beam in the bright LEDs, they are ideal for spotlighting particular areas in your case. If you want to show off a particular component, shine a couple of bright LEDs on it.

TIPS OF THE TRADE

Spreading Light

To help spread the light from an LED over a wider area, you can lightly sand the casing of the LED. This will cause the light to diffuse more evenly through it. You could also try using a translucent nail varnish. Paint it thin onto the LED casing to slightly adjust the color of light that the LED emits.

LEDs are available in a wide variety of shapes, sizes, and colors. There are also specialized "laser LEDs," which consist of a housing with three bright LEDs in it. The lights are slightly angled, so they give a wider spread of light.

HEADS UP!

LEDs often run at fairly low voltages—lower than that supplied by a PC molex connector. This means you will need to buy LEDs that are rated to run at 12 volts or 5 volts, or you will need to calculate which resistor you need to drop the voltage to a safe level. You can see how to calculate the resistor you need later in the chapter, in "Inserting an LED into the CD Drive."

It's also possible to change the LEDs in your case (for the power and hard drive activity), keyboard, mouse, or any other device. Just take care to choose LEDs that are appropriate for the job. Case LEDs are typically 5mm, while other devices may use 3mm LEDs. There is also a range of small, square LEDs for mounting onto circuit boards. Some devices may use these instead. Although it's possible to change them, they have small contact points and can make for tricky soldering.

Other Lighting

In addition to the lighting previously mentioned, there are now fans that feature types of lighting. There are a couple of different types, and, as you would expect, they are available in a range of colors. One type has a number of LEDs around the edge of the fan that light up when the fan is powered. They are quite bright, and can be used for some subtle lighting effects.

The other type of fan features a small, round, cold cathode tube that attaches to the fan. This gives off slightly more light but makes the fan a bit thicker. These fans are often UV reactive, with the cathode giving off UV light to help make them glow.

Also available are products such as EL string, EL tape, and EL sheet. EL stands for electroluminescence, and basically means that the item lights up when you provide power to it.

EL string and EL tape pretty much look as their names imply—they are both fairly flexible, and can be bent around corners and stuck to almost any surface. They don't emit much light, but can be useful in highlighting certain areas. Both products are available in a number of colors and lengths.

EL sheet is a little different. It is available in sizes similar to paper, and it isn't that much thicker. When you apply power to the back of the sheet, it emits a soft glow. The primary benefit of EL sheet is that you can cut it into any shape with a pair of scissors. As long as you leave a couple of tracks on the back of the sheet for power, it will still light up. This can provide some stunning effects. You could cut the sheet into a logo, stick it to the inside of a window, and have it light up when the PC is switched on. An alternative is to make a lighted case badge. The design could be cut straight from the EL sheet, or printed onto a transparent sheet and stuck to the EL sheet.

HEADS UP!

Neons, cathodes, and EL products generally require inverters. They convert the 12-volt DC power from the PC into the substantially higher AC voltages needed to run the lights. Some cathodes require in excess of 500 volts AC to run. This can cause you some very nasty injuries if you're not careful. Always take care when handling inverters, as they might still shock you after they have been disconnected.

More Lighting Options

Lighting effects can also be used in other areas of your PC. You can buy UV-reactive IDE and floppy drive cables or glow-in-the-dark luminous cables. There is also a range of cabling that has EL string wrapped around it, so the cables themselves light up.

If you're handy with a soldering iron, there are also many electronic kits available that provide various lighting effects. They range from a fairly simple pattern of LEDs that move back and forth, to complicated controller boards that can turn on a number of cold cathodes in a set pattern. With all of these effects available, you could coax your PC into providing a spectacular light show.

Now that you know about all the kinds of lights that are available, it's time to decide what's going into your case. Our plan is to place a blue LED in the CD drive, place some LED fans in the case, and inset a couple of ultraviolet cold cathodes.

14 MINUTES

Changing the Case Fans

Changing the case fans is the easiest job, so that's where we are starting. In the next illustration, you can see a collection of fans. The black fans are the ones that shipped with the case; the clear fans are the replacements. Each of the clear fans has four blue LEDs included to provide light.

The new fans just slot into the places where the original fans were located. Because the Lian Li case uses push pins, we don't even need a screwdriver for this step.

HEADS UP!

These LED fans are slightly chunkier than ordinary fans. Because of this, you may need to be careful when positioning them. If they sit close to other components or the edge of the case, you may have slight clearance issues.

Case Lighting

The next-easiest job is the mounting of the cold cathodes. Although it's easy in practice, you need to spend some time thinking about the positioning of the lights. They should be in a location where you can't easily see the source of the light, but the light can still illuminate the case.

HEADS UP!

Placing lights at the top or bottom of the case may light the entire case when it's empty, but when you start adding graphics cards, sound cards, and so on, a lot of the light may be blocked. Take some time to think about how your components will affect the light path.

Because cathodes get their power from an inverter, we need to be able to put power *into* the inverter. This is best done with an LED holder and a male molex connecter. The LED holder is the perfect size for connecting to the power pins on the inverter. Crimp some male molex pins onto each of the holder's wires and then align them so that the red wire on the holder will line up with the yellow 12-volt line from a PC molex. The black wire on the holder should connect to the black wire next to the yellow one on the PC side.

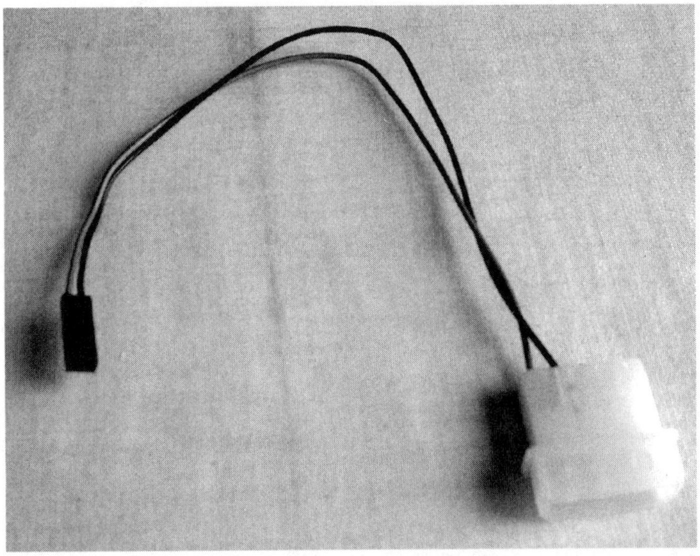

As mentioned earlier, cold cathodes need to be connected to an inverter to run. The inverters change the 12-volt DC power from the PC into several hundred volts of AC power.

Having these inverters bumping about inside your case is not a good idea! If they touch part of your case, the best scenario is that it kills most of your components and trips a fuse. The worst-case scenario is that your case becomes live, and you get a serious electrical shock. To prevent this kind of accident, we will be mounting each of the inverters in a plastic project box, like this:

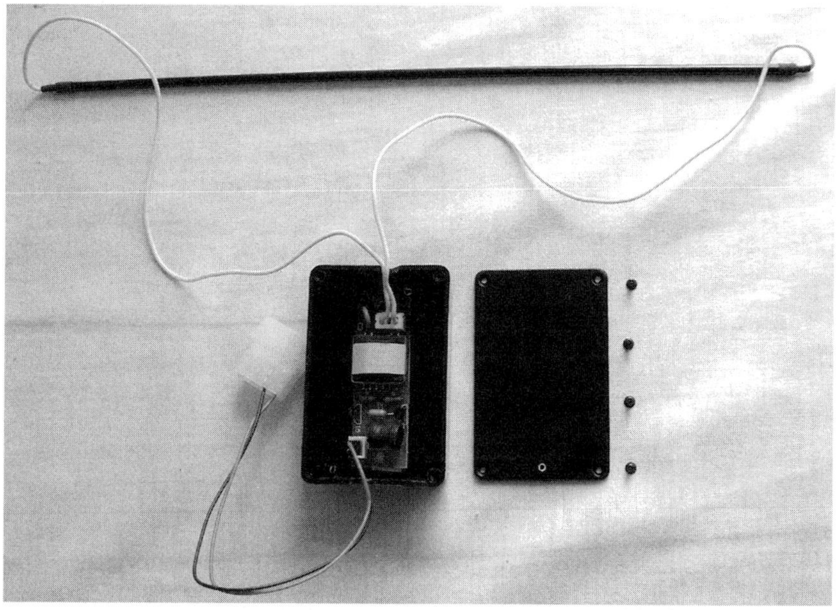

The box will keep the inverter insulated from the rest of the system. To mount the inverter, first cut a hole in each side of the box. This will allow the wires to run in and out. Next use a couple of sticky pads to stick the inverter inside the box.

Now that the inverter is safely located in its box, we can plug in the LED holder to provide power

HEADS UP!

Make sure you connect the LED holder the correct way. The red wire supplying 12 volts needs to connect the positive terminal on the inverter—often marked with a + sign. Getting it wrong could damage the inverter.

We will be using UV cold cathodes, and their effect can be diminished if they are too far away from the items they are meant to be lighting. To help get around this, we'll be using two of them—one at the top of the case and one at the bottom.

We attach the bottom cathode with a self-adhesive cable clip to the side panel just below the window. We mount the inverter box to the side of the window.

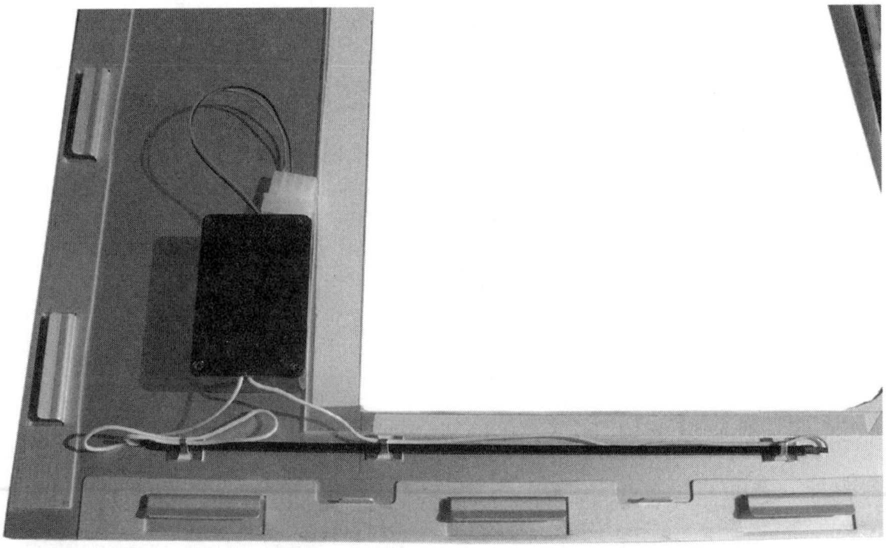

The top cathode is more problematic. The ideal placement would be above the window, but part of the chassis is in the way. After much deliberation, we decided to attach it to underneath of the power supply. The inverter box is placed on the power supply itself. This view is from the bottom of the case looking up:

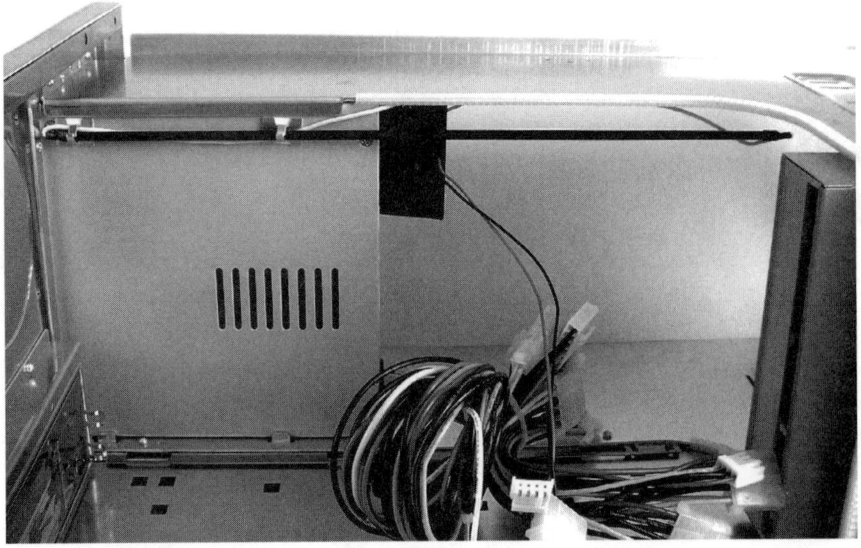

With our cathodes now positioned, we need something for them to light up. UV light looks slightly purple, but there is a significant portion of the light that is outside of the visible spectrum. If the light is shone onto something that is UV reactive (or very bright white) it will glow.

None of our components are naturally UV reactive, so we have to help them out a bit. This is a straightforward process, but it is very time-consuming.

Most fluorescent pens and markers will glow under UV light, and they are available in a range of colors. Not all colors glow equally, though. We are using the pens shown here:

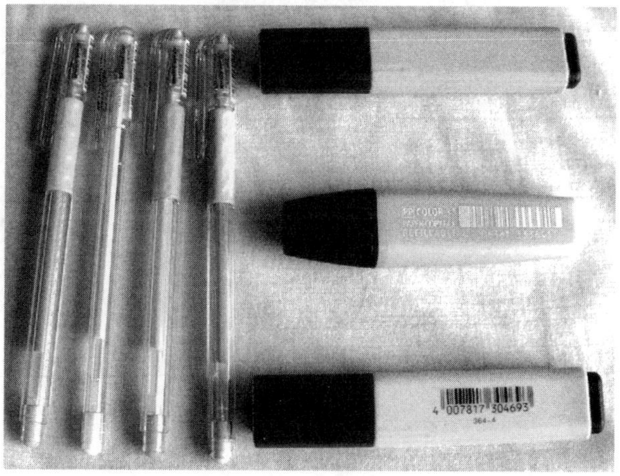

HEADS UP!

Make sure you do not use pens that have a metallic finish. They will likely cause short circuits on your components.

The pens are handy for small bits of color, and the markers make coloring larger areas easier. We are using green, yellow, orange, and pink. We tried several other colors, but they failed to glow under a UV cathode.

TIPS OF THE TRADE

UV Paints

There are also UV-reactive paints on the market. These are available in a wider range of colors when compared to marker pens, and all of the paints glow visibly under UV light. They are, however, significantly more expensive than the pens.

Using the pens, we're going to color in a number of resistors and other small chips on the graphics card and motherboard. When installed and lit by the cathodes, the colored components will give off a nice glow that looks different from most "normal" case lighting.

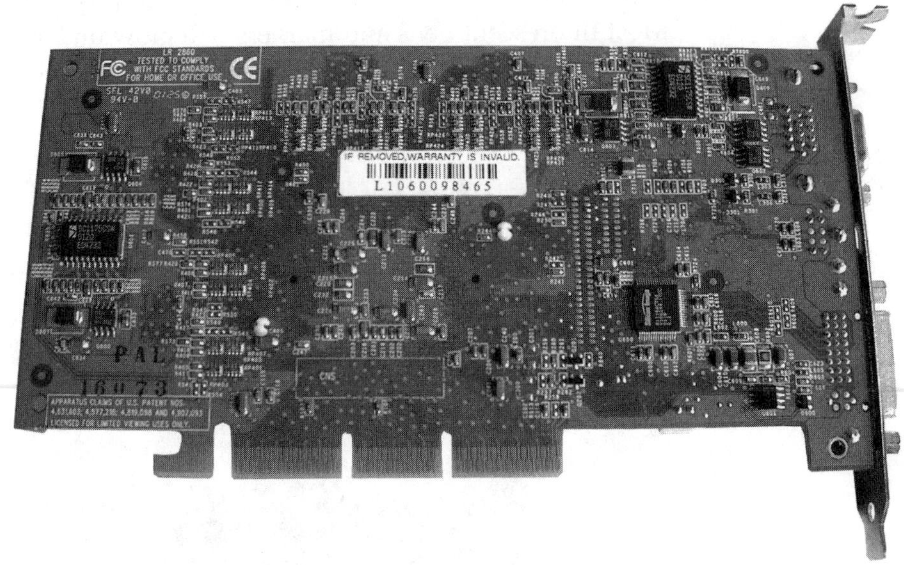

HEADS UP!

As you can see, this card has a "warranty void if removed" sticker. The chances are that the warranty will be void from the moment a marker pen touches the card!

The illustration above shows the graphics card after it has been colored. You can see that many of the small chips on the card have been colored in. The colors and patterns were picked slightly randomly, but other cards may lend themselves to a more ordered coloring scheme. It entirely depends on the look you're after.

HEADS UP!

Remember that most cards fit into PCs upside down, so you want to color the parts that are on the back of the card.

Some cards don't have that many chips on the reverse side, but all need not be lost. With a steady hand, you could trace a number of the tracks to create your look.

Once the cards are done, it's time to move onto the motherboard. When coloring the board, be aware of exactly where your other components will be placed. There is little point in coloring the chips around the CPU socket if the heat sink will cover them all. We colored a significant number of the small chips on the board, as well as the tops of the large capacitors.

You don't need to stop there, though. You can color the RAM chips, molex connectors, and power wires.

HEADS UP!

Some of the plastics may not hold the ink very well, so watch for smudges.

20 MINUTES

Inserting an LED into the CD Drive

With the case lighting sorted, we can now move on to the CD drive. The plan is to put an LED inside the drive to give it a blue glow. To do this, we will need to cut away part of the CD drive casing to feed the LED in, and create a custom power connector to power the drive and LED.

We are going to start with the leads for the LED. We need an LED holder, a 5mm blue LED, and a 470 ohm resister. The resistor is needed to drop the voltage from 12 volts down to about 3.5 volts.

TIPS OF THE TRADE

R = V/I

You can calculate the resistor you need by working with the following formula: R = V/I where *R* is the resistor you need, *V* is the forward voltage from the LED (which may be listed as Vf on the LED datasheet), and *I* is the amps required by the LED. For example, if we have an LED that has a forward voltage of 2v and requires 20mA, and we want to power the LED from the 5v line of the PC, we would use the following calculation: (5–2)/0.02=150 ohms. If we were to power the same LED from the 12v line, we would use: (12–2)/0.02=500 ohms. It's not always possible to buy the exact resistor you need, so you may need to get one with a slightly higher ohm rating. The light from the LED will be reduced a little, but you will save the LED from blowing.

First we need to solder the resistor to the LED power wires. It doesn't actually matter which wire you connect the resistor to. We are connecting them to the positive lead.

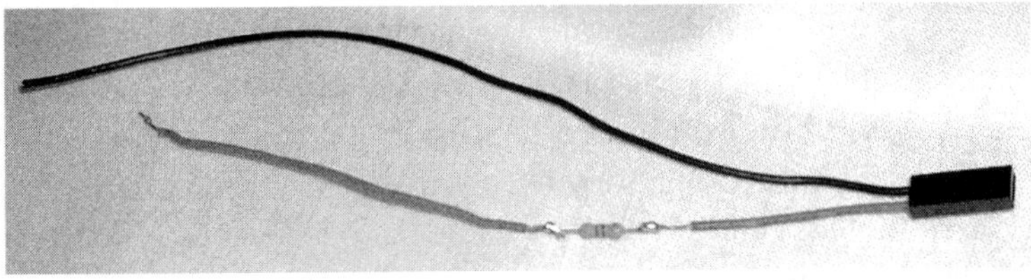

The next step is to wrap the resistor and bare wire with either heat-shrink tubing or insulation tape. This will prevent the resistor or wire from shorting out on other parts of the case of the CD drive.

The easiest way to power the LED is to grab power from the CD drive. To save any complicated soldering, we're going to create a custom power lead, which will plug into the CD drive at one end, the PC at the other. The power for the LED can be taken from the CD drive end of the connection.

We'll need some lengths of wire, cut to about 1½ inches. Although it's not essential to have the correct colored wire, it does help when it comes to wiring everything up if you have a yellow wire, two black wires, and a red wire.

Strip a length of the wire on both ends, and crimp some male molex pins onto one end of each bit of wire. Insert them into a male connector correctly so that the colors match up with those from the PC.

The red wire from the LED holder should be intertwined with the yellow wire from your molex, then crimped into a female mole wire. The black wire from the LED holder should be joined with the black wire next to the yellow, and also fitted with a female connector.

The two remaining bare ends should also have female connectors attached, then all four wires can be put into a female molex plug.

HEADS UP!

It's very important that the molex plugs are wired correctly. Getting the wires crossed could damage components in your PC. If you're not certain about which order the wires should be connected, perform a couple of test fits to make sure your wires line up correctly with those on a molex connected to the PC's power supply.

Once complete, we have something that looks like this:

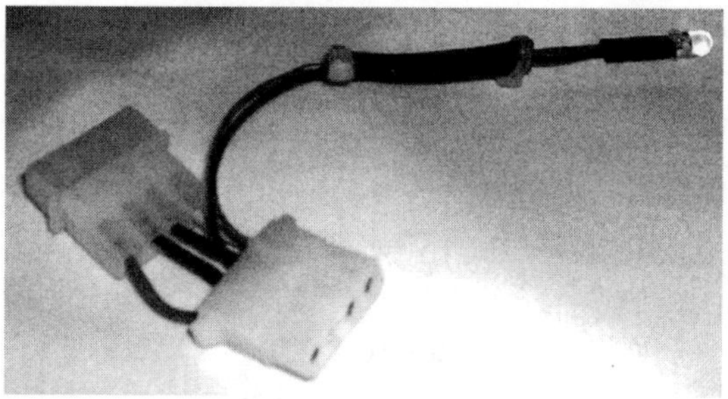

Now all we need to do is fit the LED inside the CD drive. To do this, we carve out a hole in the plastic at the back of the CD drive, making sure that it's large enough for the wires to feed out. Some CD drives (including the one we are using here) have a lip on the lid. The hole we're making needs to be large enough that this lip doesn't squash the wires when the lid is put back on.

Once the hole is made, we position the LED inside the drive and use a hot glue gun to secure it in place.

Be sure when positioning the LED that it will not interfere with the tray or other mechanics inside the CD drive.

Our CD drive is now ready and can be reassembled.

Construction Time

That's it for the interior lighting, so we can now put a few of the components in the PC, power it up, and see how things stand at the moment.

When it comes to building the PC, take your time over component placement. Remember that modding a PC is all about the look, and that could easily be ruined if you have bundles of cables hanging about in your case.

Use cable ties, twist ties, even elastic bands if you have to, but spend some serious time considering how to route cables inside your PC. It would be a shame to spend time cutting and fitting a window into your side panel, only to have the view blocked by a rat's nest of power and IDE cables.

Depending on the style of your case, you may be able to tuck extra power leads down behind the motherboard tray. If your power supply has really long wires leading to the molex plugs, take advantage of this and run the cables along the chassis so that they're out of sight. Tuck them into unused drive bays, or if you think you won't need all the extra connectors, cut them off. Just make sure you insulate any bare wires!

Spending a bit of extra time at this stage can pay off later when your work is finished.

HEADS UP!

When tidying cables, be aware of how your case comes apart and how you add and remove components. Although you want your cables tidy, you don't want to make it completely impossible to replace hardware in the future.

The side window with the lighting and fluorescent coloring gives a subtle look that doesn't overpower you with brightness. Here you can also see one of the UV-reactive IDE cables that we are using:

Looking in slightly closer, the coloring on the back of the graphics card and the motherboard starts to stand out a bit more, indicating that this is a personally modded case, and not something that has been bought.

Finally, we have the view through the top window. The blue LED fans cast an eerie glow and give us a glimpse into the inner workings of the CD drive.

But we're not done yet! There are still more things we can do to spice up the case and personalize it further. So stay with us as we move onto the next chapter….

TESTING 1-2-3

The case is now lit, and you're getting ever closer to reaching your goal. You put in some lighted fans, some cold cathodes, and an LED inside the CD drive.

The following quickly recaps the steps needed to carry out these mods:

- ❑ Lighted case fans
    - ❑ Remove existing case fans
    - ❑ Fit lighted case fans
    - ❑ Tidy away the power cables
- ❑ Case lighting
    - ❑ Place cathode inverter in an insulated box
    - ❑ Make a power lead to connect the inverter to the PC power supply
    - ❑ Select the best placement for the cathodes and fix in place with adhesive clips
    - ❑ Secure inverter box with double-sided sticky pads
    - ❑ Tidy away the power cables
- ❑ CD drive LED
    - ❑ Select a suitable resistor for the LED and power supply
    - ❑ Solder resistor in line with the + leg of the LED
    - ❑ Make a Y-shaped molex to connect to the LED and the CD drive
    - ❑ Make a small cutout at the back of the CD drive
    - ❑ Glue the LED into the cutout
    - ❑ Reassemble the CD drive
- ❑ Build the PC
    - ❑ Fit motherboard, graphics card, and other components into the case
    - ❑ Connect the case lighting and fans to the PC power supply
    - ❑ Tidy away power cables, IDE cables, and so on

Chapter 19
Internal TFT Screen

Tools of the Trade

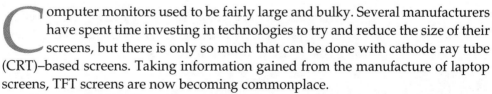

Screwdriver
Pliers
Wire cutters
Portable games console five-inch TFT screen
Plastic project boxes
Sticky pads
Insulation tape
Male molex connector

Computer monitors used to be fairly large and bulky. Several manufacturers have spent time investing in technologies to try and reduce the size of their screens, but there is only so much that can be done with cathode ray tube (CRT)–based screens. Taking information gained from the manufacture of laptop screens, TFT screens are now becoming commonplace.

TFT screens are still more expensive than their CRT counterparts, but because of the way they are made, they are available in a much wider selection of screen sizes. And size is all-important for this mod. The plan is to take a five-inch TFT screen designed for a games console and fit it into our case.

HEADS UP!

This mod requires that you have a video card with a TV-Out connector. It's also useful if the card can show a display on two screens at once. Otherwise, you'll be able to use either the monitor or the TFT screen, but not both at the same time.

Choosing a TFT Screen

There are several different types of portable TFT screens on the market. They range from small, four-inch models up to large screens with a diagonal measurement in excess of seven inches. These larger screens, which are designed to fit into cars for mobile entertainment, are too big for our needs. Their prices can also be rather prohibitive.

Fortunately for us, there are smaller, less expensive screens available. These screens are designed so that mobile gamers can connect the screen to their games console while they are in a car. These screens typically have a diagonal measurement of around five inches, and because they connect to the cigarette lighter, they are already designed to run at 12v DC.

HEADS UP!

When shopping for a display, ensure that it has a composite video connector on it. Many mobile console screens have connectors only for the console they are designed for. These connectors are very difficult to convert to use with a PC.

As it happens, the Lian Li PC-60 case has three 3½-inch drive bays visible on the front. The diagonal measurement of these bays is 5 inches, and this should be true for any case that has three bays.

HEADS UP!

When deciding on the exact size of screen to use, note the position of any components near the drive bays. Things such as intake fans, power buttons, and LEDs could wreak havoc with the placement of your screen.

The first thing you need to decide on is which screen to use. The screen we have chosen is shown next. It is primarily designed to be used with a Nintendo GameCube console, but it is compatible with other equipment that can be connected via a composite video cable. It's also designed to be used as a portable screen, so it comes with a power lead fitted with a cigarette lighter adapter.

The screen is slightly larger than needed, measuring 5.4 inches diagonally. The extra space will come in handy, though, because a 5-inch screen is actually quite small when it comes to displaying text. Luckily, it still fits in the case, and very little of the screen will be lost behind the front bezel of the case.

Turning the screen over, we can see the items that we are primarily interested in.

Here you can see the audio and video connectors and the power connector. You should be able to spot the other benefit of using this kind of portable console screen: it takes 12v DC as power. Fortunately, that's exactly what our PC power supply provides.

10 MINUTES

Replacing the Cigarette Lighter Adapter

Powering the screen from the PC is fairly easy to do. It requires that we remove the cigarette lighter adapter from the power lead and replace it with a molex. Opening up the adapter, we're met with two color-coded wires:

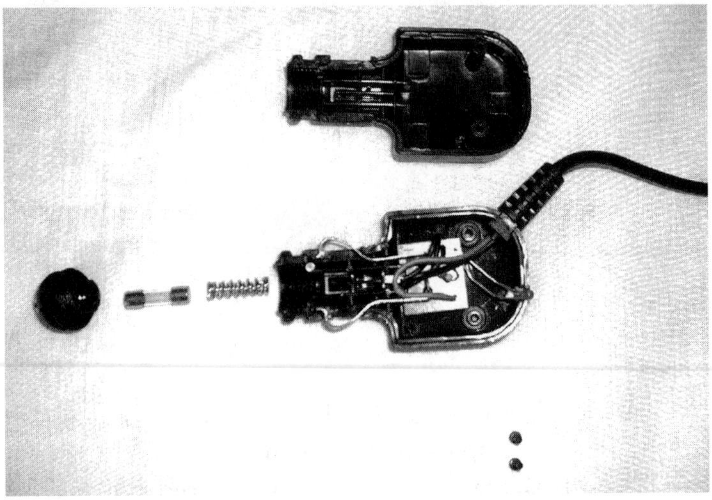

The red wire is live, and the black wire is the ground. Simply cut the wires and hook them up to a male molex connector. The red wire needs to be positioned so that it meets with a yellow one on the PC side. The black wire will slot in next to the red one.

TIPS OF THE TRADE

Careful Wiring

If you happen to have two wires of the same color, and you can't tell which is the live and which is the ground, you have a little investigative work to do. You need to carefully strip a small section of each wire, plug in the cigarette adapter, and test the wires with a multimeter. Wiring the screen the wrong way will likely destroy it!

Before we take the mod any further, we had better check that the screen works. Using our newly modified power lead and a composite video cable connected to the TV-Out connector on the video card, we can see if the screen works.

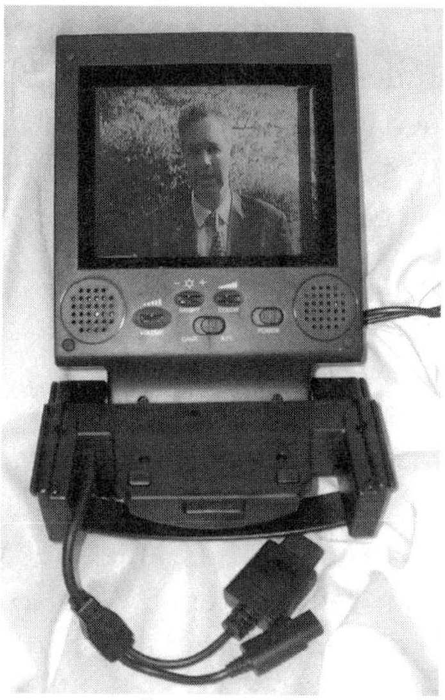

Success! That's a good start.

40 MINUTES

Dismantling the Screen

Now comes the fun part: dismantling the screen. The screen casing is far too bulky to sit behind the front bezel of the PC, so it needs to be slimmed down significantly.

This screen is fairly easy to dismantle, only requiring a few screws to be removed. Once it's all in pieces, we have the following:

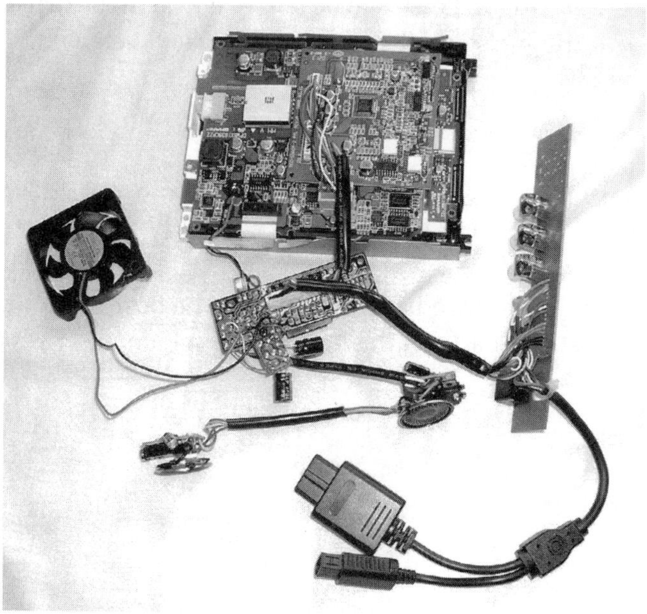

The screen is at the top. Directly beneath it is the board that has the controls on it. Just under that are the speakers. To the left of the screen is a cooling fan that was positioned behind the screen. The board to the right contains the audio and video connectors, as well as video and power connectors for the GameCube.

First we simply disconnect the speakers that are attached to the controls board.

HEADS UP!

You can leave the speakers connected if you want, but they are not very high-quality. If you leave them connected, you won't have to carry around a set of speakers with the PC.

Next we cut off the GameCube video and power connectors, as they are surplus to our requirements. We also removed the fan. The screen will have a lot more air flowing around it once it's inside the PC, and it's located fairly close to the front intake fans, which will help keep the temperature down.

30 MINUTES

Mounting the Screen

Now that the screen has been slimmed down, we can mount it. The screen has quite a few exposed circuit boards and electronics, which we need to prevent from coming into contact with the case. To do this, we cover the area around the 3½-inch drive bays with insulation tape.

We also put insulation around the board that contains the audio and video connectors. The control board was left without insulation for the time being.

With this done, we can freely move the screen to decide on the best mounting position. It needs to be fairly central in the drive bays but not interfere with anything else on the front of the case (such as the power buttons and LEDs).

HEADS UP!

It doesn't matter too much if the screen isn't exactly in the middle of the drive bays, because you can use software to adjust the image position on the screen.

Once we have decided on the best place to locate the screen, we put some sticky pads on the back of the screen and press it into place.

We are sticking the audio/video connector board to the top of the hard drive bay, with the connectors facing away. This allows the power and video cables to be routed around the back, where they will be mostly out of sight.

The last thing to sort out is the control board. This board contains the power switch for the screen, as well as the brightness and contrast controls. Once the settings are finalized, they shouldn't need to be adjusted again, so mounting them inside the case is fine. If you want to be able to control the screen from the front of the case, you could cut some extra holes in the front of the case and position the board so that the buttons poke through.

We next mount the board on a plastic project box. This box is exactly the same as the one we used earlier to house the cold cathode inverters. A couple of sticky pads will hold the box in place; they are also used to fix the control board to the box.

The mod is just about done. We only have a couple of things left to do, the first of which is to run a video cable from the screen to the graphics card. Fortunately, the motherboard we're using doesn't have a network port on it, so we simply punch out that blanking plate from the motherboard plate and run the wire through there. If you don't have a spare hole on the back of the motherboard plate, you could drill out one of the PCI blanking plates and pass the cable through the hole.

If you are planning to hook up the speakers, you can also run an audio cable through the case at this time. You need a stereo phono lead that has red and white plugs at one end and a 3.5mm jack at the other. The jack plug will connect to the speaker input on your sound card, and the red and white plugs will connect to their respective sockets on the audio/video PCB.

With the cables in place, it's time to put on the front panel and see how it looks.

The big black area of the screen on the front certainly gives the case a slightly different look from what you would normally expect to see.

We can now configure the video card to output a signal to the screen. How you do this will be dependant upon your graphics card, operating system, and the driver version. You need to tell the software that you now have two monitors, but that one of them is a TV.

Once you have done this, you should be able to use the screen as if it were an extra monitor. You can display normal Windows applications or even video on the TFT screen.

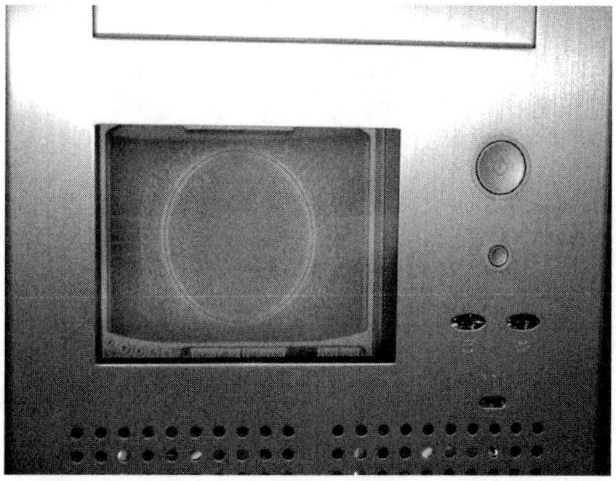

HEADS UP!

Getting video to run on the TFT screen may require some extra configuration of your video drivers. Typically, telling Windows that the TFT screen is your primary monitor would be sufficient.

The screen is displaying visualizations from WinAmp. Having this screen available will free the main monitor from a lot of desktop clutter.

TESTING 1-2-3

With the mod complete, the following is a quick recap of the steps involved:

- ❑ Modify cigarette lighter adapter to power screen
    - ❑ Remove cigarette lighter adapter
    - ❑ Fit male molex connector
- ❑ Dismantle screen so that it's ready for fitting
    - ❑ Remove screen and other electronics from casing
    - ❑ Remove any extra electronics such as speakers and wires that are not needed

- ❑ Fit screen to case
    - ❑ Insulate area of case that screen will be fitted to
    - ❑ Insulate extra screen electronics
    - ❑ Mount screen on case
    - ❑ Secure other electronic components such as screen controls
- ❑ Connect screen
    - ❑ Connect video and power cables to screen
    - ❑ Route cables so they are mostly out of sight
    - ❑ Configure Windows to use the screen

Chapter 20

External LCD Screen

Tools of the Trade

Pliers
Wire cutters
Soldering iron
Hot air gun
Jigsaw
Thin paintbrush
Matrix Orbital LK204-25 LCD screen
Acrylic sheet
Two overhead transparency sheets
Silver conductive paint and silver-loaded epoxy

Spray paint
Double-sided tape
Self-adhesive feet
Six solderless LED holders
One male molex connector and one female molex connector
One PCI bay cover
2.5mm DC power lead
2.5mm DC power socket
Yellow and black wire, about six inches long
Heat shrink tubing

Now that the case has been modded, it's time to start thinking "outside the box"—quite literally, in this case! We will take an LCD screen, mount it in a custom-made acrylic frame, then create a keypad to control the LCD screen. Our major challenges are how to power the LCD screen (because it's not attached inside the PC) and how to build the keypad. After everything is functional, we will configure the LCD screen to display various bits of useful information, such as system temperatures, news headlines, and weather reports.

Choosing an LCD Screen

LCDs are available from several suppliers and come in a variety of different sizes, colors, and capabilities. They generally fall into two main types: character and graphical. Character LCD screens are less expensive and display text-based information. Some of them support custom character sets, so you can display basic graphics on them. Graphical LCD screens support far more advanced drawing capabilities, but cost a fair bit more.

LCDs are also available with a number of different interfaces. Parallel LCDs are the cheapest option, but you are limited in the choice of software you can use to control them. Serial is the most common and the easiest to get working. There are now USB-based LCDs coming onto the market. These are the simplest to hook up. The USB cable works as both the data and power cable, so they are the easiest to get working.

The Matrix Orbital LK204-25 LCD screen we are using is a character-based screen that uses a serial connection to the PC.

HEADS UP!

Many new PCs and motherboards are shipping without any serial ports. The serial port is reaching the end of its life in home PCs, so it might be wise to buy a USB screen to ensure that you can continue to use it in the future should you change or upgrade your PC.

LCDs are essentially made of two main components. The first is the screen itself, the second is the controller. The screen displays text and graphics as dictated by the controller; the controller is the key to the LCD. You can buy screens and controllers separately, but this can lead to a few compatibility problems.

When it comes to extra features for your LCD, there are a few things to look for. The first (and most important as far as this mod is concerned) is the ability to support a keypad. The LCD we'll be using supports 25 keys (five rows of five keys), but you don't have to hook up all the keys. The keypad can be used to launch applications, flick between different screens of information on the LCD, or pretty much anything else that you can think of.

A keypress on its own won't do anything very exciting. You need to have software running that will perform an action based on which key is pressed. To do this, we will be using software called LCDC. The software is shareware; a trial version is included with the Matrix Orbital screen. LCDC allows you to create screens of information to display on the LCD. There are a number of plug-ins available that hook into various applications (such as Motherboard Monitor and WinAmp) and will allow you to configure events based on keypad events.

The keypad is obviously an input device. Output devices called GPOs (General Purpose Outputs) are also available for use with this particular LCD screen.

With the correct programming, GPOs can be used to do such things as light up LEDs when a new e-mail message arrives or when your CPU reaches a particular temperature. In fact, you could set one GPO to light an LED to let you know that a high temperature has been reached, and set another GPO to turn on an extra fan to aid with cooling.

Up to six GPOs can be configured with the LCD that we are using for this mod, but, unfortunately, they can't be used at the same time as the keypad.

The first problem we need to solve is how to power the screen, discussed next.

5 MINUTES

Powering the External LCD Screen

The screen requires 12 volts to power it, so getting an external power adapter to plug into a wall socket would be a bit messy. We would also need an extra wall socket in order to use the LCD screen.

Instead, we're going to feed 12v out of the PC into the back of the screen, to help keep things nice and easy. Power brackets similar to the one we are about to make are just starting to appear in a few electronics and modding shops. But when you consider what's involved in making one, it's much cheaper to build your own.

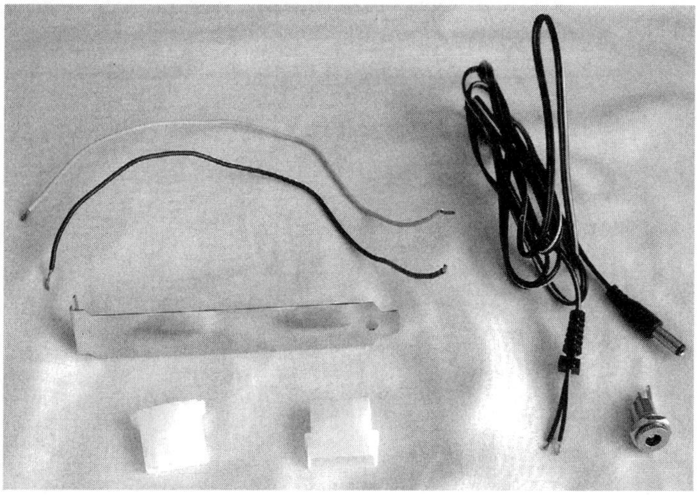

As you can see, we have a DC power lead and socket on the right to provide power to the screen, and some spare wire and molex connectors on the left to connect inside the PC.

First we need to drill a hole in a PCI bay cover and fit the DC power socket.

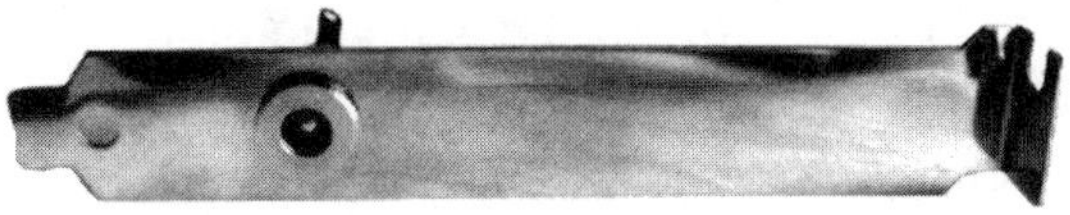

HEADS UP!

When fitting the socket, make sure you fit it the right way! It's much easier to check this now before you start attaching wires to everything.

Now we need to construct the wires that will power the socket. Taking the yellow and black wires, attach a male molex connector to one end, ensuring that the wires meet up with the same-colored ones in your PC.

The other ends of the wires need to be soldered into the DC power socket.

HEADS UP!

We have soldered the yellow wire into the center of the power socket, and the black wire to the outside. This keeps the live wire in the center of the socket where it is hard to touch accidentally.

Before you start soldering, slide a piece of heat-shrink tubing over each wire so that you can insulate your solder joins.

Once the soldering is complete, slide the heat-shrink tubing down and use a hot air gun to shrink it into place.

The last step is to attach a female molex connector to the DC power lead. Watch for the orientation of the cables, though. The wire with the white stripe is positive, and this should be positioned so that it is in the same place as a yellow wire on a normal molex. The following shows the finished power lead and power bracket:

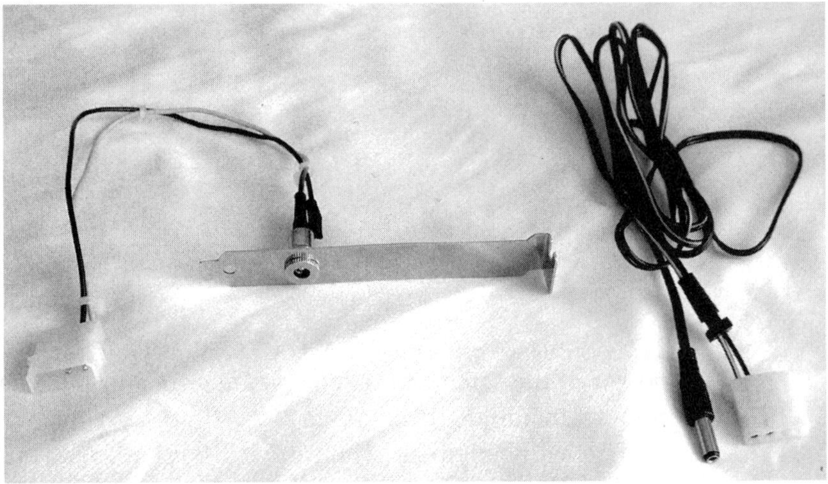

You can now fit the blanking plate into the PC and connect the molex. Then it's just a matter of plugging everything together. If everything went well, the screen should power up.

HEADS UP!

We have wired this so that it provides 12v to the LCD screen. Not all screens run at 12v, so if your screen requires 5v, make sure you rewire the molex connectors accordingly. They will need to match with the red wire inside your PC and the black one next to it.

Now we can get on with designing the stand.

25 MINUTES
To make, plus 60 minutes to paint and allow to dry

Making the LCD Stand

The front of the stand needs to be big enough to house the LCD and keypad, and the base needs to be of a suitable size so that the whole thing doesn't topple over when you press a button on the keypad.

Using graph paper, we draw the size of the LCD screen (98mm × 60mm) and then draw in lines to represent the edges of the screen and the bezel around it. The LCD screen is 98mm wide, so we have decided on a 100mm × 100mm keypad. We add a bit of extra space around the edges, which gives us a rough size for the stand of 140mm wide × 240mm tall. The base will be the same width as the stand (140mm) and 110mm long. So the final dimensions for the stand will be 140mm wide × 350mm long. Grab the jigsaw and cut some acrylic to this size.

HEADS UP!

Keep in mind the tips from Chapter 17 when you cut the windows for the case panels. Use a fine-toothed blade in your jigsaw, and take your time.

The next step is to bend the acrylic to turn it into a stand. If the acrylic has a protective sheet coving it, you need to remove it. There is a chance that this protective cover could catch fire or melt while you are heating the acrylic to bend it.

Clamp the acrylic to a workbench and gently heat it with the hot air gun until it begins to bend.

TIPS OF THE TRADE

Avoid Melting Your Mod

Don't hold the hot air gun too close or linger too long in one spot. You run the risk of melting the acrylic if you do. Just move gently from side to side.

If you are using fairly thick acrylic, you may need to concentrate a little more on the edges to ensure that they bend smoothly. Once the acrylic starts to droop, use a piece of wood to gently bend the acrylic to the desired angle. The acrylic gets quite hot, so the piece of wood will prevent you from burning your fingers.

Once the acrylic has been bent into shape, hold it in place for a minute until it cools. You can then release the pressure, and the acrylic should keep its shape.

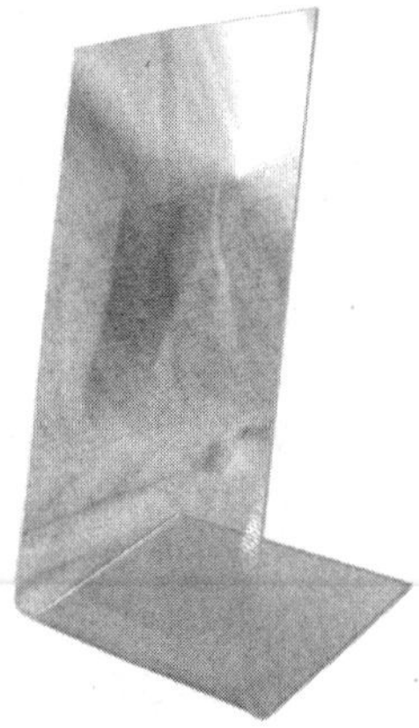

The keypad will be attached to the front of the acrylic stand, so we need to cut a couple of channels in the stand for the wires to run through. You can do this by drilling a couple of holes and then using a jigsaw to cut the slit.

HEADS UP!

Don't worry if the slits you cut for the wires to run through aren't straight. They will be hidden from sight by the keypad.

The stand itself is almost complete. The last couple of jobs are to paint it and attach some rubber feet that will aid its balance and prevent it from scratching the surface it will be placed on.

HEADS UP!

You don't need to paint the stand. You could use the off cuts from the case windows to cover the front of the stand so that it blends in with your case.

Before painting, there are some things we need to do first. The stand should be washed with a mild soapy water to remove any grease or debris remaining from cutting. This will help the paint adhere to the acrylic. Then we need to mask out part of the stand so that we can still see the LCD screen after painting. This is fairly straightforward and just involves measuring the size of the actual screen and then masking off that area on the stand.

We are using a glossy black spray paint, but you could use pretty much anything as long as it is suitable for use on plastics.

Remember that two or three light coats are better than one heavy one. Keep the can a reasonable distance from the stand to stop the paint from running. Also, spray in only one direction—spray from left to right, for instance. Once you get to the right side, stop, move back to the left, and then spray the next bit. You should also start spraying just before the stand, and move over it. Make sure you have gone past the end of the stand before stopping. Spray paint can be a little temperamental when you first press the nozzle; this technique will help ensure an even covering at the edges.

TIPS OF THE TRADE

Watch the Weather

Take notice of the warnings on the paint can for weather and environmental considerations. If it's too cold, the paint won't spray properly from the can. If it's too humid, you may have problems with the paint not settling properly. Allow the paint plenty of time to dry once you have finished.

Once the paint is dry, we can stick some self-adhesive rubber feet to the bottom. They will aid stability and prevent the edges of the stand from scratching the surface it sits on. One near each corner of the base should be sufficient.

Now we can start having fun—figuring out the keypad.

60 MINUTES

Designing the Keypad

A keypad works on a simple matrix layout of rows and columns. The rows and columns are printed onto different layers and come into contact when pressed. The hardware on the LCD scans the columns looking for a contact and then scans the rows, somthing like this:

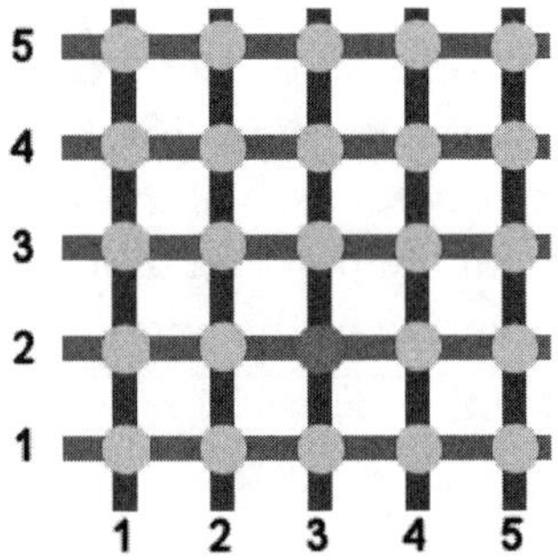

The dark circle is at column 3, row 2. This is the only key that will generate that particular set of coordinates. PC keyboards work in a very similar way—they just have a few more rows and columns.

Looking at the details for the LCD screen used here, the module is 98mm wide × 60mm high. This particular LCD also supports a keypad with up to five columns and five rows of keys. To keep things nice and simple, the keypad is being designed as a 100×100 square, with each button being a 20mm square. This should make each button large enough to press with ease, and is plenty big enough to have an icon displayed on the button front to indicate its function.

We initially drafted the keypad on graph paper, and once we had finalized it, we designed it in a graphics package, with fairly standard icons representing the various functions.

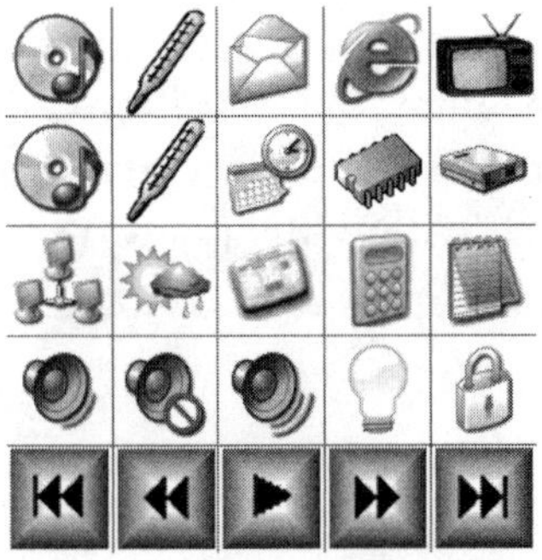

You can design your own keypad however you like. It's just an overlay, so you could design it to look like a computer panel from a sci-fi show instead of using icons.

HEADS UP!

Just because the screen will support a keypad with 25 buttons, you don't have to use all 25. You can easily design a keypad with fewer buttons instead.

Working from the top row down, the buttons in our keypad design perform the following functions:

- **Row 5** Launch various applications: WinAmp, Motherboard Monitor, Outlook, Internet Explorer, WinTV
- **Row 4** Show information screens: WinAmp details, Motherboard Monitor temperatures, time and date, RAM usage details, hard disk usage details
- **Row 3** Show information screens and launch applications: network usage, weather report, news headlines, launch Calculator, launch Notepad
- **Row 2** Access some system controls: decrease volume, mute volume, increase volume, toggle LCD backlight, pause current LCD screen
- **Row 1** Access the WinAmp controls on it: previous track, fast rewind, play/stop toggle, fast forward, next track

As mentioned earlier, the keypad works by scanning a number of rows and columns and checking whether there is any contact between the two. This means we need to create a set of columns and a set of rows to connect to the LCD. We also need an insulating layer between the two. The insulating layer keeps the other two layers apart, and ensures that there is only contact when we press a key and that only the contact of the key we are pressing is made.

To create these layers, we simply tape a transparency sheet to a sheet of graph paper and trace the lines. This is done twice, once for the columns and once for the rows. With the row and column sheets laid over each other, we mark where the lines meet. We transfer these marks to the insulating layer and make them into squares. The squares will line up right in the middle of each icon on the keypad overlay. The squares on the middle sheet will be cut out so that a connection can be made between the top and bottom layers. Our layers look like this:

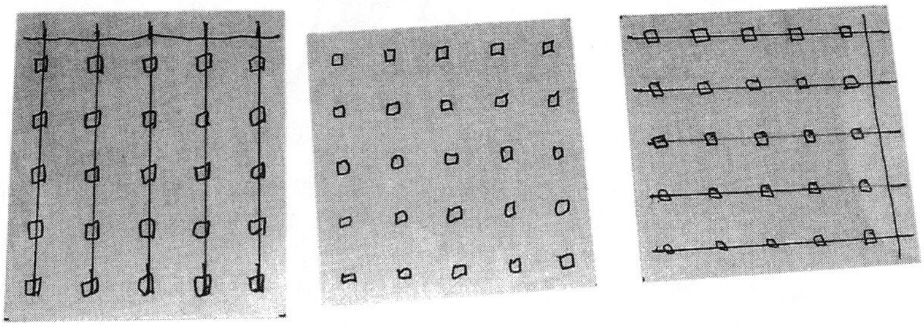

The top and bottom sheets are actually slightly wider than the keypad. This extra bit of space is to allow for wires to be connected and run back to the LCD.

The next step is to trace the lines on the top and bottom sheets with conductive paint. Where the columns and rows overlap, a square will be filled in with paint to increase the contact area for each key.

Now we need to start putting it together and connecting the wires that will lead back to the LCD screen. To do this, we will use solderless LED connectors.

HEADS UP!

These are the same holders that were used in Chapter 18 when the LED was placed inside the CD drive.

These connectors are handy for a few reasons. On one end, you have some bare wire, ready for soldering or connecting to circuitry; on the other end, you have the LED connector. For their original use, an LED will just push into the black connector. But as luck would have it, the pins are also the right distance apart to allow connection to the keypad connectors on the back of the LCD.

To attach the wires to the painted side of the sheet, you can use silver-loaded epoxy. This will help ensure that the contact remains solid and will still conduct the signal from the keypad. Because each LED connector will connect to two traces on the keypad, we will need three connectors for the columns, and three connectors for the rows. After the wires have been stuck to the sheet, they are covered with insulation tape to prevent any possible shorting.

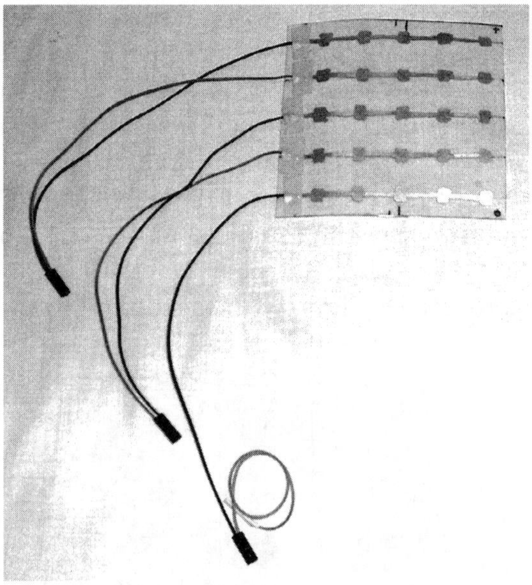

After that, we line up all three sheets and use double-sided tape to stick them together. We are making a sandwich of the three sheets. The row sheet is one side, the insulation layer is in the middle, and the column sheet is on the other side. Make sure that the painted squares line up with each other and with the holes cut into the middle sheet.

HEADS UP!

When aligning the sheets, ensure that the sheets with the painted lines on have the paint facing into the middle of the sandwich.

Once this is done, feed the wires through the slots in the stand and stick the keypad to the stand using double-sided tape, like this:

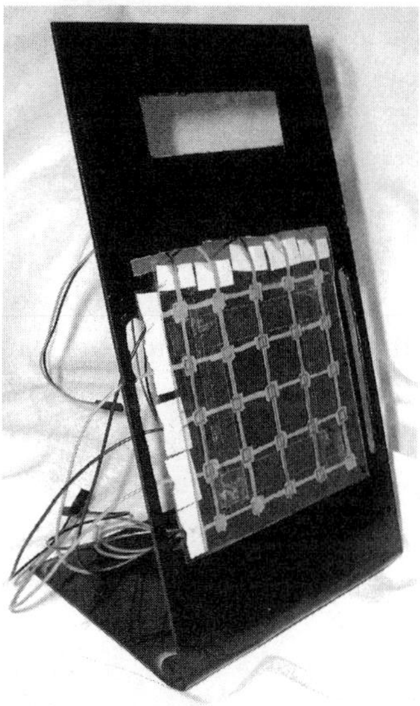

The keypad design has been printed in color on a sheet of white paper. The paper helps to hide the silver traces of the keypad so that we have an attractive front to the stand. It needs to be carefully lined up with the transparency sheets, and stuck into place with double-sided tape.

The last job on the stand is to put the LCD screen into place. This can be done with screws (if you drill mounting holes through the acrylic) or, as we are doing, with double-sided tape.

Finishing Up

With everything in place, the last job is to wire up the keypad to the LCD display. This is simply a matter of connecting the LED holders onto the pins on the back of the screen.

As you can see, the wires are all very close together, so use a couple of cable ties to stop them from becoming entangled:

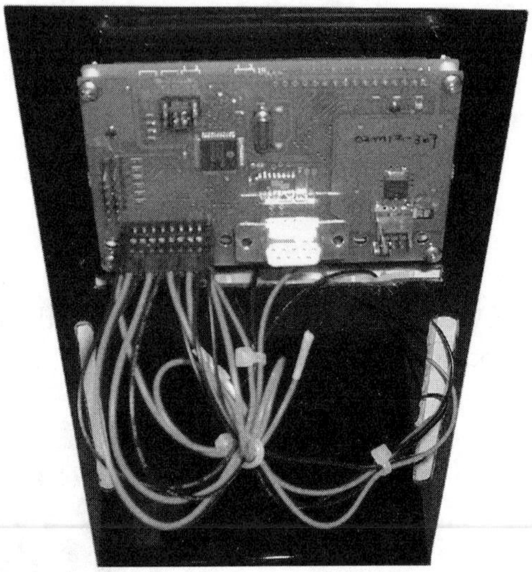

The mod is now complete—we just need to connect the power and serial cable to the screen. Before it bursts into life, however, we need to spend some time with the software to configure the various informational screens that the LCD will display. We also need to set up the software to respond to the keypad.

We are using LCDC, but there are other alternatives. LCDC is shareware and can be obtained from www.lcdc.cc.

So that's it. Time now to connect everything up and see how the final LCD stand looks:

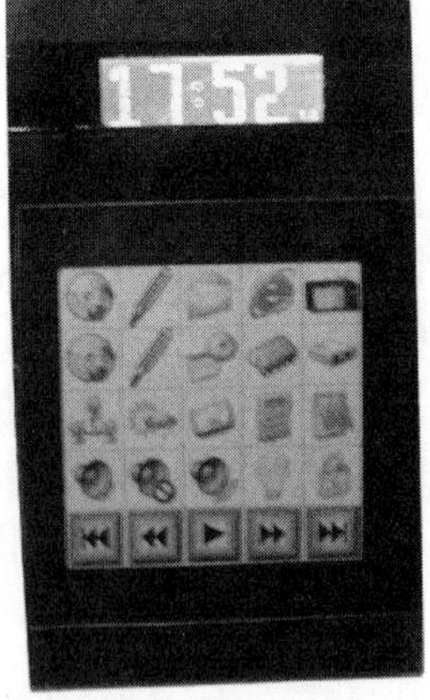

TESTING 1-2-3

There are a lot of steps involved in making this LCD stand and keypad, so the following quickly recaps them:

- [ ] Create an external power source
    - [ ] Drill hole in PCI bracket and fit the DC power socket
    - [ ] Solder wires to DC power socket
    - [ ] Fit molex to power socket wires for connection to PC power supply
    - [ ] Attach molex to free end of DC power lead
- [ ] Make an acrylic stand
    - [ ] Cut acrylic to size
    - [ ] Bend acrylic with hot air gun
    - [ ] Clean and then mask acrylic, ready for painting
    - [ ] Paint acrylic stand and fit rubber feet when dry
- [ ] Design and make keypad
    - [ ] Design keypad overlay
    - [ ] Make some "rows" and "columns" with transparent sheet, and paint with conductive paint
    - [ ] Make an insulation layer to keep the rows and columns apart
    - [ ] Stick LED holders to row and column traces with silver-loaded epoxy
    - [ ] Stick rows, insulation, and column sheets together with double-sided tape
    - [ ] Stick these sheets to the stand
    - [ ] Line up the keypad overlay and stick over the row and column sheets
    - [ ] Attach LCD screen to stand
    - [ ] Plug LED holders into keypad connectors on LCD screen
    - [ ] Connect LCD to PC and configure software

Index

Numbers

A

Y

INTERNATIONAL CONTACT INFORMATION

AUSTRALIA
McGraw-Hill Book Company Australia Pty. Ltd.
TEL +61-2-9900-1800
FAX +61-2-9878-8881
http://www.mcgraw-hill.com.au
books-it_sydney@mcgraw-hill.com

CANADA
McGraw-Hill Ryerson Ltd.
TEL +905-430-5000
FAX +905-430-5020
http://www.mcgraw-hill.ca

GREECE, MIDDLE EAST, & AFRICA (Excluding South Africa)
McGraw-Hill Hellas
TEL +30-210-6560-990
TEL +30-210-6560-993
TEL +30-210-6560-994
FAX +30-210-6545-525

MEXICO (Also serving Latin America)
McGraw-Hill Interamericana Editores S.A. de C.V.
TEL +525-117-1583
FAX +525-117-1589
http://www.mcgraw-hill.com.mx
fernando_castellanos@mcgraw-hill.com

SINGAPORE (Serving Asia)
McGraw-Hill Book Company
TEL +65-6863-1580
FAX +65-6862-3354
http://www.mcgraw-hill.com.sg
mghasia@mcgraw-hill.com

SOUTH AFRICA
McGraw-Hill South Africa
TEL +27-11-622-7512
FAX +27-11-622-9045
robyn_swanepoel@mcgraw-hill.com

SPAIN
McGraw-Hill/Interamericana de España, S.A.U.
TEL +34-91-180-3000
FAX +34-91-372-8513
http://www.mcgraw-hill.es
professional@mcgraw-hill.es

UNITED KINGDOM, NORTHERN, EASTERN, & CENTRAL EUROPE
McGraw-Hill Education Europe
TEL +44-1-628-502500
FAX +44-1-628-770224
http://www.mcgraw-hill.co.uk
computing_europe@mcgraw-hill.com

ALL OTHER INQUIRIES Contact:
McGraw-Hill/Osborne
TEL +1-510-420-7700
FAX +1-510-420-7703
http://www.osborne.com
omg_international@mcgraw-hill.com

Expanded Gaming Column!
PC UPGRADE
THE GUIDE TO BUILDING AND EXPANDING COMPUTER SYSTEMS
BUILD YOUR OWN DVD MOVIE PRODUCTION SYSTEM
DIGICAMS | KILLER GRAPHICS
PC UPGRADE
build your own digital audio workstation
RIP! EDIT! MIX! BURN! PLAY!
SNEAK PEEK | 14 WILD
PC UPGRADE
Build Your Own Killer Gaming System
PC UPGRADE
BUILD YOUR OWN
GHz
Supercompute
A Triple Dose